GIRLHOOD,
TRANSLATED

GIRLHOOD, TRANSLATED

Understanding Girls in the Age of Therapy Speak and Self-Diagnosis

DR SUZANNE GARFINKLE-CROWELL

SIMON & SCHUSTER

London · New York · Amsterdam/Antwerp · Sydney/Melbourne · Toronto · New Delhi

First published in the United States by Crown, an imprint of the Crown Publishing Group, a division of Penguin Random House LLC, 2026
First published in Great Britain by Simon & Schuster UK Ltd, 2026

1 3 5 7 9 10 8 6 4 2

Simon & Schuster UK Ltd, 7th Floor, 199 Bishopsgate, London EC2M 3TY

www.simonandschuster.co.uk
www.simonandschuster.com.au
www.simonandschuster.co.in

Simon & Schuster Australia, Sydney
Simon & Schuster India, New Delhi

The authorised representative in the EEA is Simon & Schuster Netherlands BV, Herculesplein 96, 3584 AA Utrecht, Netherlands. info@simonandschuster.nl

A CIP catalogue record for this book is available from the British Library

Hardback ISBN: 978-1-3985-4976-0
Trade Paperback ISBN: 978-1-3985-4977-7
eBook ISBN: 978-1-3985-4978-4

Brush-drawn art used throughout courtesy of Shutterstock.com / Anastasiia Hevko

Typeset by Aubrey Khan

Printed and Bound in the UK using 100% Renewable Electricity at CPI Group (UK) Ltd

FSC www.fsc.org MIX Paper | Supporting responsible forestry FSC® C013604

To my patients,
who have been my greatest teachers.

And to Aaron.
I literally can't even.

The Lord said, 'If as one people speaking the same language they have begun to do this, then nothing they plan to do will be impossible for them. Come, let us go down and confuse their language so they will not understand each other.' So the Lord scattered them from there over all the earth, and they stopped building the city.

Genesis 11:6–10

The idea that gives psychiatry the power to name our pain in the first place – that the mind can be treated like the body, that it is no more or less than what the brain does . . . reflects what is best about us: our desire to understand ourselves and one another, to use knowledge to relieve suffering, even if it results in a kind of reductionism that insults our sense of ourselves as unfathomably complex and even transcendent creatures. It also reflects what is worst – the desire to control, to manipulate, to turn others' vulnerabilities to our advantage.

Gary Greenberg,
The Book of Woe

She broke up with me. Didn't really tell me why. Luckily when you're the guy, you just tell people she's crazy. 'Hey Tom, I heard you and Lucy broke up.' 'Yeah man. Turns out, she's *crazy*.'

Tom Haverford,
Parks and Recreation

Contents

Author's Note . . . xv

Prologue . . . xvii

Introduction . . . 1

- Girls Are Not Doing Well – Right? . . . 1
- Psychiatry Words in Context . . . 3
- The Problem with No Name . . . 4
- The Language of Therapy Culture . . . 8
- Girls Just Want to Have Fun . . . with Language . . . 11
- How Therapy Speak Hurts Girls . . . 13
- The Backlash, and Where I Stand . . . 15
- Finding Our Way Back . . . 18
- Why Therapy Stories? . . . 18

PART ONE
How We Got Here

1. Diagnosed . . . 23

- I. Alphabet Soup . . . 23
  - What Is a Teenager? . . . 26
  - The Task . . . 29
  - Peer Supervision . . . 30
  - Faux Pas . . . 34

II. Duelling Narratives . . . 39
The Trauma Police . . . 44
Trust the Process . . . 46
Decoding Therapy Speak: A Beginning . . . 51

2. A History of the Emotional Female in Two Breakups . . . 54
I. Heartbreak . . . 54
Hysteria from Plato to Prozac . . . 62
II. Chill . . . 73
Chill Pills . . . 78
Prozac Feminism . . . 80
The Lightbulb Has to Want to Change . . . 81

3. Identity and the Internet Age . . . 84
More of a Carrie . . . 84
The Internet Sad Girl . . . 85
Social Media: Illness Incubator . . . 88
Social Media: Traumatiser . . . 91
Social Media: Your Psychiatrist . . . 94
The Rise of the Medical Model . . . 96
The Expansion of Diagnoses . . . 100
The Costs of Illness Identities . . . 103

PART TWO
What I'm Hearing

4. Anxiety Girlies . . . 109
Sleepless . . . 109
Having Anxiety . . . 110
What Is an Anxiety Disorder? . . . 113
Social Purgatory . . . 114
The Girlies . . . 119

The Teenage Girl Brain . . . 123
Neurosis 101 . . . 125
Tend and Befriend . . . 127
Are You Saying I Should Have a Fight with Her? . . . 128

5. Too Much . . . 132

The Queen of Quantities . . . 132
You'll See . . . 134
Eggshells . . . 138
A Lot . . . 140
The Eye of the Beholder . . . 143
Too Fat, Too Slutty, Too Loud . . . 145
Difficult . . . 147
Skills Culture . . . 149
It's Complicated . . . 153

6. Not Enough . . . 156

Best Friend Necklace . . . 156
Stressed . . . 157
What's on the Test? . . . 159
Parts Work . . . 163
Inner Critic . . . 166
This Other Weird Thing . . . 167
Mean Coach . . . 170
The Intergenerational Transmission of Not-Enoughness . . . 174
This Is Water . . . 180

7. The Curious Case of the Bitch and the Narcissist . . . 184

Watch Out . . . 184
All-American Bitch . . . 188
The Hidden Curriculum . . . 189
The Proto-Bitch . . . 191
Cocktails . . . 192

Anger Issues . . . 195
Bully . . . 197
Inner Child . . . 200

8. *Slay*-DHD . . . 204

One Simple Thing . . . 204
Deficit Disorder . . . 209
The Girl Kind . . . 214
Uphill Battles . . . 221
Steady . . . 224
Neurocosmopolitan . . . 226
Done . . . 230

9. Toxic, Etc. . . . 233

Extremes . . . 233
The Drama . . . 235
Poisoned Arrows . . . 238
Victims and Perpetrators . . . 241
Late Bloomer . . . 244
Linguistic Relativity . . . 246

10. People-Pleaser . . . 248

The Answer . . . 248
Family Stuff, Sometimes . . . 249
The Secret to a Successful Therapy . . . 250
I Feel Bad Saying Anything . . . 252
The Wisdom to Know the Difference . . . 255
Defence Mechanisms, Redux . . . 256
Family Vacation . . . 257
A Little Upset . . . 258
The Girl Self-Defence System . . . 259
Emotional Labour . . . 263

PART THREE
What Now?

11. Three Anxious Mothers (and One Confused Dad) . . . 267

My Heart of Hearts . . . 267

The Never-Healing Wound . . . 270

Helicopter, Snowplough, Therapist, Friend . . . 272

We All Make Our Choices . . . 275

A Note from the Surgeon General . . . 277

Good Enough . . . 278

Postscript: One Confused Dad . . . 281

12. Returning Girlhood to Girls . . . 284

Getting Bangs . . . 284

Turning Off the Cultural Gaslight . . . 287

Suggestions for Girls . . . 288

Suggestions for Parents . . . 292

Suggestions for Psychiatry and the Mental Health Establishment . . . 295

Now What? . . . 300

Translating Towards Health . . . 301

Acknowledgments . . . 305

Notes . . . 311

Index . . . 337

Author's Note

The stories in this book are drawn from my experiences as a psychiatrist, but the specific details have been changed to protect the privacy of my patients. The characters are composites, designed to highlight common struggles of girlhood.

Prologue

Hazel is quiet at dinner.

'How was your day, sweetie?' her mom asks.

'Um, well, Olivia and Jack broke up, and now he's with Luna,' she says, pushing her rice around with her fork.

'Oh,' her father says with a smirk. 'Jack sure moves fast!'

Hazel can't believe her dad. 'That's really *not* okay, Dad. Olivia is seriously traumatised.' She glares at him, trying to remain calm.

Her father looks confused.

'Oh. Okay. I'm sorry to hear that,' he says. 'She's a great kid and I'm sure she'll find another boyfriend soon.'

Hazel rolls her eyes. 'It's actually very complicated for Olivia,' she says quietly, placing her fork down. 'She already has attachment issues.'

Her mom jumps in. 'Hazel, I think Dad is just trying to be supportive.'

Ugh. Her parents are missing the whole point – how broken Olivia looked in first period, how Luna can just sweep in and take anyone's boyfriend she wants. And how, if someone like Olivia can't keep a relationship, what hope is there for Hazel? They just sit there, chewing their chicken. And her mom is *always* standing up for her dad, even when he's obviously in the wrong.

'You guys are giving me a full-on panic attack right now,' she says, pushing her chair back and storming off to her room. A few minutes of sitting and scrolling will help her calm down.

A year later, Hazel sits in my office for our first appointment. She adjusts her red glasses and tells me this story – and others like it. She talks about her anxiety and depression, her dysregulation, the trauma from growing up with parents who are codependent and maybe even on the spectrum? And the stress she feels having to mask it all just to get through the day.

Hazel is identifying psychiatric symptoms and conditions I know how to treat. I can use medication; I can teach her 'coping skills', as her parents have requested. All of this can get her better – but only to a point.

Because Hazel hasn't told me what her real problem is – she can't.

'Okay,' I say. 'Let's get started.'

GIRLHOOD,
TRANSLATED

Introduction

> Let's normalise not calling girls crazy.
>
> **Internet meme**

Girls Are Not Doing Well – Right?

When Taylor Swift sings, 'Every time you call me crazy, I get more crazy,' she's putting her finger on a phenomenon that's taken hold of us. About ten years ago, I noticed young women were speaking in a new way about their feelings: almost everything was evidence of a mental disorder. Therapy speak had come to dominate conversations, both in the world and in my psychiatric office. That did not seem good for anyone – not for the healthy people who were surely overpathologising themselves, and not for the sick people whose labels were losing their meaning. Most of all, it wasn't good for girls and young women, who have consistently been called 'hysterical' and 'crazy' through the ages. Now, in addition to bearing the brunt of a mental health crisis affecting teens and young adults, they seemed to be using the language of mental illness to convey all sorts of experiences, from the mundane or whimsical to the genuinely distressing. From the parents I talk to, I was hearing both dismissiveness and panic. This language needed some translating.

So, I sat down to write this book.

I soon realised the explosion of therapy speak in our culture had its roots in another phenomenon – something that had concerned me since I entered medical training more than two decades ago. At that time, I was troubled by a reductionism that had taken hold in psychiatry. With the rise of managed care in the 1990s, psychiatry had grown more medicalised and less human. Insurance companies were putting new restrictions on the type and duration of treatments they would cover, and there was a push to make a medical diagnosis and select a medication, rather than getting to know a patient as a person.

Now teenagers and young adults, especially young women, have stopped getting to know themselves – as people.

The rise of therapy culture and therapy speak has landed us in a very strange place, where many girls define themselves by their psychiatric profiles. Although identifying with a mental illness can promote acceptance and motivate help-seeking, it has been shown to have an 'engulfing' effect, obliterating other aspects of identity and making someone worse. Young people today are stuck in a cycle of learning about mental health largely on social media, self-labelling with disorders, and then posting about them.

This occurs in the wake of some progress. Starting in the 1990s, mental health awareness initiatives were helped along by the rise of the internet and a widening of access to health information more generally. These developments helped destigmatise mental illness – but also injected psychiatric language into the mainstream without much context. Misinformation and misunderstanding have now created a deeper crisis for generations of young people who have been taught to overpathologise human suffering and have lost – not gained – the ability to name and tolerate their feelings. For Gen Z (people born between 1997 and 2012), therapy culture and its situation in the broader corporate enterprise of 'Wellness' has also redefined the meaning of life as a quest to achieve 'mental health.' But what does that mean? Somehow, normalcy seems more elusive than ever: now one in five Gen Alpha children (born between 2010 and 2024) carries a mental, emotional or behavioural health diagnosis.

As you read this and think about girls today, maybe there's a tired voice in the back of your mind grumbling about the ills of social media, or misogyny, or feminism. *It's the phones! It's the politics! Atomisation! Too much therapy! Too much narcissism! AI! It's the same old problems that have burdened women for centuries,* perhaps. *It's a crisis!*

It's bullshit! Or maybe there's a specific girl you know and worry about.

I am a psychiatrist who specialises in helping young women and their parents. I also have a parallel life in the medical humanities – a field that strives to humanise medicine through reflective and creative practices like reading, writing and examining the stories we tell. Throughout my career, I have trained my eye on the line where the illness meets the person, always haunted by this question: how do categories, labels and interpretations clarify – and obfuscate – our knowledge of one another? At heart, I am a recovering teenage girl, and a mom who likes nothing more than to talk to parents about parenting. In all aspects of my work, I am a translator: a specialist in bridging communication gaps between young women and the people who care about them, and between young women and themselves.

Psychiatry Words in Context

People use the language of mental health in three major ways. The first is in a casual and often jokey fashion: 'Oh, I'm so *OCD* about my skincare routine.' 'Sorry to be completely *ADHD* in this conversation.'

The second is to use diagnosis words earnestly to describe actual mental conditions. Those with serious depression, anxiety or trauma – not to mention addictions, eating disorders, bipolar disorder, autism and psychotic illnesses – speak of their diagnoses factually, in addition to whatever cultural, identity or interpersonal meaning they carry. In other words: some people are just really mentally ill.

What do you mean, 'actual', 'serious', and 'really'? might be your next question. That one has a short answer and a long answer. The short answer is that real mental illness is debilitating. But, of course, that answer raises more questions; for example: how does one separate what's 'real' from what's misinterpreted, misunderstood – or just a lack of willingness, fortitude or grit?

The answers to questions like that one are entirely case-specific. They are clinical questions and can only be addressed in the context of a thorough evaluation of a person and their life. In a full psychiatric assessment, we take what's known as a 'biopsychosocial' approach. Psychiatric conditions are not like other medical illnesses. They include, often in equal measure, complex biological, psychological and social forces. The question of what is 'real', what's truly debilitating, where the line is between *can't* and *won't* – these are the questions of our daily work as clinicians.

If it's tricky for mental health professionals to find the best answers, it's even more confusing for young women who now, thanks to therapy culture, interface with this language all the time.

This brings us to the third major way people use therapy speak and the language of diagnosis: to figure out who they are and why they are having a hard time. Therapy speak, in that third sense – and the girls who use it – are the subject of this book.

The Problem with No Name

Why do adolescent girls and young women struggle so much?

As generations of writers have described, being a woman is impossible. That 'impossible' feeling begins in adolescence.

First, there is your body, which metamorphoses on its own schedule, fully disregarding your preferences. Hormones bring on dark moods and intolerance of others like you've never known. You are surrounded by peers who are also in chaos. You don't fully grasp that you feel unstable in part because your world is populated by immature actors with mercurial tastes and little life experience, peddling delirious joy and freewheeling cruelty. You are being driven by feelings – more intense than you've ever felt – all under the shoddy supervision of brains that have not finished forming. This, while everyone is underslept and spending long days doing thing after thing they must do very well – because, future – and which, by and large, they did not choose to do at all.

Some people say that teenage girls should be having an easier time than ever. After all, girls in Europe and (until recently) in America have experienced more rights, more physical comforts, more freedoms than ever before – and have surpassed their male counterparts in academic and professional achievements. It's never been more possible for women to access independence and power; they are so dominant in higher education that some US universities are now practising affirmative action for boys, handing out 'bro-chures' advertising male-friendly collegiate activities. Furthermore, adolescence has gradually expanded in our culture as a developmental period of time: less is expected of our teenagers, and for longer. *Don't be silly,* parents tell girls nowadays. *Of course you can have it all.* And *of course you're perfect the way you are.*

But society sends a different message, continuing to hurt girls disproportionately. To be clear: boys and men have their own burdens. They are more likely to misuse substances and to die by suicide when they attempt it – and they are far less likely to seek help or discuss their problems in public. Indeed, men more than women experience a pressure to appear strong. Young men today may also identify with a psychiatric diagnosis. Therapy culture and the identities it underwrites are not unique to females – but they are more pronounced among young women. In the words of the writer Lisa Appignanesi, it's 'as if psychology, that whole business of understanding the (troubled) mind and relations, were a uniquely feminine undertaking'. Indeed, a recent study by Pew Research Centre found that girls are more concerned about teen mental health, mothers are more concerned than fathers about the mental health of teens today, and parents of a teen girl are more concerned than parents of a teen boy.

In recent years, girls have experienced a decline in confidence while their anxiety has climbed to new heights. Despite their academic prowess, more than half of girls still stay away from leadership roles for fear of being 'bossy'. Today, 83 per cent of US high school girls report feeling they are going to 'explode' from pressure and more than half of girls say they are not sure if they are smart enough for their dream career. More than two-thirds of girls claim that they don't say what they are thinking out of concern for being disliked. Three out of four girls in the US say that boys their age are disrespectful towards them, a dynamic that increases sharply from fifth grade (69 per cent) to high school (84 per cent).

Ever heard of the 'Hot Crazy-Matrix: A Man's Guide to Women'? It dictates (only ever so jokingly) that you have to be at least 'a five' to be fuckable, at least 'an eight' to be datable, and that your 'craziness' (defined in this system as an inherent property of the female) is only tolerable if you're hot. Like many viral concepts, this one reflects an enduring truth: one video on the subject has comments by both men and women, saying, '*This is so real.*' So, at the same time as girls are diligently outperforming their male classmates in advanced history, they must also answer to another set of rules – and they know it.

In 1994's *Reviving Ophelia,* psychologist Mary Pipher described a 'girl-poisoning culture', blaming the toxic trio of 'sexism, capitalism and lookism'. In other words, in order to earn her rights in the kingdom of humanity, a girl has to manage her appearance and vibe pretty aggressively. What teenage girl doesn't want to be sought-after? What human being doesn't want to be valued? Pipher detailed how those problems played out at the end of the twentieth century: before social media, before smartphones and before the internet.

Girls today were born in the aftermath of major waves of feminism that tried to reconcile some of these tensions, expanding the kind of person a girl could be. But, as the possibilities grew through the decades, the conflicts and contradictions multiplied. 'Progress is confusing,' Pipher writes. That's as true now as it was in 1994: for example, the body positivity movement was not lost on Gen Z, but spend ten seconds on Instagram and you'll see that neither was it entirely successful.

Some say 'go back'. Recent years have seen a polarisation in young women's concept of what it means to be fulfilled and whole. Just as variations and fluidity in gender and sexuality were becoming more accepted and even encouraged, a wave of traditionalist female movements took hold: Southern sorority girls and tradwives emerged, strident and unapologetic about wanting classic domestic comforts – the things many girls are ashamed or afraid to admit they covet as well. On the surface, ours looks like a world where girls can now do anything and be anything, including a size 16 or a childless cat lady. But ask a teenage girl how that sounds to her.

If you're a teenage girl today, our culture's ambivalence about you becomes part of who you are. You spend a lot of time feeling confused and bad, and you'll likely even develop some psychiatric symptoms – which is what happens when human beings feel confused and bad. It's also par for the course to experience psychiatric symptoms in adolescence. Mood swings that would make an adult look bipolar are often part of the ordinary repertoire of the fourteen-year-old. Anger outbursts, anxiety meltdowns, self-esteem spirals, brooding, rumination, friend drama, family conflict, moments of jaw-droppingly poor judgement, body image and skin-related freak-outs: all normal. Internal conflicts create anxiety, and anxiety can rage in the healthy adolescent. Newly strong needs that can't be met at home produce a sense of general emotional instability and frustration; it is easy to feel distracted, irritable and restless. There's so much exhilaration in finding one's true self, but that's invariably tied to an inchoate sense of loss, having to part with the idealised version of one's parents and childhood. It's therefore normal for adolescents to feel depressed and not know exactly why. None of that feels especially good, and it's so easy for kids today, steeped in social media, to read these emotions as signs of disorders – especially because sometimes, they can be.

If you're a teenager, you're likely to want to make sense of those feelings and symptoms. You're looking for your *story*. As a kid, your parents and others around you had a lot of say over who you were and what your experiences meant. But now, you get to tell that story yourself. Separating from your family is a narrative act as much as a behavioural one. Identity formation is about language and power: who gets to be the author; who gets to decide.

What is at best an identity challenge and at worst an identity crisis is waiting at the gate of adulthood for most girls. It's then that they step into the 'girl-poisoning culture'. *Reviving Ophelia*'s title references the female ingenue in Shakespeare's *Hamlet* who was a happy child until she hit adolescence and was immediately caught in a panicked – and ultimately, tragic – effort to feel loved and important.*

It's worth noting that teenage girls have been contending with this simultaneous construction and destruction of the Self for as long as adolescence has existed. They are the victims in fairy tales – the ones who are cursed and persecuted by stepmothers and fated to perish. As Denis Diderot, who lived in the 1700s, famously said to a female friend: 'You all die at 15.' Simone de Beauvoir called it the moment when girls 'stop being and start seeming'. It's the beginning of what Betty Friedan called 'the problem with no name'.

The name we give that problem really matters.

The Language of Therapy Culture

So, teenage girls: welcome to therapy culture.

Have you been having a tough time? What makes life uniquely challenging for you? Therapy culture will embrace you, bathe you in concepts that make sense of your pain, offer you tricks to help yourself and others in your life. It will teach you a whole new language that will explain what you're going through – and you can post all about it. Here is an overview of what you will learn.

There are, of course, the psychiatric diagnoses. But therapy speak goes far beyond those. It draws concepts from various schools of thought, including psychiatry, psychoanalysis, developmental

* Ophelia is obsessed with appeasing the men around her: father, brother and Hamlet himself. When the main character rejects her, her mind and sense of self disintegrate. She goes fully crazy and drowns herself in a stream full of flowers.

psychology, attachment theory, cognitive therapy, addiction treatment and behaviourism. Popular terms can be organised into a handful of categories. In addition to the diagnoses, there are *family of origin* and *early experience* concepts: 'attachment style', 'inner child', 'issues', 'boundaries', 'generational pain', 'trauma', 'gaslighting' (Merriam-Webster's Word of the Year in 2022), and how you 'show up in relationships'. There are *defence mechanism* words like 'projecting', 'coping mechanisms', 'avoidance', 'repression', 'denial', 'inner critic', and 'impostor syndrome'. There are *thought pattern* words like 'positive thinking', 'catastrophising', 'ruminating' and 'affirmations'; *behaviour* words like 'trigger' and 'skills' and having 'tools in the toolbox'.

There are *drive* or *instinct* words like 'needs', the notion that pleasure is important, that sex is important, that being true to one's inside self is important. There are *developmental* words like 'emotional maturity', 'journey', 'work in progress'; *uncovering* or *revelatory* words like 'unpack'; *sacred relationship* words like 'trust', 'emotional safety', being 'present', 'holding space', feeling 'seen' and privileging vulnerability, such as using 'I feel' statements; there are *affective* and *self-state* words like 'validation', 'self-esteem', 'dysregulation', 'unstable', 'capacity', 'bandwidth' and being in a 'good place' or a 'dark place', and the notion of 'sitting with discomfort'. Therapy speak also refers to certain *practices:* 'talking', 'sharing', 'opening up', as well as 'analysing', 'reflecting', 'processing', and 'metabolising'. There is the lexicon of damage and healing like being 'scarred', engaging in 'self-care,' and 'wellness'. And there are words that seek a connection with Eastern spirituality like 'mindfulness', 'energy', 'synchrony', 'intentionality' and 'manifesting'.

Therapy culture also references the expansion of *spaces* where mental illness, personal trauma history and psychological diagnosis are discussed: on the internet, in school, in the workplace, in the playground, in academia, in politics. And in therapy culture, the *types of relating* one might find in a therapeutic environment become expected everywhere. 'Validation' and 'emotional safety' – originally technical terms describing special features of a therapeutic setting – are now sought out from the soccer field to the subway to the C-suite.

This is not an entirely new phenomenon. Therapy concepts have been creeping into the culture for more than a hundred years, since the birth of psychoanalysis. We can see it in the idea that dreams are meaningful, that sexuality drives our decision-making, that one's early experiences are formative, or that someone might be 'repressed' or 'in denial', have 'control issues' or an 'inferiority complex' or an 'addictive personality'. As W H Auden wrote of Sigmund Freud, 'To us he is no more a person / now but a whole climate of opinion'.

Make no mistake: therapy words have infiltrated so deeply into the English language because they are useful – we don't even realise how thoroughly we rely on them. Therapy speak has helped us understand ourselves and one another, and its expansion has made the world, to some degree, a better place. For generations, people were made fun of for experiencing pain and vulnerability. Nowadays, it's no longer cool to mock someone for having a diagnosis, taking medication or talking to a professional. Therapy culture has encouraged us to bring more empathy and openness to our personal relationships, to expect to be treated fairly and with concern for our mental well-being in school and work, on the street and at home. Therapy speak is also brimming with great inventions and powerful memes that blend so well with internet culture that it's nearly impossible to separate the two. A few examples: 'trauma dumping', 'main character energy', 'love bombing', 'weaponised incompetence'.

Labels and organisational systems make human beings feel safe. It can be healing to find a way to describe what's troubling – especially for those in powerless positions. Being young is a form of powerlessness. So is being female. The ideas of therapy culture have helped girls see and liberate themselves, at times. For example, the elevation of the term 'gaslight' from obscure movie reference to common parlance, while easy to mock, has helped millions of women recognise and resist manipulative behaviour, and has raised the bar for how they expect to be treated.

But therapy culture is also a Tower of Babel. Suffering and symptoms are multifactorial, created by overlapping processes and described through many different schools of thought. A person's insomnia, for example, might occur because of circadian rhythm dysfunction, anxiety, excessive screen time, relationship stress or failed sleep training long ago. A cacophony of psychoanalytic, cognitive behavioural, biological, dialectical behavioural, and various other theoretical traditions rattles in our ears. A person with a problem wants to know: 'Which is it?'

Girls Just Want to Have Fun . . . with Language

The jumble of therapy speak is well suited to teenage girls because it offers a colourful palette for self-expression. And young women's speech, commonly known as 'girlspeak', is nothing if not colourful. That's one of the reasons I have always loved working with them.

Most of the world does not see it that way. For decades, teenage girls have been made fun of for classically 'female' ways of talking. How many of us have been reprimanded for saying 'like'* too much, ending statements as if they were questions (known as 'uptalk'), or adding 'tag questions' like 'you know what I mean?' From feminists

* The most vilified word in the girlspeak lexicon is probably 'like'. I think, like, almost every girl has been told to use it less. I know I have. When people say that to me, I'm, like, *please*. The word 'like' is uniquely geared towards conveying a multilayered experience. When you say 'and I was, like . . .' the word functions as a mixture of what you said, what you thought and what you felt. What follows is entirely context dependent. One must read body language or tone of voice to infer if you actually said what you were 'like', or if you're describing an internal response. 'Like' also functions as a 'discourse marker', meaning it's equivalent to 'I feel like', as in, 'this is, like, my favourite meal'. It would mean something different entirely to say 'this is my favourite meal', but in girl-land, the meaning is clear: You like this meal so much. It makes you happy. It's more about the *feeling* it gives you than some objective comparison to all other meals. Despite its bad reputation, the word 'like' is a powerhouse of understanding and being understood.

to misogynists, critics have denigrated these forms of speech as sounding too insecure and too deferential, with an implied message that if a girl wants to get anywhere in life she had better start speaking more like a man. Even in clinical psychiatry, teenage girls are known for their 'circumstantial thought processes' – a vaguely pathologising descriptor that's part of the mental status exam, our equivalent of the physical exam. The 'healthy' standard for 'thought process' is 'linear and goal-directed', whereas a 'circumstantial' person includes too many details.

I've never felt that way. I love the details: the meandering stories, the pockets of description, feeling, backstory, drama, excitement, gossip. Packed with artful abbreviations and slang – *literally the worst, literally can't even* – girlspeak is so vibrant and full of life.

The real superpower of girlspeak is that it tends to be *playful,* buzzing with neologisms and sophisticated slang that capture complex feelings and relational phenomena never named before: 'hangry', 'frenemy', 'situationship', 'bromance'. There's the classic 'mansplain', but also countless others: 'fratriarchy' (a social structure in which power is held by a brotherhood that 'objectifies and dehumanises those on the outside') and 'floordrobe' (where your husband keeps his clothes) are two of my recent favourites. Playing with language is not just fun, it's subversive: it's a time-honoured form of social resistance.

In fact, research has shown that girls tend to acquire vocabulary earlier and faster than boys,* and that as a whole, young women are about a half generation ahead of their male peers in linguistic progress. Female language is also marked by certain types of intelligence. Compared to male speech, which is 'competitive' – monologuing, grandstanding, info-dumping, argument-making, directive-giving – female speech is communal and cooperative. Women tend more

* The neurobiology of female adolescents supports these observations, as girls tend to develop grey matter (brain cells) earlier than boys in the areas of the brain where language and social experiences are integrated.

often to acknowledge what others are saying and to build on it, generating intimacy through consensus. Even the 'weak language' of hedges, disclaimers and tag questions has been shown to help women attain raises and promotions, and to make uncomfortable demands on people.

Yes, girls are the language pioneers,* shaping the culture the rest of us will inhabit. Filled with irony and flair, girlspeak is most subversive because there's so much you can get away with when nobody knows how serious you are.

How Therapy Speak Hurts Girls

Isn't it a shame, then, that therapy speak has taken over, filling every space in which a girl could speak *as herself*?

The problem is even darker than that. As George Orwell describes in 'Politics and the English Language', once one has turned to clichés, one has stopped thinking.

We in psychiatry are partly to blame. Decades ago, we set up a categorical system that emphasises external symptoms and disease labels rather than a continuum that reflects the broad spectrum of human emotions.

In this book, I will tell some of that history, how the lexicon of psychiatry grew from the medical model of mental health: organising people's emotional pain into symptoms and diagnostic categories, and coming up with an elaborate – and often very effective – system of treating that pain as disease.

Fed in part by psychiatry's desire to stand alongside the other medical sciences, multiple economic and social forces created and now sustain the prevailing medical model in our field. In the US, insurance companies require that any patient in therapy needs a

* As linguist Gretchen McCulloch writes, 'The role that young women play as language disruptors is so clearly established at this point it's practically boring to linguists who study this topic.'

diagnosis from the *Diagnostic and Statistical Manual of Mental Disorders* (*DSM*) in order to receive coverage. The global antidepressant market, dominated by North America, is forecasted to reach $18.29 billion by 2027. Pharma funds most clinical trials in psychiatry and relies on the *DSM,* which, in its most recent edition, created even more diagnoses that are even easier to make. It's as effortless for doctors to diagnose and prescribe as it is for patients to take pills and feel better. The tyranny of wellness culture, and our collective frustration intolerance, has led to an epidemic of superficial, medically based thinking.

With young women as its target population.

Mental health authorities and young women have been stuck in a centuries-long situationship, marked by codependence and troubling power dynamics – but also off-the-charts chemistry. Hysterical girls were the original psychiatric patients; serious, fatherly older men were their doctors. Females turn to psychiatry for treatment more often than males, and psychiatry welcomes their suffering with open arms.

In the present, doctors are more likely to diagnose depression in females compared with males who have the same symptoms. Women are more likely than men to be prescribed psychotropic medications. Women experiencing physical health problems are more likely than men to receive diagnoses of mental disorders instead. And young women accrue more psychiatric diagnoses than young men do, especially of depression, anxiety and stress-related disorders.

These gendered dynamics encourage a young woman to attribute whatever problem she is experiencing to a defect in her own brain – to make herself into the 'identified patient'.

In the cases I describe, you will see how medicalising one's pain helps girls do something else they've been conditioned to do: to dramatise and minimise their emotions at the same time. The female effort to be light and pleasant is not new. We still like girls better in pretty packages – vulnerable, but not too demanding. Girls read that room, sugarcoating themselves in lighthearted speech and demeanour, disguising their feelings even from their own consciousness – a process I've come to think of as 'the Girl Self-Defence System' (GSDS). At some point, they realise how invisible they have become, so they up the ante using medical terminology in order to receive validation and help. Girls are indeed human beings, after all: they would rather be ill and attended to than ignored and alone. In other words, society sets a girl up to transform herself into the cliché of the hysteric, overstating her problems and 'being dramatic'. It's a vicious cycle – one might even say . . . 'toxic'.

These language patterns develop at a critical period. In adolescence, one's identity is taking hold in the brain. The words a girl uses to *describe* herself are part of a neural network that is actively being built.* It's the same system that lights up when she compares herself to others and thinks about who she is in the present, past and future – her 'eras', if you will. The words a girl uses during this time – whether 'crazy', 'toxic' or 'ADHD' – play a big role in shaping what she will view as the enduring truth of who she is.

The Backlash, and Where I Stand

In the past few years, people have been weighing in on therapy culture – and increasingly pushing back on it. Popular books and discussions on forums like Reddit express criticism and even contempt for young people who self-diagnose and identify with mental disorders. They blame therapists, patients and would-be patients for promoting weakness and self-indulgence.

Some of the messages I can get behind. Yes, people need to think about one another and not just themselves. Yes, there is more to life than being a patient. Yes, sometimes we just need to do hard things

* The brain is also laying down myelin, a lipid sheath around frequently used neurons that makes their pathways thousands of times more efficient, while neurons that receive less traffic are pruned away.

with discipline and grit. And, yes, sometimes we even need to stop talking about our feelings and just *deal*.

But the pushback has grown into a full-on assault against the fundamental values of the mental health profession. Some even go as far as to argue that time-tested, evidence-based psychiatric treatments are *causing* the mental health crisis. They suggest eating more protein, focusing on family, getting outside more. Nothing wrong with pursuing personal goals and a healthy lifestyle, but that is not the answer for many people. It's human nature to be tormented by difficult feelings, and it is common to experience psychiatric symptoms. We all have private problems, and we are all capable of getting in our own way. No matter how we lead our lives, people need other human beings who can offer a special kind of listening – and, sometimes, medication.

The temptation, when one grows exhausted by therapy culture, is to react with two forms of impatience: dismissiveness, on the one hand, and panic on the other. Some people – parents, for example – might try to help by normalising a young woman's suffering as just 'typical drama' that she'll get over. And, spoiler alert: normalising feelings is part of what I'm going to recommend when I get to the what-to-do. But the risk of normalising too reflexively – 'don't worry, it's fine, this is what kids go through' – is that you might miss something important about how a person feels. If you do that over and over again, you risk making her problem much worse – even if it's true that the underlying problem is 'normal'.

On the other side, parents often live in fear of their teenagers' strong emotions. They don't want to be neglectful and, of course, they don't want their child to harm herself, so they take therapy speak too literally. ('Blake is having anxiety – call the doctor!') This reaction is also counterproductive. Not only does it contribute to overpathologising, but it skips the essential step of connecting with the child: asking 'gentle questions' (as a patient of mine once put it); joining her feelings; figuring out what the problems are underlying the symptoms and helping her think through it all; giving her reasons to feel hopeful; sharing your own difficult experiences; trying to understand; and continuing to see her as a full human being whose symptoms may, in fact, make sense. Adults must continue to do this, even if their child is also working with a mental health professional.

And then, some people who are sick of therapy culture can be fully unsympathetic and even kind of mean. 'Back in the old days, nobody spoke like this.' 'Look at people living in poverty, in war zones.' The message is: those people have *real* problems. We can see this kind of thinking in the rise of 'Fuck Around and Find Out' (FAFO) parenting, which rejects the focus on feelings and emotional safety promoted by the 'gentle parenting' movement.

This change in the tide away from emotion is notably gendered. Concerns about therapy culture are curdling into ancient misogynistic ideas – for instance, that women, in their focus on feelings, have ruined the workforce.

Shaming girls – sending the signal that *I have no desire to engage with your feelings and refuse to take them seriously* – can only push them to find other ways to make their troubles seem valid. And the best way for them to do that is to present their symptoms as diseases: 'You can't ignore me if I have a *medical diagnosis*.' And around and around we go.

Gen Z has already distinguished itself through a laser focus on mental health. Several studies report that they've deemed it their *number one social issue,* above climate change and racial inequality. But they report feeling discounted by the adults they know, and on the list of sources they trust about mental health, they place their parents dead last. Access to care and affordability remain major issues for this generation – as they are for many Americans – and so they find themselves turning to social media for guidance. But they quickly become overwhelmed by the cacophony of voices, the random assortment of good and bad information. Meanwhile, Gen Alpha has grown up exposed to the highest degree of mental health awareness in history, and they will likely benefit from its destigmatisation. But the well-documented forces that have impacted Gen Z's mental health may take an even greater toll on them.

Finding Our Way Back

It's time to move beyond the reflexive and ubiquitous use of therapy speak. To parents, teachers and mentors: I hope that this book is going to help you listen. When girls speak this way, it's meaningful. They are trying to illustrate what they are going through, and a lot of that is hard to describe. But it does mean something is not okay; your job is to keep up your curiosity and your drive to understand.

To the young women who rely on therapy speak: I hope this book is going to help you get heard. Whatever ails you, the people you are trying to reach – your parents, your teachers, your friends – should listen to what you are saying. In this book, I'm going to try to help you learn how to speak in a louder, clearer and more personal voice. The capacity to be a good translator – to know and express one's mind and to engage with the minds of others – is the secret to emotional health and good relationships, generative work environments and thriving societies.

Why Therapy Stories?

The stories in this book show how girls can grow to understand themselves better and find relief. They demonstrate the uneasy process of young women developing increased self-compassion and a decreased drive to pathologise their pain. And they take place in therapy because that's what I do – not because that's the only way to grow and change.

Still, there is value in portraying the therapeutic process. Sceptics have good reason to wonder what goes on in the clinic, and the office, past the noise machine and the soundproof door. From a bird's-eye view, our collective mental health has only got worse over time.

Could it be that our treatments aren't working? (And, yet, the same is true of our physical health. Diabetes and heart disease and cancer continue to plague the modern body, and that's not because we don't have good doctors or good medicine.) Do we direct patients towards illness labels for themselves, their loved ones and their relationships?

As I've listened to therapy speak over the years, I have observed that these terms often do the exact *opposite* of what we aim for in a treatment. Therapy culture can be judgemental, distancing and disempowering. I am hoping these stories can clear up some of the differences between therapy culture and therapy itself.

And so, you're going to see what it's like to be in the therapist's chair, as I react to my patients and hope that something I say lands, get excited when it does, and frustrated when it doesn't. I do this intentionally. The process of individual psychotherapy is awkward and intimate. It has to be, in order to work. It's about two people being authentically close in a way that's usually not possible out in the world because of the way people keep themselves hidden.

These stories also show forces in the culture that cause my patients to struggle. Please note that the patients I describe in this book have certain kinds of problems. There are many problems they *don't* have. They are not the young women dealing with the most serious mental illnesses. They are not the ones struggling to put food on the table, or raising younger siblings because they have a single mother who is working four jobs. Some of the major social determinants of mental health – poverty, racial discrimination, access to care – are beyond the scope of this book.

I will depict the pressures girls feel – to perform, to be happy, to be fulfilled. You will see how our tolerance as a society for messy emotions and inefficiency has remained meagre. Human suffering continues to show up in forms as varied and protean as clouds in the sky.

And, of course, not everybody needs therapy. Research also shows that teenagers can derive some of the same benefits from positive relationships in many contexts – with friends, with teachers and through ongoing connections with their primary caregivers. One can grow from a relationship with a religious community, a sport team or a fandom. The task of adolescence is to figure out how you feel and who you are because of it, and I think we can do a lot better for future generations than leading everyone to believe there is something wrong with their brain. But they need meaningful relationships in order to do that work. They need listening, understanding and translating. These days, here in Babel, that's more important than ever. I'm hoping this book can help.

PART ONE

How We Got Here

1

Diagnosed

Sometimes it's good to know and to name things, don't misunderstand me. But this, it's like, everything is labeled. So in effect, you never say what you feel.

Esther Perel,
Where Should We Begin?

Translation takes time, and it is time, concentrated. This is its gift.

Cristina Rivera Garza,
'A Stacking of Translations and the Affect of the Here-and-Now'

I. Alphabet Soup

Violet is seven minutes late for our first appointment. I sit in my therapist chair, staring out the window onto the tree-lined Manhattan side street. It is June. A young couple shares a sandwich on a stoop. A police officer saunters towards a double-parked car. A dog lifts its leg to pee on a pile of garbage bags.

Then the buzzer sounds. I hear footsteps on the stairs. She knocks softly on my office door, and there she is: petite, messy blond ponytail, tattered tote bag. She gives me a solemn once-over as if she still hasn't decided whether to go through with this or not. After a pause, she walks in.

I seem to have passed the first test. But not by much.

Violet settles into the chair opposite mine, manspreading, then reaches into her bag and takes out a banana. She peels it, breaks off a large piece, and begins to nibble sideways, looking absently around the room. Then she puts both the peel and the half-eaten banana on my side table and wipes the thin, sticky residue on her cargo pants.

'Sorry, I don't know why I'm so gross,' she says.

'That's fine,' I say quickly. With any new patient, those first few moments are crucial. I'm going for nonjudgemental, reassuring. It's easy to get off on the wrong foot with a teenager and never see them again.

'Well,' she sighs. 'I guess I should tell you about my OCD.'

'OCD?' I scribble in my notebook and look up at her.

'And my PMDD. And my ADHD,' she adds, wearily. 'And my depression.'

Violet is seventeen. Before this appointment, her parents told me she had seen a few doctors – a psychoanalyst who told her she was 'hysterical', a behavioural therapist who provided breathing techniques, and a psychopharmacologist who moved away – but no treatment took hold long enough to help her now. In the process, she accumulated a pile of diagnoses. She is like so many young women I see these days, who either receive multiple labels from elsewhere or identify them independently off the internet and apply them to themselves. By the time they get to me, those labels have often grown quite . . . sticky.

When I hear Violet's litany of diagnoses, I am reminded that a doctor's first obligation is to 'do no harm'. If I confirm these diagnoses and follow evidence-based practice, Violet will need a cocktail of medications, including, at minimum, a high-dose antidepressant that can target her OCD symptoms, and a medicine for ADHD, likely a stimulant – a long-acting one for the school day, as well as a short-acting booster dose for the homework hours, both of which could possibly make her anxiety symptoms worse and might affect her sleep, which would in turn worsen her psychiatric issues across the board. I don't like to medicate teenagers for sleep, but if she's massively helped by the stimulant, one could argue, why not just treat the sleep, too? What matters is how she feels, and how she functions. Birth control would also probably help with the PMDD, or premenstrual dysphoric disorder.

But that's just the meds. As they say, 'Pills don't build skills.' In addition, she will need a variety of therapies. For her OCD, the most evidence-based treatment is exposure and response prevention. It consists of gradual exposure to the anxiety-producing stimulus, whatever that turns out to be for her, coupled with coping skills like breathing, to help her increasingly tolerate the discomfort of the exposure. She'll need executive function coaching for her ADHD, which teaches her the organisational skills she lacks: how to plan, triage work tasks, estimate how much time they will take, and set achievable goals. Apart from that, she would benefit from cognitive behaviour therapy for her depression, helping her identify and combat the automatic negative thoughts telling her bad things about herself, with the goal of entering a more positive cycle. And if that's not enough to help her feel normal, okay or like herself again, she will also require general talk therapy with a supportive or psychodynamically informed therapist to put it all together, help her reflect on her life, her family and her relationships, and to salvage some narrative about who, underneath all of this, she is. That ought to do it. But where will she find the time? She'll have to quit most of her activities, just for a while. I'll write letters to the school, the coaches, whoever needs to hear from a professional: she's struggling; she's ill. But she's 'getting the help she needs', right?

There must be a different way of fathoming human suffering than through this alphabet soup of pathologies. Surely, there is something that hurts in Violet, something she is trying to communicate to me through this medical language. But its excesses – in number of diagnoses, in implied degree of disability, and in these words as substitution for actual descriptions of feelings or stories in her life – make me uneasy. And that's a tough way to begin a therapeutic process.

What Is a Teenager?

Adolescence was first named as a distinct stage of life by a psychologist named G Stanley Hall in 1904, and since then experts have had a lot to say about it. Sigmund Freud saw it as the final stage of a developmental course oriented towards reproduction, filled with new levels of inner conflict between a person's emerging desires and their sense of right and wrong. According to psychologist Jean Piaget, adolescence ushered in the final stages of intellectual and imaginative capacity, giving the mind a profound sensitivity to the world and an unchecked fascination with one's own thoughts. Lawrence Kohlberg and Carol Gilligan connected this intellectual growth to the refinement of the teenager's moral sense, and Anna Freud noted how the fluctuation of personal and emotional qualities – '*more idealistic, artistic, generous, unselfish than he will ever be again, but also the opposite – self-centred, egoistic, calculating*' – would be '*deemed highly abnormal at any other time of life*'. It was these extremes of intensity that drove Hall to label adolescence as a time of '*sturm und drang*', or 'storm and stress'.

Ambivalence – including loving one's parents one moment and hating them the next – is also par for the course. Teenagers are the world's biggest hypocrites. They'll show fascination with a topic one day, and be totally uninterested the next; they'll admire and wish for success, but appear allergic to doing the basic things that will bring it to them; they'll express an almost religious reverence for things that are 'real' or 'matter', but grow preoccupied with trivialities and can seem content to lie to others and themselves. They can be demanding yet cold, arrogant yet ignorant, concerned with nothing but friends yet entirely self-focused, obsessed with directness yet passive-aggressive. This is because they are facing new frontiers of emotion and newly complex life problems, and also because they are trying to solve these new problems on their own, and wind up regressing to a toddler-like state in which their wants seem to require immediate gratification, and their frustrations are quick to bring out controlling behaviour if not full-on tantrums.

Those emotions can be disorienting, and teenagers can sometimes feel quite miserable. Scientists have observed that, over the span of a week, adolescents are more euphoric and more depressed than adults. Their positive feelings are shorter-lived, and their emotional responses are glued to the social world. As they contend with this instability, they are also compelled to withdraw from their family and place their trust in the often less reliable – but singularly important – hands of peers.

The adolescent brain develops in a sequence that explains typical teenage behaviour. The emotional centres of the brain mature rapidly during this time, providing a structure to propel the tumbling hormones set in motion by puberty. Meanwhile, the prefrontal cortex, the seat of executive functions like planning, self-regulation and impulse control, is still being built. The adolescent is uniquely poised to feel sharper and deeper excitement, love and pain than at any other time in life. This asynchrony is not a developmental malfunction; it's likely an adaptive setup for later flourishing. The intensity of these experiences drives motivation and creativity, and provides the necessary burst of energy to launch a person out of childhood and towards becoming who they are.

A teenager is obsessed with who she is. That may read to some as being 'obsessed with herself'. I'd put it a bit differently: she's obsessed with her *Self*. This is the central task of adolescence, according to psychoanalyst Erik Erikson, who conceived of human life as a series of tensions specific to each developmental stage. Identity is not an abstract concept; it doesn't just mean who you 'are' in some vague sense. It's an emotional experience of daily life: it means *Why are you important?* (And implicit in that: *Are you important?*) She looks to the world to help her form a self-concept that is accurate, useful and whole.

One thing that differentiates adolescence from other stages is that it's culturally determined. A child's body becomes an adult's body, but it's culture that dictates what is expected of that person at various stages. Different groups have struggled with how to mark entrance to so-called adulthood with ceremonies like the Bar or Bat Mitzvah, the quinceañera and the Sweet Sixteen, but those who have traversed these milestones have years and sometimes a decade left to live before anyone in their right mind would say *This is an adult*. When does that time come? When you get a driver's licence? A bank account? Know how to make chicken? When you start paying for your own phone contract? When you can shoulder your own rent? Some say it's when you become a parent yourself. And what if you never do any of those things: what is the measure of growing up? Decades ago, adolescence was considered over when a person turned eighteen and presumably moved out of the childhood home. Now we know that the prefrontal cortex develops into at least the mid-twenties, which helps to explain why adolescence lasts longer than the teen years. As a culture, we have increasingly made room for this lengthy developmental course. Spanning (conservatively) from ages twelve through the mid twenties, the adolescent phase and the forming of the adult Self occupies at least ten years of a person's life.

If adolescence keeps getting longer and is marked by a unique fascination with one's emotional Self, that may partly explain why therapy culture takes up ever more real estate – and why therapy speak has become the lingua franca of the young woman.

I sit there with Violet, my head cocked to the side, milking the slow, silent nod that is the hallmark, and the secret weapon, of the psychiatrist. We wisdom-signal; we cultivate an atmosphere of calm reflection, while inside, we deal with our own blundering reactions: *What is up with all these diagnoses?*

Violet speaks in a soft voice with a hint of gravel; her apparent coolness glows with inner desperation. I don't know much about her yet, but I picture artsy parents who are always on the verge of getting divorced and share a home well stocked with pistachio milk and piles of old *New Yorkers*. After about thirty minutes of talking, it's clear that Violet has absorbed the vocabulary of hypereducated, urban girlhood – she's a simmering cauldron of privilege and guilt. She is fluent in post-colonial, post-structural, post–fourth wave feminist, post-Freudian, post-everything, and if you say the wrong thing she will take you right down. And yet, her eyes check in with mine for a millisecond here and there, as if she's awaiting my approval. It seems exhausting to be Violet. I find myself wishing I could just take her out for ice cream, give her a bit more time as a little girl.

The richness of Violet's monologue draws me in, but just as she begins sharing a personal story, she circles back to her diagnoses: *I guess I get stuck in these spirals because of my OCD . . . sorry I'm so all over the place, I just have really bad ADHD . . . Last week I was just feeling so depressed and I know this happens to me mid-cycle from my PMDD . . .* A cascade of medical problems tumbles out, unfolding layers of broken upon broken. She's here, in my office, supposedly trying to invite me into her world, but with each acronym, I feel like I know less and less about her.

The Task

Occam's razor, or the law of parsimony, guides medical practice. Popularised by William of Ockham, a fourteenth-century English philosopher and theologian, it states: 'Entities are not to be multiplied beyond necessity,' or more commonly, 'The simplest explanation is usually the correct one.' The theory has been upheld as a model for philosophers, mathematicians, statisticians, physicists and physicians. In medicine, we use the adage 'When you hear hoofbeats, think of horses, not zebras.' Parsimony is necessary to be effective as a clinician. Sitting with a patient, you can only examine one problem at a time.

One would think that, when a psychiatrist and their patient sit down and talk, the task would be clear. But one of the most confounding aspects of psychiatry is that so often the opposite is true. For example, with Violet: Is she coming by choice, or because her parents forced her? Does she believe she is here for medication, therapy or both – and who should decide that? We must establish what she believes is causing her problems, and what I believe, and find a way to agree. We will not succeed unless she is coming to do some form of *work* on herself. This is called the 'therapeutic alliance' – a shared sense of the task and commitment to the effort it entails. It's especially important – and tricky – to establish this alliance with teenage girls.

Many patients in therapy know *why* they are there, but couldn't tell you *what* they are working on, exactly. The truth is, doctors don't always know, either. Even if the patient and doctor agree the problem is, say, 'depression', they have to decide which of the many potential causes of the depression they are going to focus on. Is it a genetic or biological problem for which medications are the most obvious solution? Would a behavioural approach, like discussing the value and logistics of sleep, nutrition and exercise, be better? Perhaps unhelpful thought patterns need to be interrogated and modified. Maybe it's unprocessed rage at loved ones that the patient has turned against herself. And even when doctors and patients agree on all of this, patients aren't always ready to do the heavy lifting required.

My response to Violet – 'That's a lot of diagnoses' – does not land well.

She takes a laboured sigh. 'Yeah . . . I don't know.' She looks around the room. She eyes the painting to my left, the diplomas to my right, unmoved. 'So I guess we'll be meeting at this time next week?'

Peer Supervision

A few days later, in my weekly peer supervision, I am eager to tell my colleagues Zach and Eloise the story of my first meeting with Violet.

Therapists supervise one another throughout our careers. In supervision, mental health professionals review and discuss cases, analyse each other's thinking about patients, and also examine the emotional responses that can make our work so challenging.

Over the years, as my work with teenagers and young adults has deepened, these meetings have become a lifeline for me. They've given me support when I hit a wall with a patient, and help me track what's going on in the *transference* and *countertransference*. 'Transference' is when someone in the present, such as the therapist, brings up old feelings the patient has towards someone else. 'Countertransference' refers to what feelings come up in the therapist around the patient, and what that says about the patient herself. An emotionally charged reaction to a patient is information that can guide the treatment.

The three of us gather in my office and pull the chairs into a closer circle. Zach is an MD psychiatrist like me, who almost became a surgeon, but then realised he would rather have a job where he could really get to know his patients. Plus, he decided he'd prefer to spend his life reading journal articles about the human condition than about the latest developments in suture technology. Eloise is a few years older than Zach and me. She's a PhD psychologist, not a psychiatrist. After graduate school she spent several more years becoming a psychoanalyst. When Zach and I became pals in residency, Eloise was finishing her analytic training at the same hospital. We worked together on a case conference and hit it off as a group. Now we all see patients in New York City, and we all think day and night about the biological, psychological, and social factors that cause symptoms and suffering.

But our differences are what keep us engaged in an ongoing conversation that is practical, philosophical and, at times, emotional. Zach is always the pragmatist and tends to favour the biological and medical model of psychiatric care: 'You can't argue with results,' he likes to say. Eloise sees some of her patients multiple times a week. They lie on a couch in her office, talk about their dreams and fantasies, and she offers interpretations. And as for me, I am somewhere in the middle, always trying to, well . . . suture it all together – to translate back and forth.

I fall into my chair and start to tell them about Violet.

'She's so smart and articulate. She's funny, and self-aware, and *compelling*. But almost immediately, the main thing she emphasises is that she is a sick person – not to mention, a "gross" person.'

'Maybe she *is* a sick person,' Zach says. 'Maybe these are just her diagnoses.'

Right away Zach and I are representing two camps. He's on Team Psychiatry: that there are brain diseases that people have, that we diagnose them by examining their symptoms. Things are as they seem. He is also taking the position that she *knows* what her illnesses are. The famous physician Sir William Osler would probably agree. He said: 'listen to your patient. He is telling you the diagnosis.'

On the other hand, I have a nagging feeling that both of those points are wrong in this case. First, the idea that these diseases are *things* – entities existing in nature that just are what they are. I've never been so sure. Psychiatric symptoms cluster into what we call illnesses, and these can be extremely debilitating for people. But they are not as clear-cut as medical illnesses. We have no brain scans or blood tests to diagnose them, and most professionals would agree that they are complex entities – products of the interaction between biology, psychology and culture.

And to the second point, maybe Violet *is* sick, in all these ways. It scares me to imagine missing how sick she might be. As a psychotherapist, you must be aware of your own blind spots, and one of mine is mistaking intelligence for health, especially when I think someone is cool and interesting. But what is the difference between a high-functioning 'sick' person and someone who is just suffering a lot and not coping well?

'It's something about the way she uses these diagnoses,' I say. 'The *passivity* of *having* illnesses. The *helplessness* of being someone with so many afflictions.' This is my countertransference, telling me there might be more going on.

Zach and Eloise both nod.

What I'm getting at is that these words are being used as *defences*. Defences, also known as 'coping mechanisms', are all the many things we do in our personalities to protect ourselves from feelings we don't like having. They are typically picked up in childhood and become involuntary and automatic, making up the masks we use to meet the world. Defences protect us from feelings that are difficult for us, usually feelings we see as 'negative', like sadness – or feelings in conflict with one another, like being disappointed in someone you respect. Getting too close to difficult feelings can cause anxiety, so defences function to ward off both the feelings themselves and the anxiety they produce. When defences function well, they help people accept and deal with reality. When defences do not function well, they help us avoid reality or deal with it poorly.

Often, people's problems in life are caused by using defences that don't quite work as they get older. Some of these include black-and-white thinking, self-blame and helplessness. As awful as it might be to live in a world of self-blame, for example, at some point the person using this defence decided it was the lesser of two evils. The other, worse alternative, was probably feeling rage at a loved one early in life. Because we love our parents and caregivers, we – especially children – don't want to be too angry at them. A child might choose to suppress that angry feeling and decide everything is her own fault instead. She would rather sacrifice herself and protect her parents from that feeling inside of her.

One of my main jobs as a therapist is to get to know a patient's defences and to help her get to know them, too. Defences are necessary to function as a human, so the goal of therapy is not to take them away, but rather to see if the current ones are serving the person well. I'm wondering if Violet is using psychiatric labels not only as an attempt to find the truth about herself but also as a defence against it.

'It's too early to know what the diagnoses mean,' Eloise says, peeling the foil top off her yoghurt and setting it on my side table. 'You're just at the beginning of this treatment and you have to establish a therapeutic relationship first. Just let her keep talking.'

Faux Pas

Violet and I are now meeting weekly. She's always late. And she always starts with an opening monologue that goes something like this: *Yeah, so this week was pretty crazy for me . . . I was feeling kind of agitated and manic on Wednesday, and the next morning I just woke up feeling like everything around me was just kind of menacing and dystopian . . . and then I just kind of went downhill from there, I don't know* . . . And then, she drifts off.

What should I say in response? I ask some questions about timelines, triggers, context, any actual events, current or past, that might be related to her distress. What are her friends like? Who is she to other people, and how does she feel? What is family life like? Does she have specific ambitions in life? What does she *want*? But when we get close to anything that makes sense to me, she drifts away to another day, another fragment of a story.

'Violet . . . this is all a little . . . vague . . . do you know what I mean?' I say.

Her dull eyes flash: 'That's obvious.'

'Okay, then. So, what would you like us to focus on?'

But she sighs and offers a withering critique of those who feel the need to focus.

Week after week, the same thing. I am curious about what happens when we take the conversation in different directions. Sometimes you can learn a lot about a patient by moving away from the more anxiety-producing 'therapy' material. Violet is quite charming. We exchange praise of new novels and TV dramas. She relaxes, seems freer to express her quirky opinions.

'I love it that you're drinking a Diet Coke,' she says with a warm smile. 'That is *so subversive*.'

But every time, after I feel the high of these exchanges, an emptiness sets in. The conversation is pleasant, but ephemeral – it's a word cloud: 'iconic'; 'derivative'; 'devastating'. I lose my bearings; I'm not sure what we are talking about or what the subtext is, except that this is starting to feel like a Beckett play. Are we doing therapy, or avoiding therapy? Is she very sick, or not sick at all? What was our agreed-upon task again?

I recognise this is all part of my countertransference, those feelings that are induced in me by being in her presence. She must feel a certain high when she's in angst-ridden intelligentsia mode, because *I* feel it. She must feel an emptiness underneath it, because *I* feel that, too. She must feel lost and afraid in other relationships just like *I* feel, so far, in ours.

And so, in every session, our riffs dissipate into thin air. That's when she refers to her MDD, or her OCD, or her PMDD, or her ADHD, or some combination thereof. When I ask for an example of how these illnesses manifest, she squirms and scowls: I am putting too much pressure on her; I am thick-skulled for needing it all spelled out. As the sessions go by, my thoughts, like the treatment, like Violet, become Escher staircases, artfully going nowhere.

Months have passed, and Violet is late again. And when she does arrive, it starts like this: *Yeah, so last Thursday I was feeling really bipolar so I wound up going for a long run, which kind of just made things worse, and then I was just hyper and couldn't focus on anything – just kind of an ADHD meltdown, you know? [Sigh.] But then I got my period, and I was, like, fine for a few days, but then on Saturday I just got really depressed and started spiralling again.*

She may have arrived physically in my office, but she is still not here. How can we move forward – in this session, or ever?

Finally, towards the end of our time together, I can't take it anymore. 'Violet,' I say, 'the thing is . . . I don't think you are depressed, exactly.'

Silence. Violet looks shocked, as if I've slapped her. Then, rhythmic sniffles, a reddening face, then tears, then rage: 'This is what always happens to me!' she sobs. Her voice is raw and urgent. 'Nobody ever understands how I feel.'

This is it: the real emotion, in a context that makes sense, towards *me,* a real person. Except, not even: without either of us knowing it, I have just become someone really bad to her – a *kind* of person who has hurt her in the past. She is having a transference experience. These are the heated moments in therapy where everything is on the line: this could be the end of the treatment, or the beginning. And here we are at the end of the session. What can I say, except what therapists always say when time is up?

'Violet, what you're saying is very important. I hope we can discuss it more the next time we meet.'

She gets up and walks out. She did not refuse this offer, but she did not accept it, either.

I notice the licked yoghurt foil still lying on the side table from the peer supervision session. *Just let her keep talking,* Eloise had said. At a certain point, though, you no longer get that chance.

As I'm walking home through the park near my office, feeling the light hollowness of failure, I realise why it is such a challenge to connect with Violet: *She's* the one telling *me* what the diagnoses are – but aren't I the doctor? Strangely, her passive, dreamy behaviour and her use of therapy words have been mobilised towards control. When I said '*I don't think you are depressed*,' I was taking control back. Deprived of the protection that control had provided, her real fears came out: that I was going to misunderstand her, not take her seriously. Without knowing it, through her way of speaking and acting towards me, she had provoked the very response from me she feared the most.

The session immediately following a bad one feels like the morning after a night of drunken mistakes: nobody is quite sure what happened, if bridges were burned or if life will continue as it was before. Somehow, Violet and I carry on in the basic way that therapists and patients do: she shows up.

On time, she sits down with a determination on her face that I've never seen before.

'You're just like everyone else, Dr Garfinkle,' she spits. 'You're just like my mother.'

Finally: something real. I'm not even upset. I just want to know everything. That's exactly what Violet begins to tell me.

Story #1: 'My weekend was horrible . . .' Tears spilling down her face. She's silent for a few beats. (She never takes a tissue, and she hates it when I offer.)

I wait.

'We hosted this holiday party for my dad's colleagues. I was doing my usual thing . . . holding court, entertaining all of my parents' guests. But I was also just feeling like kind of weird and empty the whole time – just like tired, you know? . . .'

'Yes.' I soften towards her.

'Anyway, so my dad pulls me aside and is like, *"What's with the frown, kiddo? Do you need me to put on a cartoon in the other room?"* He thought it was funny. But then I was so annoyed. Like, my parents just care about impressing all of these people, but these people don't care about them. They're all just bad people, you know? – and maybe my parents are, too. Does that make *me* a bad person for thinking that?'

'No, it doesn't.' I wish I could give her a hug.

Story #2: 'Last spring I broke my ankle. I couldn't really move for several months and the pain was horrible . . . and my mom was like . . . totally weird about it. I would tell her it hurt, and she would . . . like . . . almost get mad at me. Like she was *allergic* to me. Like it was almost . . . disgusting to her.'

Gross, even.

Story #3: 'This girl on Saturday said it was "intimidatin" how I always keep my coat on at parties. She was like, "Why do you never seem to care about anything?" and it just so happened I was having a horrible night. It was immensely alienating.'

I know those people who keep their coats on at parties, as if they have somewhere else to be, always one foot out the door. *Like she is, here.*

'Alienating?'

'Just like' – and now she starts to cry again – 'no one has any idea about my social anxiety.'

It's all starting to make sense. This kid fiercely hides her vulnerabilities and feels so alone.

Story #4: 'Have I ever told you about my relationship with Finsta?' (This is 'Fake Insta', a secondary, private Instagram account where teenagers share more personal information.) 'Well, last night I had had this deeply traumatic interaction with my ex, and after that I was strangely agitated and I posted this wildly dissociated rant . . .'

On the dark pages of social media, she connects with strangers who give her support, but her friends in school are confused by these posts and keep a distance the next day. She's embarrassed, sensing she has gone too far. She feels hopelessly alone.

There are forces in her family that I don't yet understand. I'm hearing that she has been raised to feel that her vulnerabilities are embarrassing for some reason – whatever caused it, she's at war with herself. She's not able to translate ordinary feelings into ordinary words. On top of that, I hear the slew of culturally sponsored insecurities most girls encounter at one time or another: feeling self-conscious about eating and her body, feeling misunderstood by others and socially unsure – but she does not have the perspective to accept these experiences as part of life.

Violet just might have a raging case of Modern American Girlhood – marked with the insignia of her own temperament and family history. In her tiny subculture, there seems to be an emphasis on performance and appearances (of the sophisticated, boho variety), and a discomfort with vulnerability and need. These family dynamics have repeated thousands, millions of times, as they do for all of us, and created in Violet various beliefs, expectations and frustrated longings. In her own unique context, she's playing a role that befalls many girls – especially those who are smart, sensitive and articulate. She's learned to tune in to what's expected of her rather than listening to her own wants, reactions and opinions – and it's reached a point where she no longer knows what those are. As a means of survival, her mind has found a million ways, and a handful of words, to keep her from being present.

These problems may cause her various symptoms, but I'm starting to see how her myriad diagnoses serve – rather than describe – her problem. When a person can't name or express her painful feelings, they get worse. And when others don't take that pain seriously – because of her difficulty describing it, or their own issues responding to it, or both – she has to scream it louder. A diagnosis allows a girl to convey how very serious the pain is – how much she wants comfort and care – without having to know what she feels. A diagnosis can bring power and attention to her pain while allowing her to keep avoiding it.

Thankfully, we have plenty of time to work this out together.

II. Duelling Narratives

Chloe's mother is possibly the most likable parent I have ever met in my practice. She has shining eyes and an unfussy, glamorous style; her warm smile and relaxed laugh make our initial consultation feel like a social visit she is genuinely enjoying. She compliments my décor; she loves my dog (a Cavapoo who sometimes comes to work with me). She is the kind of mom who probably has loads of best friends.

It is no surprise that she and her daughter Chloe are close. It was often just the two of them at home when Chloe was little, as her mom was an elementary school teacher who finished work in the afternoons, while her dad, a successful restaurant owner in Brooklyn, often worked until late at night.

A few months ago, Chloe's dad, as she put it, 'got Me-Too'd'. One of his waitstaff came forward reporting he had been approaching her sexually – then several other women who had worked for him spoke up about similar experiences. He ultimately had to close down the restaurant, and everyone in the neighbourhood knew why.

Like her mom, Chloe is confident and social. But unlike her mom, Chloe is short, with big eyes and frizzy curls fading from what appears to be a rosy hair-dye experiment. Also unlike her mom, she finds this incident with her father to have been a deal-breaker. In her mind, the family unit has been permanently destroyed.

I am impressed by Chloe's fierceness, her moral righteousness and her loyalty. But just as Chloe is trying to call the shots with her parents, she also comes to therapy with marching orders for me.

Despite being a straight-A student at a rigorous high school, she feels there are problems with her executive function and that she must have ADHD. A recent battery of neuropsychological tests did not find her to have ADHD, but despite that, she consulted with another psychiatrist who offered to prescribe stimulants. Chloe also feels she is anxious and depressed. She wants medication for each of these conditions. And above all, there is the trauma.

The trauma from her father did not begin with the sexual harassment incident; rather, that was the breaking point for Chloe. Her father is a volatile man: he can be warm and generous with Chloe, but tone-deaf – like the time he had her room redone, head to toe in *Frozen,* even though she had moved on months before from Arendelle to Hogwarts. He is also quick to anger when he and Chloe disagree. Chloe remembers when he would come home after long hours at the restaurant and yell at her as a small child for making too much noise and leaving her toys in the living room. To this day, they butt heads about everything from what type of groceries to keep in the house to whether or not she has to work over the summer. Chloe is a strong-willed person who usually manages to get her way, but life has been a constant power struggle between the two of them, with her mom in the middle. Worst of all has been what Chloe describes as his overt display of sexuality – sharing stories about his past exploits; flirting with 'all of my friends' moms' in Chloe's presence. There has been no physical abuse, no known sexual abuse, but many moments that surpass ordinary discomfort.

'She says it's trauma, Dr Garfinkle,' her mother pleads, 'but it isn't. Sure, he's a flirt – and yes, he can be moody. But he means well, and he's been through a lot and he loves her. Chloe has a good life.'

Chloe, however, tells a different story. She feels it as a stiffness in her body when he passes by; she feels it when she wakes up from nightmares, her throat dry from screaming. And her mother's dismissal of it is what upsets her most of all.

The word 'trauma' has thrown the cultural conversation about emotional health into crisis. Trauma became a focal point in 2014 when its bible, *The Body Keeps the Score* by Bessel van der Kolk, was published – and even more so in 2021 when that book rose to number one on *The New York Times Best Sellers* list (where it has remained since). Thousands of podcasts have the word 'trauma' in the title, and the 'trauma plot' has become a core Hollywood trope. A wide world of TikTok therapists provides freewheeling advice about what trauma is and how to manage its effects. Social media reverberates with trauma, trauma speak, trauma narratives, trauma dumping; #trauma has 9.2 billion views. In 2022, *Vox* named trauma 'the word of the decade'.

Critiques of what some people call 'trauma culture' – that it's excessive, that it's ubiquitous, that it's stupid – are widespread. The most common one is that trauma is overused as an explanation of any and all problems. Journalist Abigail Shrier makes this case rather bluntly in *Bad Therapy,* where she appears to mock van der Kolk: 'Can't concentrate? Trauma! Trouble forming relationships?

Trauma! Tightness in your chest? Trauma! Cancer, substance abuse, sexual promiscuity, stroke, irritable bowel syndrome? Trauma, trauma, trauma, trauma!'

There is much confusion about what 'counts' as trauma, compounded by the wide variety of tones in which the term is employed, from the very serious to the very tongue-in-cheek. Is there a household in America or Europe where children, new to irony as they might be, have not bandied about the term in the course of complaining that a brother's song is annoying, or that a sister has had too long a turn on the PlayStation? Even when used with humour and hyperbole, it's understood that this word confers power.

Young women occupy both ends of the continuum. On the one hand, if you texted your classmate that the professor's outfit is traumatising, it would be reasonable to expect a good *lol*. On the other hand, girls and young women are the main targets of sexual trauma and abuse – the kind that often drives them to long-term psychological dysfunction, self-harm and suicide.

The truth is, life is filled with potential traumas, large and small. And depending on genetics and temperament, degree of adversity and presence of protections, the brain can experience trauma quite frequently, or not at all.

There is the trauma of giving birth and the trauma of being born. There is the trauma of feeling hungry and the trauma of learning you can't feed yourself – the trauma of depending on others for survival. There is the trauma of realising those others are at best imperfect. There's the trauma of not being able to walk, and then the trauma of being able to walk, and finding yourself small and helpless and on the other side of the room from your protectors. There's the trauma of going to school and the trauma of realising your parents may love you but also love other people besides you. There is the trauma of strict teachers, or apathetic teachers, and walking into a lunchroom and not knowing where to sit; there is the trauma of the forced cheerfulness of summer camp and lonely afternoons at home.

There is the trauma of boredom and the trauma of being so busy that you never get enough rest. There is the trauma of being gifted and the trauma of realising you are ordinary. There's the trauma of mother issues and the trauma of father issues and the trauma of having two parents with different views, or two parents with the same views, and the trauma of having only one parent. There is divorce trauma and holiday trauma and birthday trauma. There is the trauma of gender and the trauma of friendships and sexuality and heartbreak. There is the trauma of having, or not having, social media. There is the trauma of being popular and the trauma of not being popular. There is the trauma of finding out that sex even exists, let alone that people you know have done it, let alone that you might do it, or worse, that you might not. There is the trauma of how your body smells and how easily it can get hurt and that people and animals can die. And that's all if nothing out of the ordinary has ever happened to you.

The decades-long controversy around trauma, in fact, hinges on one word: 'usual'. Trauma was first defined by psychiatry when PTSD was codified as a mental illness requiring an event 'outside the range of usual human experience'. But this definition was soon recognised as too limiting. Feminist groups, for example, noted that sexual violence was, unfortunately, well within 'the range of usual human experience', so in the *DSM-IV,* qualifying events had to involve 'actual or threatened death or serious injury, or other threat to one's physical integrity . . . or a threat to the physical integrity of another person' accompanied by 'intense fear, helplessness, or horror'.

What about purely emotional trauma, or psychological abuse? Theorists got to work expanding the category further. In 1992, psychiatrist Judith Herman published *Trauma and Recovery,* coining the term 'complex post-traumatic stress disorder (c-PTSD)'. This new diagnosis captured the experience of the many people who suffer chronic psychological or 'developmental' trauma, such as neglect by a parent throughout the course of childhood. When the *DSM-5* came out in 2013,* a person could now be traumatised by simply hearing a detailed description of a horrific event from a close family member or friend. This overlapped with another increasingly recognised category: 'intergenerational trauma'.†

And so, all traumas are not the same – and one of trauma's increasingly defining features is that it cannot be determined by outsiders: trauma lies in the body of the beholder.

I am haunted by thoughts of that stiffness Chloe feels in the presence of her father, but I'm not sure what to make of it yet – or how to help her and her mom resolve their differences.

The Trauma Police

My supervision group is back again, thank God.

Zach hardly shows it when something is wrong, but there are telltale signs: glasses instead of contacts is one.

I give him a hug.

'My sleep could be better,' he says. Zach's wife has a very busy job working for the city, his mom is showing signs of early dementia, and they have twin boys in third grade.

Zach covers his face with his hands. 'I've tried using all those sleep hygiene techniques we recommend to patients – but it's hard trying to get to bed by eleven. I've cut out caffeine after three and I keep my phone on that nighttime setting. Early morning light exposure . . . everything. Aren't we supposed to be the experts at this?'

I notice he hasn't mentioned medication. 'Want me to prescribe you some Klonopin?' I say, half jokingly.

'Ha ha. Don't think I haven't thought about it. But all that new

---

* This edition devoted a new section to 'trauma- and stressor-related disorders'.

† 'Intergenerational trauma' was coined in the 1960s by Canadian psychiatrist Vivian Rakoff, who noted high rates of distress in children of Holocaust survivors.

data about the long-term risk of cognitive effects . . . my brain needs to keep working for a long time.'

I'm not going to push it. But I think about how the consequences of *not* treating problems are a factor we often don't consider in psychiatry. I was struck by a study years ago about women with depression in pregnancy. Of course, we try to avoid psych meds in pregnant women, but it turned out the impact of maternal stress hormones on the foetus may be just as harmful as any medication effect.

And I'm also reminded that we can be such hypocrites, as psychiatrists. For example, years ago a senior colleague mentioned she had observed that psychiatrists recommend behavioural treatment and medications to patients but, for ourselves, we tend to seek psychoanalysis or its cousin (the kind of work that I mostly do), psychodynamic therapy. That has tracked with my experience as well.

'Anyway.' Zach scours his eyes. 'You guys talk.'

Eloise and I look at each other and shrug.

'Okay . . .' I begin. 'I have another interesting case.' And I tell them about Chloe, first about the ADHD question.

'Another kid misled to confuse her anxiety for ADHD.' Eloise twirls her hair.

Zach scowls. These two couldn't be more polarised on ADHD. We could easily spend the whole hour on this topic, but there's more I want to get to today.

'I'm conflicted about it, but I'm leaning towards letting her try some ADHD medication,' I say.

'Why are you frowning?' Eloise asks me. 'Why are you conflicted? Like, intellectually, or are you having a conflicted *feeling*?'

'That's a really good question,' I say. Eloise has a knack for going deep.

'Oh,' I sigh. 'Partly the usual. Just how these kids all come in expecting a quick fix. But in this case, for some reason I feel like saying yes, and it's not because I'm blown away by her ADHD symptoms. And . . . this is hard to pin down, but I also feel ever so slightly annoyed. Even though I like this kid so much.'

'What is it that's annoying you?' Eloise asks.

'You know what it is?' I feel myself forming a mad face like a small child. 'She's being *bossy*.'

'Interesting.' Eloise nods. 'Go on.'

'I'm glad she wants to take charge of the treatment, but, like . . . *aren't I the doctor*?'

My colleagues smile knowingly.

'Just trust the process,' Eloise reminds me. 'Listen to that feeling. And be patient.'

Patience has never been my strongest attribute, and I'm grateful for Eloise. I look at the clock, glad we still have a few minutes.

'But here's the other thing with Chloe.' And I tell Zach and Eloise all about the whole trauma debate. 'I'm in the middle of this language battle between the mom and the daughter.'

'The trauma police! We've all been there,' Zach says.

'Why do *you* have to be the one to decide if it's trauma or not?' Eloise asks.

'Yes, and how come they can't just agree to disagree?' says Zach.

'Good question,' I say. And that's when it dawns on me – something I'm starting to see about Chloe that might be the key to helping her.

Trust the Process

Chloe is right on time for her next appointment.

'So I was thinking about it, and I'm also concerned about anxiety,' she begins, broad smile like her mom's. 'I think I've always had that, too.'

Maybe so. 'Tell me more.'

Chloe describes how she grew up always wanting her mom close by. She never went to sleepaway camp. If her mom ever travelled to go to conferences, Chloe was certain her mother would die in a plane crash.

Classic signs of separation anxiety. And she comes by it honestly:

having a warm, cosy parent and an overwhelming and sometimes terrifying parent would make any young person afraid of what lies outside the apron strings.

'There's also my OCD. When I make up my mind, things have to be a certain way. Like when I was a kid and decided not to do soccer anymore, there was no talking me out of it. When I decide on an outfit, *that's* what I'm wearing. No discussions.'

When a child feels overwhelmed by either internal or external stimuli, one natural response is to try to control oneself and one's environment. I'm wondering if that's what she means by 'OCD' here. Historically, OCD has been considered an anxiety disorder,* and there are many theories of what causes it: biological factors, including genetics, infections and abnormal brain circuits, and also psychological factors, like a need to control one's environment because all of the stimuli coming from both inside and outside just feel like too much.

OCD often gets used colloquially as a synonym for perfectionism or being a control freak. The reason this is usually not describing real OCD is that people with the disorder are deeply bothered by their obsessive thoughts and compulsive behaviours.† What Chloe is talking about here is just being rigid, and it's unclear whether she thinks there is something wrong with that. Rigidity, in itself, is a personality trait. One can see it in the autism spectrum, anxiety disorders and even ADHD as a way to deal with cognitive and emotional chaos inside. The chicken-egg diagnostic issues are impossible to disentangle at this early stage.

But Chloe is insistent about wanting her diagnosis and treatment

* This was changed in *DSM-5* (2013), and OCD is now listed under 'Obsessive-Compulsive and Related Disorders'.

† Someone who is simply a 'control freak' would be more likely to have the lesser-known 'obsessive-compulsive personality disorder' (OCPD), in which people are very particular and believe they are simply right and everyone else is wrong. They do not usually present for treatment, however, because they do not feel that they have a problem.

a certain way, and right now. With some patients, my gut might tell me to push back. With Chloe, my instinct is the opposite.

'And what about my depression? Can we treat that?' she asks.

I give this one a moment. 'Chloe, I believe you are very sad. And you definitely have some symptoms of depression.'

Chloe looks at me askance. 'And the trauma?'

I'm getting a clearer sense of what's going on, and what Chloe needs. Maybe 'trusting the process' is working. 'Yes,' I say, gathering all the resonance my voice can find. 'I hear you. Let's stop there for today.'

The next time my supervision group meets, we all make it to my office just as one of those summer storms rolls in, where the sky suddenly gets very dark ahead of distant thunder and terrific rain.

We stare out the window as a gusty downpour batters the tree.

As Eloise watches the weather, her curls look especially luxurious. She snaps out of her reverie. 'So how's your patient from last week, the one who wants the meds for ADHD?'

'I'm not sure ADHD is what Chloe has,' I say. 'But she's sure she has it, and I think if I push back too hard this kid is going to go get the meds somewhere else.'

'And you can't treat a patient who isn't your patient,' Zach adds.

It's hard to hold that line between scepticism and immediately gratifying what patients ask for. I have to be in two places at once: fully with her but also apart from her.

'Right,' I go on. 'And this girl, like so many young women, is used to not being taken seriously. I think she'll do better if I convey my genuine ambivalence about the diagnosis but go with her request – and keep her in close follow-up, eyes open as we move forward.'

'Sounds reasonable,' says Zach.

I look at Zach. I look at Eloise. 'Guys,' I say, 'this case is all about *control*.'

'Ooh, do tell,' says Eloise.

'Let me back up. I've learned some more since last time we met. For example, she and her mom are extremely close, and I think she's struggling with some separation anxiety. They could use a bit of breathing room.'

'So, do you think she's more of an OCD kid? I'm wondering where this is going,' Zach says.

'Funny you should say that. We did talk about OCD – but no, I don't think that's her problem.'

I explain to Zach and Eloise how I believe the control issue relates to her insistence on these various psychiatric diagnoses. Chloe is leaning extra hard on her chosen words to define herself – on her own terms.

'Interesting!' Eloise turns her chair to face me head-on.

'So, I can educate Chloe about those psychiatric syndromes, but I don't want to stomp on her budding autonomy.'

'Yes,' says Eloise.

'I mean, she's used to feeling unheard,' I continue, 'so the most important thing is for her to feel like I'm listening.'

Eloise smiles. 'Sounds like you are getting somewhere.'

A few days later, I see Chloe's mom for an appointment. 'I feel for you. I do,' I tell her. 'But it's Chloe's treatment, so I think she should decide. If she says it's trauma, let's call it trauma.'

Her mom looks down.

I get it. It's hard for this mom to imagine a doctor siding with a notion she views as extreme. Moreover, she's reluctant to swallow her pride about the family she has worked so hard to hold together, and to let go of her wish that the family life had been easier. The word 'trauma' forces her to look at her own marriage in ways she had not expected in sending her daughter to therapy, and to see things she has not wanted to see.

The next day I get a phone call from an unknown number. When I pick up, a male voice introduces himself. It's Chloe's dad.

'Look, I know my daughter can be very convincing,' he begins. 'But really . . . *trauma*? We are a very loving family. I am concerned that she is going to use her therapy to turn against us. I'm hoping you can give her some skills to handle this differently.'

'I understand your concern,' I say, trying not to sound like customer service but very conscious to hold a boundary for my patient. I don't have Chloe's permission to have a full conversation with her dad yet, but I feel obligated, ethically, to connect with parents – to offer them some preliminary understanding. I believe that most parents, whatever their flaws, are trying their best.

'Sometimes kids use language that's imprecise. I don't know Chloe well enough yet to say. But at least early on in a treatment, I try not to argue back too much.'

'But I don't understand,' he continues, in anguish. 'Are you saying she's traumatised and it's my fault?'

I take a deep breath. 'Here's a story that might help clarify how I work,' I say, taking the phone off speaker and holding it to my ear. 'Yesterday, I accidentally dropped a bowl into my sink and broke it. I dropped it because I was unloading the dishwasher quickly – probably too quickly – and then my dog barked suddenly and I jumped. So it could have been me going too fast, or the dog – but ultimately it doesn't really matter. Whether or not the broken bowl was my *fault,* it is my *problem*.'

Silence. Maybe I should be more direct.

'For me, therapy is not about blame. It's about recognising a person's experience.'

More silence.

'You know what I mean?'

I hear him let out a big sigh. Like how it would sound if a bear sighed.

'Yes, Doctor,' he says. He sounds a bit more relaxed.

At our next appointment, Chloe barely settles in the chair before she starts describing the latest interaction with her father.

'Last night at dinner he's literally going on about the plight of men *ageing,* and how he feels the need to prove his *virility*. He literally used that word. To me.'

I think my facial expression is enough.

We are talking about a piece of 'the trauma'. We have said that word aloud on several occasions in this session. We sit there, holding it together, like a radioactive orb.

But *now what*? There are a lot of lousy parents, and even more imperfect and deeply flawed parents. Except for extreme cases where actual crimes were committed, there is no trauma jail. It's up to an individual patient to grow and process, to make sense of what happened, to feel there is someone who has witnessed and understood, and then to decide what she wants and needs next.

Decoding Therapy Speak: A Beginning

As therapists, we do not take words at face value. We react to them, and then we analyse those reactions. How do the words make us feel? And what does that tell us about *how* someone is using them?

In Violet's case, I came to understand that she was using diagnosis labels to make her true feelings invisible, to put distance between us. She needed that distance until she could begin to trust me. But the words also held a symbolic space, telling me loud and clear that she seriously needed and wanted my help.

Chloe, I learned, was using those words for control. She was a person who felt helpless and afraid, and found power through diagnostic language. She was ultimately able to shift from this place, but I had to meet her where she was, first.

There is a theory therapists reach for, usually when discussing younger children: the concept of 'transitional objects'. When a young child transitions from the safety of home into the outside world, they often rely on a concrete symbol of their loved ones – a teddy bear on the first day of preschool, for example – before their brains can keep this comfort inside. (My friend's son used to carry around a pair of pants everywhere he went – his 'security pants'. He had five pairs of the same pants, in case he left one somewhere.) A psychiatric diagnosis can also function, in adolescence, like a transitional object. It's something concrete that explains or excuses or contains your pain, and it demands a certain respect: teachers get what a transitional object is. They allow children to have them. Nobody worries that the child will be carrying the teddy bear to high school.

A small child uses a teddy bear when they are migrating from the care of their parents, grandparents or babysitters to the chaotic world of other children and other grown-ups. When a teenager clings to a diagnosis, she is moving from a childhood where she basically knew who she was to an adult world where she is not sure who she can be. The diagnosis is a signal to this new world: *Take care of me.* In therapy, she is using the diagnoses to protect herself from the awkward and forced intimacy with me, while inviting me in at the same time. My job, then, is to hang in there and understand the function that language is serving for each girl – not to yank away her teddy bear before she is ready.

A kindergartner might cling to that teddy bear on day one, keep it nearby on day two, and leave it in their cubby on day three. It turns out, that's what happens with both of these girls and their psychiatric labels.

As the months pass, Chloe focuses more on her inner life, to make sense of the past without being mired in it. She eases up on trying to control me and instead shows a beautiful ability to collaborate. It helped that I went along with her wish to try medication. She stays on it for several years but ultimately decides for herself that she doesn't need it.

Violet keeps the diagnoses in circulation for a bit longer, but they evolve and take different forms. After a few months, I learn she has felt incredibly anxious showing up to her therapy sessions. Her highly sensitive temperament has been a liability in a family that's uncomfortable with *need*. The mere act of arriving in my office declares a need for help, and this leads her to anticipate all kinds of judgements from me – some of which I've inadvertently validated. But once we identify this pattern, we can help her over the threshold.

One day, several months into treatment, Violet is a few minutes late, as usual, but it's fewer minutes than it used to be. I want to comment on her lateness, like always. Why does she continue to not show up for herself, or to do so half-heartedly? But I know if I do, I'll quickly become a critic and an enemy in her mind. I also know I don't need to; it's implied in the silence.

'What kind of state do you find yourself in right now?' I ask.

'I don't know . . .' Her voice stretches itself thin, translucent.

'Are you able to think clearly?'

She scrunches her eyes closed. 'Things are kind of foggy.'

'Your thoughts get foggy when you're overwhelmed. Do you think it's making you anxious, being here with me right now?'

She takes a deep breath and fights back tears. 'Yeah. I was late. I figured you would say something.'

I pause. 'And how is it now, talking to me here, in this moment?' I am speaking softly and gently.

'It's okay.' Her eyes are still closed. She is nodding.

I stay quiet.

'It's better,' she says. 'I'm here now. I'm here.'

2

A History of the Emotional Female in Two Breakups

> The determining male gaze projects its fantasy onto the female figure, which is styled accordingly.
>
> **Laura Mulvey,**
> 'Visual Pleasure and Narrative Cinema'

> In truth, naming a disease had always been a greater sign of power than the ability to cure it.
>
> **Alexander Kriss,**
> *Borderline: The Biography of a Personality Disorder*

I. Heartbreak

Hazel is depressed. She told me so herself, in our first meeting, two months ago: 'I think I'm depressed' was what she said as she sat in my office, adjusting her red glasses. It had been that way since Marcus dumped her – or rather, *texted her,* after eight months of steamy, clumsy 'homework' sessions in his bedroom, hanging out nights and weekends at play rehearsals, even planning a shared directing project for next year, all of which ended with him literally making her a playlist in which *every single song* had the word 'love' in it (she counted). And after all that, one day he just texts her – *texts her* – that he needs 'space'.

There's never been a Marcus before. There's never been anyone before, in all of her sixteen years on this earth. Hazel is not the kind of girl boys notice, she says. She's not one of the cool, skinny, perfect girls. She thought it would take forever for someone other than her friends to appreciate her. But then, along came Marcus: also a misfit, also an intellectual. She had never felt pretty around any boy until she felt herself in his gaze. Even Poppy, the cool girl who got the lead in the play, who had never before acknowledged Hazel's existence, noticed how special it was. 'Nerd love is so cute,' she said one time, watching Hazel sit on Marcus's lap at rehearsal. His *lap*. Hazel had felt like she was living someone else's life. 'I'm literally jealous,' Poppy had said.

Now Hazel stays up at night examining her mistakes. Sometimes, she lies awake before school, dreading facing the day. She goes over and over the way things ended, the way things started. What did she do wrong? It's impossible to think about anything else. History, bio, practising the violin . . . Are you freaking kidding? Why does any of that even matter anymore? And no, she doesn't feel like eating – if there's any silver lining, she says, at least she dropped a size. No, she's not going to kill herself, but there are days, many days, especially in English class, when Marcus sits with his friends and Poppy, and ignores Hazel, that she'd rather not exist. Saturday nights, she does wish she could just skip to the end of her life.

Eventually Hazel's parents recommend she see me. It's been three months since the fateful text, and Hazel and I have devoted our sessions to the topic.

It's 4:00 P.M. and in the past hour, my office has grown dark. Endless, dreary winter. Outside the window, the branches rattle. I set down my steaming mug of tea and turn on the lamps. Hazel should be here any minute.

There is a loud knock. Usually Hazel buzzes in and quietly takes a seat in the waiting room; today she arrives like a cop in a movie, ready to break down the door.

Hazel heads straight for the chair and falls into it with a scowl. I wait.

Then, huge sobs. Massive, slurpy inhalations. She grabs a small stack of tissues from the box on my table and blows her nose a few times. Crumples the wet wad, tucks it under her leg.

'I'm deleting Instagram,' she says.

'What happened?'

'He said he needed to hang out with his friends more, but I didn't realise he was suddenly *best friends* with Poppy, and the whole world.'

Apparently, there were pictures from a party.

'Why is it that he's all I can think about, but he doesn't need me at *all* anymore? He's having the time of his life.'

I let out a deep sigh.

'I don't know who I am without him. It's like he changed me, and then he broke me.' Hazel draws her knees up to her chest and cries softly into them. She looks at me with puffy brown eyes. 'Do you think I have a chemical imbalance?'

'What do you mean by that?'

'There's something wrong with me. I should be over this already. And depression runs in my family. It's genetic, right? I think my mom used to take something.'

I nod along as she speaks. I can't say depression doesn't have a genetic component. But that fact will not necessarily take us in a helpful direction for her.

'I'm a disaster. My parents tell me I should just take it easy. They bought me these lavender bath bombs – they said they're supposed to be relaxing, but I just sit in the bath obsessing about what my problem is.'

Would medicines help her feel better? she wants to know. Could it be a good idea to try them?

I have a hard time finding a reason why not. And yet, when I mention I have to discuss this with her parents – she is sixteen, after all – I'm relieved that we have to give the decision some more time.

When Hazel comes back the following week, I can see she is trying to feel better. She's wearing a cute pleated skirt and a wool sweater. As she sets down her backpack, I hope for a brighter report.

'Did my parents tell you?' she asks.

I've heard nothing. 'About what?'

'We had a huge fight last night. I figured they would've texted you.'

I pick up my phone. Indeed, there's a text from Hazel's mother from five minutes ago: 'FYI: Hazel very irritable – worsening depression?'

Apparently, Hazel went off on them about owning a car in the city. She tells me she screamed that they were 'climate-disinterested capitalists', 'selfish one-percenters', and now she feels bad and confused: Does she actually believe this?

'Marcus made me doubt things.' Hazel sits very still.

'What do you mean?'

'Like . . . I don't know, my ideas, my family, my values. He was so *critical*. I guess the whole car thing came from him; he thinks owning a car in New York City is completely immoral, and he was always like, "You don't agree with them, right?"'

'Sounds like you're trying to figure out what *you* think.'

'I don't know. It's complicated. I like the car – and it's a hybrid and everything . . . I mean, I saw his point, but – I'm not sure. And then last night my parents kept talking about this camping trip they're planning for this summer and I was getting so annoyed because I don't want to go anyway.'

I let this hang in the air for a moment. This is a big pivot: moving away from self-doubt and towards her feelings. This is good.

'How do you feel about what Marcus said?'

'I don't know . . . it just made me think, like, maybe my values are wrong. Maybe I'm not actually a good person.'

As I listen, my head fills with 'maybes' of my own. Maybe this is the self-attack of depression. Maybe this is just typical teenage girl self-doubt, or an attempt to stay linked to Marcus by hanging on to his opinions. Maybe Hazel is scarred by Marcus's judgements, or maybe she has been inspired to examine her values in a way that could be useful to her – key tasks for a healthy adolescence, part of separating from her parents and beginning to see herself as an independent person.

But whether there are blessings in disguise or not, Hazel's sense of self has slipped away. She's not the first girl to encounter this problem, and I'm not the first doctor to wonder what makes the identity of the teenage girl so vulnerable to the opinions of others. I wonder if 'depressed person' seems like an identity that could replace the one she has lost.

March winds have given way to April rain. I kick off my yellow boots and fold up my soggy umbrella, one prong sticking to the side. I know it would dry faster if I opened it, but the little girl in me is still superstitious about opening umbrellas indoors. Amazing how much of our behaviour is guided by old beliefs we don't bother to challenge.

Hazel drags in, looking tragic. Her hair hangs down in strings and her jeans are soaked at the bottom.

'Sorry, forgot an umbrella,' she says, taking off her damp sneakers in the doorway.

She treads in, sits down and begins to ask the same questions about depression and medication, this time more insistently. Looking down at her socks, she adds, with many pauses, 'Plus . . . Nobody wants to hear it anymore. I was feeling really upset in math yesterday so I texted my friend Izzie who always looks at her phone so I know she saw it but she didn't respond all day and finally at bedtime I get a response and she's like, "Hazel, I really think you should try to move on."'

Part of any great pain is being told to get over it on someone else's schedule. I mention this.

Hazel looks at me and says, with some relief, 'Yes.'

This begins to explain why Hazel is so fixed on getting a depression diagnosis. She's mad at the world right now, Marcus most of all, and that's a difficult feeling to sustain, let alone keep expressing; instead, she is turning against herself. Hazel is grieving several losses at once: the *actually datable* view of herself through Marcus's eyes; the feeling of kinship between oddball intellectuals; the newfound attention from the cool kids that couple status had conferred; a lap to sit on at lunch; and *plans*. Weekend *plans*. And now, her friends are losing patience with her. Their empathy is basically gone, and their sympathy is not far behind. Without the relief of their support, she's running out of oxygen. Her parents are trying to be helpful, but the kind of 'self-care' they recommend is just not doing the trick; their obvious desire for a simple fix betrays that they're also growing impatient with their child's suffering.

Everyone wants Hazel to move on, get over it. But she is not ready.

A depression diagnosis: now, *that* cannot be dismissed. With a depression diagnosis, her parents would be forced to see how ridiculous they look, buying her a bath bomb. Her friends would feel guilty asking her to live by some stupid societal timeline. Everyone would have to recognise this is real, medically sanctioned pain, not the temper tantrum of a toddler or a hysteric.

I have tried to give the issue time, but I recognise that Hazel needs an answer to the question she is asking.

'Well,' I tell her, 'you are clearly having a hard time. And you certainly have some symptoms of depression. Very understandable symptoms. Do you want to see if you qualify for the diagnosis, and we can talk about what that might mean?'

'Yes.' She exhales.

I click my pen, shifting into medical mode. I feel mixed about moving away from the immediacy of her experience into this more removed stance, but I think I've made it clear this is a temporary pause for some data-gathering.

The list of depression criteria is etched into the minds of psychiatrists as the acronym 'SIG E CAPS': Sleep, Interest in activities, Guilty thoughts, Energy level, Concentration ability, Appetite, Psychomotor symptoms (being generally 'slowed down' or agitated) and Suicidal thoughts or behaviour. We run the criteria. Check, check, check. She's had each of these symptoms, to varying degrees, for almost six months, so that's long enough.

Depression is a serious illness. As William Styron puts it, it's 'a condition of helpless stupor in which cognition [is] replaced by that "positive and active anguish."' The brain stops working as it should. I have no hesitation medicating major depression when I see it. As a friend of mine who got very depressed in high school told me during her hospitalisation: 'Depression is the one illness everyone keeps telling you to just get over.' But depressed people are in no position to do that.

Of course, every psychiatric condition can come in severe or milder forms – and perhaps Hazel is experiencing a mild or moderate depression. But despite her positive screen, I'm still not convinced that's what this is. What I'm wondering about, instead, is grief. Grief and depression can feel and look quite similar. Before 2013, the *DSM* depression criteria held an exception for bereavement, meaning if a person seemed depressed while they were grieving, it didn't count as depression. But in 2013, the *DSM-5* removed the bereavement exception. Those in favour of the change argued that depression sparked by grief was often overlooked and untreated.

But critics saw this as psychiatry turning a normal reaction into a medical problem. Research shows that a misplaced depression diagnosis may even exacerbate and prolong grief symptoms. (Notably, the bereavement exception – when it existed – only applied to death, not to other devastating losses, like losing the affection of your favourite person.)

It's almost spring break, so Hazel and I agree to give it another week and then decide about meds. Maybe some time away will help.

Nope! Spring break was lonely and awful, as she predicted. 'I talked it over with my parents and they agreed I should try an SSRI.'

At this point, I'm not sure I disagree. I understand Hazel's desire for relief, and as our first phase of therapy comes to a close, it seems like a logical decision to ease her pain in any way we can. I tell her as much.

'So, you think it's depression?' she asks. 'I guess I was bound to get it sooner or later.'

I take my glasses off and look at her. She literally sits on the edge of her seat, awaiting an answer. She seems, perhaps even more than wanting the meds, to be yearning for a certain narrative: *Her suffering is valid.* Diagnosis invites much-needed compassion from others and from Hazel to herself. And, yes, it opens up the medicine cabinet, where she will likely find help. So, the next steps should be obvious – this is what I was trained to do.

'Okay, Hazel,' I say. 'I see medicine as optional for you, but I do believe it will help you feel better.'

Even as I prescribe medication, I remain conflicted about it. In asking to reframe her predicament as a mental illness – not heartbreak – Hazel is unwittingly writing herself into the latest chapter of another longer and more troubling story. For millennia, girls have been told they are irrational, hysterical and crazy. The labels have evolved over the ages, and in modern times have been largely supplied by the field of psychiatry. It is psychiatry that produces our catalogue of diagnoses and decides who is sane and who is insane, who is healthy and who is ill. But psychiatry has been influenced by a struggle to define *itself* and its place in the medical establishment, falling through the cracks between medicine, philosophy, the social sciences and even religion. Our field has shifted its positions and priorities from one era to the next, in a kind of endless identity crisis of its own. Sometimes, we have taken an open, expansive posture, loyal to the gods of curiosity, exploration and uncertainty. At other times, we have lurched into reductionism, desperate to label, classify, categorise and claim the authority of medical science. In addition to our goals of healing and helping, we have grabbed on tightly to whatever authority we can find. Vulnerable young women have provided an ideal partner for our uneasy and, yes, patriarchal profession since its beginnings.

In other words: even if Hazel were a textbook case, who wrote the textbook?

Hysteria from Plato to Prozac

Do people suffer because they are sick, or bad? *Bad* was the first answer. People felt upset because the gods were angry – or so we thought for centuries, until Hippocrates, the father of medicine, said maybe that was incorrect. What if troubles with our bodies and souls had a purely physical cause? Perhaps there were four 'humours' (melancholic, choleric, phlegmatic and sanguine) that coursed through a human being, and perhaps their balance was what determined how we feel. *Not bad,* Hippocrates said. *Sick.*

If you were a girl, though, whatever ailed you was likely influenced by a buildup of bad humours in a specific part of your body: your *hystera,* or uterus. According to Plato,* the womb of a young female grew 'vexed and aggrieved' when it was underutilised. A teenage girl who had started to menstruate but had not married and had sex was therefore likely to become 'hysterical'. Whatever physical or emotional problem ailed her, the explanation was the same.

* Plato was famous for his hatred of women. He believed that weak and bad men were punished in the next life by being reborn as women.

There was no such thing as 'therapy' as we know it until the twentieth century. But back in ancient Greece, they had some thoughts about how to heal problems of the soul. The Greco-Roman physician Galen, who is famous for mapping the circulatory system, had the novel idea that some problems of the spirit – which notably did not include hysteria at that time – could be treated through conversation. This groundbreaking notion came with an explicit gender bias: the healer had to be a male, preferably of an older, wiser age, and free from the control of the passions.

Those ideas endured over the next several hundred years. In the Middle Ages, experts started to think very differently about human suffering. Maybe it wasn't the body, but the devil – not physically driven illness, but a sign of being possessed by evil. This change occurred in large part because medicine had proven unable to contain the bubonic plague, and increasing paranoia elevated priests as the new authorities on human mysteries. In other words, the answer changed again, from *sick* to *bad*.

Misogyny flared in this context, as it often does under times of social strain. This is when people started to live in fear of witches. The most renowned priests channelled the Aristotelian notion of male superiority, spreading this fear by pointing out how women were physically and spiritually defective: as the Italian priest Thomas Aquinas famously said at the time, 'A woman is a failed man.' Moreover, women were seen not just as patients, but as the *causes* of certain diseases. If a woman was moody or spirited or in any way confounded men, the odds were even higher that something wicked was involved. Even a woman's sadness was not to be trusted: 'When a woman weeps, she labours to deceive a man,' said the *Malleus Maleficarum,* the extremely popular book that spread terror about witches throughout Europe. Some witches were old, and some were young. A girl experiencing the normal teenage surge of hormones, for example, had reason to be very afraid. Throughout the Middle Ages, young women rightfully lived in fear of their inner lives, while the patriarchy sat in judgement.

Now let's fast-forward to the early modern period, circa 1600. Expertise was shifting from spiritualism back to science. René Descartes explained that the soul was linked to, but distinct from, the body. In Europe, thought leaders reengaged with an age-old question: why did women feel so much, experience mysterious physical symptoms and behave so strangely? A doctor named Thomas Sydenham led the charge investigating hysteria. He believed hysteria was the rule, rather than the exception, for females, especially 'those to whom either nature has given a soft and weak governing of mind, or . . . rendered so by a long series or continuance of diseases.' Despite the judgy language, Sydenham was the first to decouple hysteria from witchcraft and launched our understanding close to where it remains today: female suffering results from some combination of inborn temperament and adverse life experiences. Not bad: *sick*.

The early 1800s saw a renaissance of medicine and the birth of neurology, which focused primarily on physical aspects of the brain and nerves. A handful of physicians studied the mind and called themselves 'alienists', from the French term for madness, 'aliéné'. By the early nineteenth century, they began to argue, like the Greeks, that insanity was a medical problem. It was exactly at this time that the term 'psychiatry' was born. Derived from the Greek, it means mind or soul ('psyche') and healing ('iatreia').

But wherever there was 'lunacy', there was stigma, too. Medicine was known as a 'gentleman's profession', and even doctors are sensitive to social stigma. Psychiatrists found themselves perpetually on the fringes of medicine, managing very ill and seemingly incurable people, and wondering whether they were destined to function merely as 'innkeepers'. It was the neurologists who were treating the less severe and more palatable 'nervous disorders' in pleasant outpatient offices. If psychiatry was going to become a respected medical specialty, it needed a patient population that was less disturbed, more responsive to its interventions, and more socially acceptable.

Meanwhile, word was travelling of a young woman named Maria Theresia von Paradis, who had inexplicably gone blind at a young age. Bloodletting and purging failed to help her, but when she reached adolescence, her family took her to a doctor who was supposedly working miracles: Franz Anton Mesmer. Mesmer wore a long purple robe and carried a wand. He studied the cosmos and put his subjects into trances. Amazingly, the cure seemed to work:* Maria temporarily regained her sight.

Mesmer and Maria were a good team. And their dynamic recapitulated an archetypal duo: male visionary and fragile muse. That trope drives the Greek myth of Pygmalion, in which an artist sculpts his ideal woman, bringing her to life and falling in love with her. It appears again in the 1894 novel *Trilby* about an impressionable orphan girl who is manipulated by the hypnotist Svengali into carrying out his grand artistic dreams and eventually dying of a nervous condition. The same tale has been told across the ages – including in the musical *My Fair Lady* (1956) and in the movie *Pretty Woman* (1990). These myths reflect a central organising fantasy of the patriarchy.

A generation after Mesmer, his legend found its way to a physician in Paris named Jean-Martin Charcot. Perhaps hypnosis could help the hysterical patients at the asylum where he worked – the Salpêtrière. Equally talented as doctor and showman, Charcot hosted weekly spectacles where he (literally) mesmerised young women.

* Humans are heavily influenced by the kind of suggestive techniques Mesmer performed – a fact that has been demonstrated steadily over time. For example, the placebo effect is to this day one of the most powerful forces in medicine: so powerful that the gold standard for medical research requires the presence of a placebo to distinguish the true effects of whatever is being studied. In addition, entering a trance state, as one does while being hypnotised, can have a relaxing and restorative impact on the nervous system. These factors are amplified in the presence of a healing relationship with a trusted expert. Mental health theorists have agonised about exactly how and why this works ('a corrective emotional experience' and 'a transference cure'. to name a few notions), but whatever the precise mechanism, the singular value of the therapeutic relationship has stood the test of time.

They grew sleepy and swooned before entering a state of supreme suggestibility. Audiences went wild.

Enter: Blanche Wittman, a pretty girl born in poverty and battered by life – a violent father, a frail mother, childhood illness and abusive employers. By the time she found Charcot, she was suffering from extreme hysteria: out-of-control behaviour and dramatic seizure-like episodes. But under his hypnotic spell, she was docile: she would do *anything*. Throngs of doctors flocked to watch as the beautiful Blanche gathered her skirts and ran from suggested snakes, or removed her clothes and pretended to take a bath. Together, this male visionary and fragile muse were the King and Queen of Hysteria. After Charcot died, Blanche never had another hysterical attack.

Charcot was a serious doctor: his legacy in medicine is not one of quackery. In fact, he was the first physician to locate the source of hysteria outside the uterus: he called it a 'dynamic lesion' of the brain, triggered by emotional factors. Whether his seminars were more science or more performance art, a powerful medical technique or a social manipulation, something fundamental about psychiatry's identity as a profession was established during this period of time. The masterful male physician and the lovely ingenue patient were a perfect pair. This was not lost on Sigmund Freud, who drew from Charcot's teachings to create psychoanalysis, the basis of modern-day psychotherapy. Most of Freud's early patients were young women, and his text *Studies on Hysteria* (1895) laid the groundwork for the modern era of psychiatric practice.

Hysteria had reached its 'golden age', flourishing as an icon of the flamboyantly gendered Belle Epoque. Most women carried a bottle of smelling salts* in their purses. Although men could also have nervous breakdowns and a new cousin of hysteria called 'neurasthenia'. those were thought to be caused by external stressors. A woman

* These were to be used for swooning, which was a sign of emotional arousal. It was still widely held that the wandering uterus was the cause, and that the pungent odour from the smelling salts would send it back to its place.

would unravel because of her *nature*. This belief was tied to a larger cultural obsession with gender differences and their biological origins. Charles Darwin and his followers were on a mission to prove that women were mentally deficient, helpless in the face of their unwieldy reproductive systems. Once again, menstruation was seen as the start of the trouble. As British alienist-psychiatrist Charles Mercier wrote in the nineteenth century, 'Few women pass through this period of their development without manifesting signs of disorder.' The sanitorium, previously home to the male lunatic, grew popular as a place for disgruntled fathers and husbands to park unwanted females – the disagreeable, the disobedient, the intellectual and the moody. Authority over these young women gave psychiatry the validity it needed to move closer to the medical mainstream.

But psychiatry was still not keeping up with the rest of medicine. While other specialties were making landmark discoveries – microbes, aspirin and the X-ray, to name a few – psychiatrists were still scrambling for answers about what hysteria was and how to treat it. Perhaps women developed hysteria because they were having sex too often – or not often enough. Perhaps it was 'horseback riding, and taking train journeys while menstruating'. Perhaps girls ought not look at books – especially girls with long eyelashes.

But as this absurdity burgeoned, something new started to happen: women began to speak for themselves. They couldn't be doctors, but they could be writers. Drawing on the work of Charlotte Brontë, Jane Austen, George Eliot and even the famous nurse Florence Nightingale, in 1892 Charlotte Perkins Gilman published the iconic short story 'The Yellow Wallpaper', portraying how social roles assigned to the Victorian female could lead to restlessness, melancholy and even madness. (Nightingale, who suffered her own share of mental health troubles, had been particularly prescient. She was moved by the myth of Cassandra, the prophet who was never believed, and composed her own essay entitled 'Cassandra' about a woman who realises her creative energy is being drained by a life filled with idle domestic tasks. This protagonist encourages women to fight for a more fulfilling existence but, like the original Cassandra, she is written off as crazy.)

One of the most telling symptoms of hysteria, common to many cases, was *globus hystericus,* the sensation that a ball was rising in the oesophagus. It was not until a new treatment revolutionised the field that doctors began to recognise one of the hallmarks of hysteria: losing the ability to speak.

In 1880, Bertha Pappenheim (aka 'Anna O') was brought to Dr Josef Breuer, a colleague of Sigmund Freud's, because around the time of her father's illness and death, she had lost the ability to talk. Breuer found that she was a bright girl who was frustrated by her role in a restrictive family; her daily life was lonely and dull. As her speech returned, and through their months of conversations, she recalled frustrations that she associated with the onset of her hysterical symptoms. Making these connections seemed to ameliorate her symptoms, and she eventually went on to become a feminist leader and anti-Nazi crusader. Although the specifics of her case are controversial (whether organic causes were involved, how well the treatment ultimately worked), elements of this treatment took hold – above all, the therapeutic benefit of talking and remembering. Breuer and Freud experimented with several of these hysteria cases, and together they invented 'the Talking Cure'.

Psychoanalysis allowed and invited women to speak: for all of Freud's oft-bemoaned limitations understanding women, it was he and his colleagues who reversed much of the pathologising and mistreatment of young women in emotional pain. He pioneered the idea that it was therapeutic for his patients, most of whom were women, to tell their own stories. And he believed – at least at first – that psychological symptoms were produced by unacknowledged trauma, usually in the form of sexual abuse.* Psychoanalysis inaugurated a long (and still incomplete) process of normalising female sexuality in an entirely repressive culture. The Talking Cure began to redefine what it meant to be mentally healthy: instead of living life solely by society's rigid moral structure, true emotional wellness depended on friendly relations between the body and mind, a private honesty about the full range of one's own true feelings – even the unacceptable ones.

As popular as he and his techniques would become, Freud hardly reflected psychiatric culture at the turn of the twentieth century. Rather, psychiatrists were dealing with a crisis of public health and plummeting confidence in their field: asylums were growing overcrowded and conditions were deteriorating. At the same time, the profession was criticised for not making use of the laboratory the way neurology did. By 1900, psychiatry was a laughingstock. 'Who becomes a psychiatrist?' wrote one German physician, answering his own question as follows: those who are 'physically inadequate . . . not up to the exertions of a rural practice, maybe not even an urban practice', or 'intellectually inadequate, who instinctually seek out an asylum because they will stand out less there'.

A paradigm shift was needed, and German psychiatrist Emil Kraepelin had an idea. He believed the most important task for a doctor was to be able to offer reliable prognoses. He began sorting what he saw in his patients onto note cards, and he organised and classified the various syndromes. Several decades later, Adolf Meyer, the leading psychiatrist in the United States, picked up Kraepelin's mission, laying the groundwork for the creation of the *DSM,* which

* Eventually, under pressure from the political and medical community, Freud revised this theory to suggest most of the trauma was generated by repressed sexual and aggressive urges – a decision that has invited more than a century of controversy and debate.

we still use today and is updated about twice per decade. For some thought leaders, labelling diseases appeared to be the most useful contribution psychiatry could make.

The *DSM* empowered psychiatrists to decide who was and was not mentally ill. As the twentieth century progressed, a predominantly female patient population continued to be diagnosed, researched and hospitalised by a 90 per cent male profession. In the 1940s, '50s and '60s, women disproportionately viewed themselves as prone to 'nervous breakdowns'. Fun fact: the term 'shell shock' was invented because doctors found that veterans were returning from war displaying symptoms of what had previously been called 'hysteria'. But, they reasoned, they couldn't possibly use the word 'hysteria' to describe such a masculine problem.

Women were also receiving a new message about mental illness from the broader culture: mid-century Hollywood began projecting a glamorised image of female insanity. From *Gaslight* (1944) to *Rosemary's Baby* (1968), pretty girls were losing their minds. A new version of Ophelia – the postwar Sad Girl – had become a ubiquitous stock figure: a tragic, beautiful, white innocent, struggling with some highly gendered form of psychiatric disorder.

Despite the public's increasing fascination with mental illness, the field of psychiatry was still under threat, criticised for a lack of scientific rigour and proof of outcomes, until a revolution began, prompted by a series of accidental discoveries in pharmaceutical laboratories rather than consulting rooms. The surgical anaesthetic chlorpromazine was found in 1952 to have calming effects on patients and turned out to be the first ever drug to be effective against psychosis. A psychiatrist in Switzerland who couldn't afford sufficient chlorpromazine for his patients tried to make a related antihistamine in his own lab as a substitute. It didn't help the schizophrenics, but worked wonders for depressed patients. The drug was imipramine (Tofranil), the first antidepressant, which hit the market in 1957, followed by lithium in 1970 and, in the 1980s, the SSRIs.

With the arrival of these blockbuster drugs, which offered fast and powerful treatments for depression and nervousness, years of duelling between social/psychological theories of mental illness and biological theories began to produce a clear winner.

It's perhaps no surprise that young women, already the population most likely to see psychiatrists, would become the main market for the new world of antidepressants, and for the diagnoses that supported their use.

It figures that Hazel, my patient who was suffering depressive symptoms in the lengthy aftermath of a breakup, would see herself as the ideal candidate for an antidepressant. A month after starting Prozac, she feels lighter and less burdened. She can see Marcus horsing around with his friends in the hallway and not have to run to the bathroom and sob in a stall.

Hazel sees herself as a heroine. She 'advocated for herself'. She was unafraid to recognise her mental illness; she got herself 'the help she needed'. Or at least, that's one version of the story.

But is there a cost she must pay for the relief that comes with the diagnosis and its medication – beyond any stigma or potential side effects? I fear that somewhere along the way – maybe even before Hazel and I knew each other – we both bought into a narrative that was developed by men who made some pretty negative assumptions about women, and especially about teenage girls. We are living in the direct lineage of patriarchal psychiatry, and our review of its history reveals powerful forces that have pushed adolescent girlhood towards the teen mental health crisis of the present day. How did we get to a point where someone like Hazel is so eager to be diagnosed with a psychiatric disorder? There's psychiatry's century-long quest to establish its own list of disorders that could be categorised and cured, just like the rest of medicine. There's the clockwork chaos of adolescent girls and their feelings – shaky new bodies and unfinished selves – the exhilaration of a crush fulfilled, and the kaleidoscope of pain that accompanies first love's sudden and unwanted departure: despair, disappointment, confusion, emptiness, helplessness, aching loneliness and not being sure who you are for a while. I wish we could let Hazel's problem be all of those feelings, rather than helping her towards a view of herself as someone with a medical condition.

I have ways of finding comfort with my decision to offer her medication. One is a principle called 'psychological justice', the notion that the world is not set up to support everyone's emotional needs, and that even short of medical illness, one can use medicines, carefully and deliberately, to bridge that gap. Neuron for neuron, breakups are harder when you're young and possibly more disruptive for girls than for boys; high schoolers live in small bubbles that are genuinely constraining, and the lack of life experience, perspective and options acts with full force on the teenage heart.

And yes, the medicine is a Band-Aid of sorts. But that's not necessarily a bad thing: Band-Aids protect a wound so that healing can take place. I'll monitor her closely. We will reassess periodically and plan to try to taper off the meds when she is ready. We will make sure her psychotherapy is engaging and purposeful.

Of course Hazel wants to feel better; of course she wants a reason to be hopeful; of course she wants to circumscribe her pain and signal to all that it is not her fault. I know the diagnosis 'depression' provides some of that for her. But that does not fully explain the mindset of Hazel and so many other young women today. Propped up by every corner of culture and medicine, by the end of the twentieth century, the long-germinating identity of the 'teenage girl as mental patient' became something that girls increasingly adopted and took upon themselves – and which, with the dawn of the internet, went viral.

II. Chill

Kaia's auburn bob frames her face, and when she looks at you, you can't look away. I'm not sure what it is: the crystalline blue eyes, the dark lipstick; when you zoom out and notice the combat boots, it becomes very clear who's in charge here.

Kaia wants to be a CEO. She is a sophomore in college and plans to major in finance. She has a silver ear cuff that looks so chic I wonder if I should get one.

'I'm *completely* mentally ill,' Kaia begins. This is the first time Kaia has ever been dumped – and worse, Natalie totally blindsided her.

'So now I'm having a full OCD meltdown – or something. I'm all about control.'

Everything had been going great, Kaia tells me. From the first night they met at the dorm party, Natalie was dazzled by Kaia, how 'together' she was; Kaia was charmed by Natalie's sweetness. It was instant chemistry. They were each the most amazing person the other had ever met, and Kaia has no idea what went wrong.

'I never thought in a *million years* she would pull something like this.' Kaia's voice is soft but very, very steady.

So, what happened?

'She just tells me the other day, *It's over.* She's like, *I'm not doing this anymore.* So, I was just like, *fine*. It's fine,' Kaia says.

I note that it does not seem to be fine with her.

'No! Low-key, it destroyed me. But, you know, I don't want to give her that.'

I love the use of 'low-key' and 'destroyed' in the same sentence, and it helps me get closer to what Kaia means by 'completely mentally ill' and 'OCD meltdown'. She already knows about her need for control and can see it's a problem. But she may not see how viewing herself in such pathologising extremes keeps that problem going.

As we get to know each other, Kaia also describes herself repeatedly as a '*chill* girl'. The worst thing, as far as she's concerned, is to be needy, weak or *desperate* – she says with a shudder – which is how she feels now, more and more, every day she doesn't talk to Natalie.

'I'm not talking about it. I haven't told my roommates. I haven't even cried.'

'Wow,' I say. This genuinely baffles me, and I'm hoping my reaction will help her see the problem (a technique called 'therapeutic alarm'). 'So, what do you mean when you say it destroyed you?'

'I'm just having anxiety.'

I learn for Kaia this anxiety takes the form of panic attacks and some scratching of her inner thighs with her nails, where no one can see. She says this relieves stress. She cleans her room a lot. She manages her Instagram story like it's her job, giving the illusion of a life that is cool and enviable. Ditto with her online communications. Kaia never double-texts. And Kaia *never* gets dumped.

That all checks out. But I'm confused by a few things. Kaia is a puzzle of contradictions: every silvery piercing, every lash heavy with mascara, every dark angle of her presence says, *Life is pain*. And yet, she seems so afraid to hurt.

When I look at Kaia, I see a girl who has succeeded at coming off as 'chill'. I recognise what an accomplishment this is. 'Chill' is a synonym for good, safe, cool, acceptable. 'Don't worry, she's chill,' a kid will say. This phrase paves the way for a new member of any social group. It puts your peers at ease when your mom (if she's nice) walks in unexpectedly. 'Chill' means someone who is not going to freak out or otherwise be annoying. I find it's mostly a word used to describe females. It is females who are most often told that they 'need to chill'.

I think of my friends who have got dumped by guys the moment they no longer seem blithe and independent. I think of how girls teach one another to 'play it cool', especially in the beginning of . . . everything. I think of a dating book that came out when I was in high school: *The Rules: Time-Tested Secrets for Capturing the Heart of Mr. Right*. *The Rules* advised, 'Don't Stare at Men or Talk Too Much;

Don't Call Him and Rarely Return His Calls.' Of course, back then I knew the book's message was 'egregious', and the girls of my generation all voiced our outrage – while secretly reading the shit out of it anyway.

These lessons seemed gallingly outdated then, and would seem even more so today, especially in this case involving two women dating. (Of course, once a girl succeeds in coming off as 'chill', she quickly faces another set of dismissive social categories: the ice queen, the disaffected stoner, the manic pixie dream girl.) But still, Gen Z girls seem no less convinced than their mothers and grandmothers that being *chill* is, somehow, the key to a certain kind of social acceptance and romantic appeal.

The damn lightbulb is out. I'm scurrying around my office, getting ready for Kaia's next appointment. I turn on the three other lamps and stick the sparkly magic wand back in the box on the shelf, combing its neon streamers down like a lock of long hair. The bell will ring any minute.

But after the lamps are on and the wand is tucked away, I realise I don't feel calm. I wonder if my tension has anything to do with the patient who is about to arrive for her second visit.

When I open the door, Kaia strikes me all over again as imposing: tall, with her hair pinned up, in cat-eye glasses and a black unitard. She sits down, takes out a notebook and a pen, and jumps right in. 'So, I'm trying to make a game plan for what will happen if I run into Natalie.'

I picture the strategy diagrams football coaches draw, arrows curving in all directions.

'How does it make you feel, to imagine running into Natalie?' I say, trying to redirect Kaia back towards her own psychology.

She rolls her eyes, then catches herself and offers me a pleasant smile. 'I just want to make a plan.'

Kaia is asking me to help her with what to *do*. This would be a behavioural kind of help, rather than a psychological one. I get it: I'm a planner, too, and a problem-solver by nature. But tempting as it is to conduct therapy that way, that approach often comes at the cost of deeper work that will help a patient figure out what to do on their own.

'You mentioned last time you like to be in control. If we came up with a perfect strategy, that would give you back some control, right?'

Kaia shifts in her seat. I see her jaw clench and her whole body tighten. She sits up with perfect posture.

Which makes me aware that I am slumping back into my armchair. *You are only as old as your spinal column,* says a chalkboard sign outside a Pilates studio in my neighbourhood. I sit up tall like Kaia, who stares at me with glassy blue eyes, stone-faced.

'Yeah, I guess,' she says absently, tucking a strand of hair behind an ear and staring into the middle distance. 'Me and my control issues.' If she had a cigarette in her hand, she would take an *insouciant* drag right now.

Issues. The perfect word to describe partial self-awareness. If something is an 'issue', maybe it's a slight problem – a deep problem, even – but maybe it's a trait that makes her a captivating person. Maybe it's a reason to be in therapy, but maybe it's just something to accept. People are serious and private about their actual *problems,* but often simultaneously public and casual about their *issues*. *Problems* demand direct attention; *issues* call for a more laissez-faire approach: 'anger issues', 'trust issues', 'boundary issues'. The word 'issues', in some way, captures the worst of therapy culture: psychological troubles are chic, vague and inevitable – conversation pieces rather than troubles that can be helped.

'*Control issues?*' I repeat.

She takes a deep sigh and leans back in the chair. 'Do you think I have OCD, by the way?'

I have not heard a compelling story for OCD, but we run the

criteria since she brings it up. She has a few symptoms of OCD (some cleaning, a lot of ruminating), but nowhere near the full syndrome.

'Let's call them *traits,*' I say.

I get a thumbs-up from the disaffected person who is still reclining. Seems like she wasn't super invested in that diagnosis.

By the end of session two, I am not sure we are on the same page yet. We are poised at a crossroads. We have gently identified Kaia's preference for control and are gradually starting to challenge it in a few different ways. One way of controlling things would be to affix psychiatric labels to her problem: if we could diagnose 'OCD', that might bring a reassuring path towards cure. But we have peeked down that path and can see that is likely not our answer. And at this moment, we are pushing back on another possible means of control: using our in-session time to try to choreograph Kaia's behaviour, or to help her continue to manipulate other people's image of her. It might take some time to see if she gets on board with doing the opposite: helping her experience and tolerate vulnerability.

Why is Kaia like this, anyway?

I have a few guesses, which we will examine when she is ready. I learned from her mother in our initial intake that Kaia's father died of heart disease when she was little. Maybe her abandonment fears run deep, and being aloof helps her protect herself from getting hurt again. My sense is that Kaia's mother is a very expressive person, and I know that they are close; I'm wondering if Kaia ever felt overwhelmed by her mom's emotionality, and resolved, somewhere, to be the opposite. I'm also wondering how Kaia feels about her sexuality. Sure, these days college students in New York City feel more accepted than ever for a broad range of gender and sexual identities and preferences, but being anything other than cisgender and straight almost always includes experiences – or at least fears – of stigma and shame. I wonder if that creates extra pressure to guard her needs and vulnerabilities.

Before we end our second session, I have one last question for

Kaia: 'And what if you weren't the chill girl?' I ask her. 'Who would you be then?'

'Crazy.' Kaia doesn't miss a beat. 'I'd be a crazy motherfucker.'

Chill Pills

From their first introduction to the public, psychiatric drugs bore the promise of easing females into their societal roles. In 1912, when phenobarbital came on the market as a sedative, its makers dyed the medicine pink; many women carried a bottle around in their handbag to use as needed. The 1950s ushered in 'minor tranquilizers' like Miltown and later Valium. These were advertised primarily to women, promising to help them maintain the appearance of a perfect, controlled life of fulfilled feminine destiny. Frigidity, singlehood and failing to be an industrious-enough, loving-enough or calm-enough mother were commonly displayed problems calling for the panacea of benzodiazepines. The pages of *Cosmopolitan* and *Ladies' Home Journal* alerted women to wonderful new treatments for their anxiety, depression, nerves and fatigue. 'Now she can cope,' says the 1964 advertisement for the tranquilizer Butisol that displays a woman in a cheerful housedress playing with a little girl in front of a stove. After only one year on the market, Miltown became the most popular drug in the United States, dispensed at the rate of one prescription every second. And until Prozac, Valium was the single most successful drug in history.

Meanwhile, young women continued to contend disproportionately with emotional stress. In 1967, there was 'more mental illness among women than men from every data source'. Whatever ailed a woman, the drug companies droned, the problem lay within her fragile self: And so, 'whatever the cause, it helps to add Miltown to her treatment'.

The antidepressants of the 1950s, called tricyclics, had many side effects and were therefore only used in serious cases. However, they provided the scientific launching pad for what was to come, by way of the 'catecholamine hypothesis', which suggested that neurotransmitters like norepinephrine might be involved in depression.

In the 1970s, Eli Lilly began experimenting with derivatives of Benadryl that might improve mood symptoms without the side effects of tricyclics, and which might target a new neurotransmitter – serotonin – rather than norepinephrine. The novel compound was named 'fluoxetine' in 1975 and studied until 1987, when it was released to the public as 'Prozac'.

Within a few months, sales took off, and by 1990 Prozac had become the bestselling antidepressant of all time. Its increased safety and tolerability led to much wider use, which in turn decreased stigma. Taking an antidepressant was no longer something to be embarrassed about.

The more the *DSM* broadened the definitions of mental illness, the more drugs pharmaceutical companies could sell. Me-too antidepressants appeared in rapid succession. And a new story was being told to help sell them: depression was caused by a 'chemical imbalance'. This narrative, originally promoted by Pfizer in a 1992 ad for Zoloft, found its way into America's dinner conversations. Not only was depression easy to diagnose and easy to treat, it also came with a convenient explanation that relieved people of responsibility for its existence. It wasn't your fault. It wasn't your mother's fault. It wasn't because of mistakes you made, or bad habits, or tough experiences, or self-destructive behaviour: it was just chemical.

Psychiatrists also benefitted from the change. In a sea of non-MD therapists competing for patients, MD psychiatrists could stay more relevant if they were treating 'real' illnesses rather than life problems. Moreover, psychiatrists held the exclusive ability to establish new *DSM* categories that would occasion the production of new drugs, which in turn they alone could prescribe. This offered the eternally tenuous field of psychiatry a hard-won and heady combination of validity and prestige.

Prozac Feminism

Five years after the release of Prozac (fluoxetine), 80 per cent of its consumers were female. As with Valium, Big Pharma targeted the drug to women by encoding a strong social message about how it could help them fulfil their feminine roles. And that message was easier than ever to convey. Prior to the 1990s, the FDA maintained strict regulations about the conditions for advertising drugs. In the 1980s, it even required pharmaceutical companies to list on benzodiazepine labels that these drugs were not to be used for 'ordinary frustrations of daily living'. But in 1997, direct-to-consumer laws were relaxed, and by 2007, pharmaceuticals became the second most advertised type of product in the United States behind automobiles.

Prozac and its cousins came onto the scene when stories of empowerment and self-positivity filled women's magazines, alongside the more traditional emphasis on beauty, thinness and consumerism. 'What few people know is that Susan, forty-four, needs a little chemical help to be a supermom,' said *Time* in 1993, portraying a self-described workaholic who gets irritable around her period and once threw her wedding ring at her husband. 'Power that speaks softly,' said a 1999 ad for Zoloft, showing a young mom in a business suit strolling joyfully with her kids. Unlike the 1950s and '60s advertisements for Valium, which featured women being calm and serene at home, Prozac enabled women of the 1990s to hyperfunction. They could make the choice to live with less pain, so why shouldn't they? They could be 'empowered health-care consumers'. Starting as early as their teen years, the ads suggested, they were doing something good for themselves by taking these medicines.

In the 1993 bestseller *Listening to Prozac,* psychiatrist Peter Kramer argued that taking Prozac might function as a new form of feminism by 'free[ing] women from the inhibiting consequences of trauma'. He also saw the potential benefits of 'cosmetic psychopharmacology', or making oneself 'better than well': 'Since you only live once, why not do it as a blonde? Why not as a peppy blonde?' The freedom to live your best life on these drugs became known as 'Prozac feminism'.

But the Prozac ads were sending a distinctly regressive message to girls. Women had long been taught by the media that their ability to succeed at femininity required constant self-surveillance and discipline. 'Mental health' was now considered a feminine issue, and mental distress was being presented as yet another unattractive thing girls had to fight off, like acne or sun damage. Taking Prozac could speak to both messages: affirming your femininity, while helping to conceal your blemishes.

As hordes of young women started taking Prozac, some people started asking: are they taking this drug for an illness, or as a kind of Brazilian wax of the personality?

The Lightbulb Has to Want to Change

I putter around my office in stocking feet, waiting for Kaia to arrive, turning on the lamps, one by one. Didn't I bring a spare bulb? I grab my tote bag and draw one out of the thin cardboard box. *How many psychiatrists does it take to screw in a lightbulb?* I laugh to myself.

As I straighten the chair where Kaia last sat, her words echo in my mind: Kaia, the *chill girl* with the *control issues,* who is *completely mentally ill,* who is *a crazy motherfucker.* Kaia, who lost her father as a little girl. Kaia, who never gets dumped.

Kaia comes in wearing a big winter coat. She's carrying a large coffee and she sits down, keeps her coat on, places her coffee on the table. She's quiet. I notice she's wearing sweatpants and no makeup today. She looks softer.

'It's midterms.' She rubs her eyes. 'I'm exhausted.'

'I see that,' I say. 'Where should we begin?'

'I don't know.' She unzips her coat and settles in, revealing an oversized hoodie that matches her sweatpants. She still looks intimidatingly cool, but there's something more accessible about her. Some molecules have shifted.

'Well, what do you think you'd like to accomplish today?' *Just one, but the lightbulb has to* want *to change.*

Kaia meets my eyes. 'This is the time Natalie and I met last year, during midterms.' She looks down. 'I miss her.' Kaia takes a very heavy sigh.

'Of course you do,' I say softly.

And then, for the first time since the breakup, Kaia starts to cry. 'I'm sorry,' she says as she takes a tissue. 'This is so embarrassing.'

'You're having a feeling, Kaia. What's embarrassing about that?'

'I just don't want you to freak out and think I'm like depressed or anything.' She takes a sip of her coffee.

There she goes again, managing my impression of her.

'Why would I freak out about how you're feeling right now? It seems perfectly understandable.'

She looks at me and nods.

For the first time since meeting Kaia, I feel like we are really together, sharing this moment. I've had to dodge so many of her attempts to put distance between us: diagnosing, labelling, dismissing, judging, trying to get me to control her, trying to control me. We are now just two people, sitting here with the lights on. During the time that Kaia sees me, she gradually unpacks her fears and vulnerabilities, especially when it comes to loss. She eventually realises that missing her relationship will not actually make her go crazy. She never winds up asking for medication, and I never think she needs any.

Kaia is a masterpiece of modern culture. The girl who is 'chill' but perpetually adjacent to a dark world of serious mental health issues, living in fear that she belongs there, or that others will believe she does. She's figured out that our society celebrates this sort of girl – a girl who does not burden others with her opinions or emotions or desires, who is not 'too much', but who's also convinced she might be nuts. Over the past few months, Kaia has learned she can get attention and help without adhering to the bargain so many girls have unwittingly made with the patriarchy: that in exchange for feeling better, they must first commit to being sick.

3

Identity and the Internet Age

The tradition of psychological curiosity has been dying a gradual death. . . . These days, psychiatrists are less interested in 'why' and more interested in 'what'.

Daniel Carlat,
Unhinged

Now we are never not posing.

Melissa Febos,
Girlhood

More of a Carrie

My favourite song in high school was '32 Flavors' by Ani DiFranco. The title references the Baskin-Robbins ice cream selection, but it's a song about identity – about being made up of many differ-ent 'flavours'. Back then, when I looked around, everyone else seemed so constant: happy, perfect girls were happy and perfect; edgy, alternative girls were edgy and alternative. What was wrong with me?

I remember confessing this to a friend – and feeling so relieved to hear that she related to this song, too. To be thirty-two flavours 'and then some', as the song went, was a shocking notion – blasphemous, even. Somehow, we had internalised the message that we were supposed to be this type of girl or that type of girl, and that being more than one thing violated the social order. Worse, that it was a shameful secret.

I was hungry to find myself in a pre-cut category. Throughout my childhood it had been horoscopes – those uncanny notes in the back of the teen magazines that just *saw* you. They declared the truth: that I was a Scorpio – that deep down I was honest, passionate and determined. That this somehow explained my affinity for blackberry lip shine and – *oh my god, how did they know?* – existential angst.

As I strove to figure out what type of person I was, pop culture (*Beverly Hills, 90210,* for example) functioned as a living horoscope. Was I more of a Brenda or more of a Kelly? (Let's be real, Andrea.) What about which Spice Girl? (Um, next question please!) *Sex and the City* offered some better options. (Carrie, with a hint of Charlotte. How about you?)

My attempt to resolve this uncertainty did not end in high school. In college, I worked on the school newspaper. Working late into the night under the fluorescent lights, sitting in front of clunky desktop computers, I'd go on Yahoo.com and take quizzes: What is your spirit animal? (Dolphin); Who's your *real* celebrity crush? (Adam Sandler, duh); What's your style – comfy, boho or classic? (Still deciding). It would be decades before my children would help me learn the real truth: I'd been a Hufflepuff all along.

I had narrowly escaped the internet; it was already nipping at my heels, saying, *Come, ask me your questions . . . I know you.*

The Internet Sad Girl

Picture this: it's the year 2009, and you've had the worst day. Tenth grade at your school deserves its own special zip code in hell. Fuck that girl Anna from the school newspaper. And why do Gigi and her dumb friends in the other room have to be so loud right now? You wonder if your dad is still dating that lady Jennifer. Whatever. At least you're finally alone. You curl up in bed and open Tumblr on your laptop. Scrolling through blogs, you pause to stare at a captivating photo with a vintage filter. It's posted on a page you like, by a girl who is just like you, but hotter – one of the girls with runny mascara, lazing about in black lingerie, thinking about hurting herself. Like you think about doing sometimes. It would help if you could just go tell everyone off, but then they would just think you're a huge bitch. Which maybe you are. You scroll down and like a bunch of the posts. Under the cloak of your alias, Sadgirl15, you post about how depressed you are and how no one understands. Thank God nobody you know IRL has found out about your Tumblr page. It's the only place you can be honest.

Sadgirl15 and others like her had no idea about this, of course, but the pull towards mental illness identities came from two very separate culture shifts that took place just before she was born: the arrival of the internet and the rise of the 'medical model' of mental health. Both were propelled by a deeply American push towards self-determination and the democratisation of knowledge.

The embryonic internet was a haven for teenagers who felt misunderstood, lonely and stressed-out. In this new space, you could privately explore whatever was on your mind, ask questions you'd never breathe to another human, draw on the wisdom of crowds. There were communities, mercifully anonymous, for whatever you felt and whoever you said you were. No matter how badly real life betrayed you, there was a world of infinite strangers online luring you with an irresistible message: *It's okay to be fucked up*. In fact, in this world, that's what made you someone worth knowing – or worth clicking on, whatever. And the darker, the better. For teenagers who felt like outsiders, this was a dream; it's no surprise that more than half of the original users of social media were under twenty-five years old.

When it came to their identities, girls of the early Internet Age had even more to sort out than those in past generations: there were the next-level paradoxes of post-feminism, a growing awareness of intersectionality, and ever-widening class disparities, all of which served both to connect and to isolate young women from one another.

Conversations around power dynamics, privilege, class, race and gender were this generation's soundtrack. For some, these issues became a passionate focus; for the rest, a set of vague directives: be kind, be guilty, be humble, be empowered. Girls had heard all about objectification and knew it was important to be in command of your own body and your own story – to engage with the world, including the world online, on your own terms. What should those terms be?

Cool, alluring, and allegedly empowered, the Internet Sad Girl made her debut on Tumblr, but she'd been rehearsing for decades – especially in the one just before she arrived on the scene. If you were a girl in the nineties passing through a bookstore, surely you would have noticed the bedroomy cover of *Prozac Nation: Young and Depressed in America:* a doe-eyed Elizabeth Wurtzel, long hair a-scraggle, arm bent in a floppy headlock. It's a portrait of coming of age off-kilter, that moment where pain converts girlhood into something sexy.

Wurtzel's candid, ruminative memoir recalled her childhood as the brilliant, volatile only child of divorced parents, who makes her way to Harvard only to blow apart in a hurricane of tumultuous relationships and academic pressure. Increasingly battered by her own mind, she seeks help from a psychiatrist and ultimately finds Prozac, the one thing that provides her with some 'breathing room.'

The seismic nature of this discovery is not lost on Wurtzel. What does it mean to be a person who relies on a pill? How does that shape her identity? Does a 'chemical imbalance' define her? Whatever the answer to these questions, Wurtzel is willing to pay any price for an explanation of her suffering – for the existential balm of *meaning*. Generations of young women followed in her footsteps: they read the book, and they tried the pills.

'We weren't bad or lazy or stupid; we were sick,' wrote Laura Delano in a reflection on *Prozac Nation*'s impact. 'The meaning that we were seeking had been right in front of us all along in psychiatric patienthood. By leaning into personal defect as destiny, we'd finally get what we'd been searching for: feeling seen, and heard, and special.'

Wurtzel was far from the first to combine sickness and sexiness – but *Prozac Nation* injected the Sad Girl deep into the mainstream. This girl-depression could bring help without pity, sympathy without ostracism; mental illness could even make you cool. Better yet, it could make you hot.

As the nineties ended and the new millennium began, the All-American Sad Girl was perfectly poised to take centre stage. Then the technology arrived to make her a star.

Social Media: Illness Incubator

As the Sad Girls on Tumblr multiplied, the messages grew layered, and confusing. No line was drawn between mental *illness* and mental *suffering*. Was a Sad Girl just someone having a bad day, seeking support, making a statement, or clinically depressed? Some Tumblr accounts began to actively promote food restriction, self-harm and suicide. Users were seeing darker and darker content, and this took a toll on an already fragile demographic. Just as Tumblr banned blogs encouraging these harmful behaviours, the world changed again. New platforms launched – Instagram (2010) and TikTok (2018), both of which enthralled adolescent girls – and everyone got a smartphone. The hypnotising algorithms driving these apps made sure that anyone whose browsing indicated an interest in mental health would be pummelled with videos of other teens suffering similar or worse symptoms, making kids feel they were part of a growing and important community of mentally unwell peers. It was a living experiment in social contagion.

The new technology arrived in time to augment other aspects of the cultural moment in the mid-2010s. From the halls of academia to the silver screen, everybody was talking about *trauma*. Trauma and its healing processes – disclosing and witnessing, telling and listening, narrating and decoding – captured the public's attention. A surge of memoirs and novels appeared, describing alcoholism and drug abuse, eating disorders and depression, as well as societal traumas of racism, sexism, poverty and other forms of cultural disenfranchisement.

Young people from wide-ranging backgrounds began to recast their painful experiences in line with this new cultural conversation. The feeling was that they would never be seen or acknowledged (or even, as I've heard more than once, have a good story for a college essay) unless they could claim some form of trauma. As the years passed, these concerns generalised in the minds of teenagers: if you don't have a psychiatric diagnosis, nobody will care about you.

It wasn't just mental illness identities that were being transmitted on social media: it was symptoms, too. 'Emotional contagion', a subset of social contagion, is 'the tendency to automatically mimic and synchronise expressions, vocalisations, postures, and movements with those of another person and, consequently, to converge emotionally'. 'Mood transfer', or (amazingly) in German, 'Stimmungsübertragung', can be as simple as a tender moment of empathy, as dangerous as an angry mob, or as benign as the Christmas Spirit. Of note, women are more given to emotional contagion than men.

History is filled with colourful examples of emotional contagion, from the dancing plague of Strasbourg in 1518, to the Tanganyika laughter epidemic of 1962, to, less humorously, the Salem witch trials. Perhaps most famously, the publication of Johann Wolfgang von Goethe's 1774 epistolary novel, *The Sorrows of Young Werther* – which depicted a young man who took his own life in the context of unrequited love – produced some of the first documented copycat suicides, as men shot themselves while dressed up as the main character and left a copy of the book at the scene of their death.

Centuries later, this 'Werther Effect' persists. In 2017, the Netflix series *13 Reasons Why* told the story of Hannah, who commits suicide after being bullied and leaves thirteen tapes behind explaining her reasons for ending her life. Death is the ultimate power grab for Hannah, who gets the final word and revenge from beyond the grave. Critics worried about the potential impact of the show, and they may have been right: suicide rates increased by 28.9 per cent among teens in the United States in the month following the show's release. In fact, suicide has been found, time and again, to be tragically contagious.

Waves of emotional contagion tend to arise in times of adversity, and although both positive and negative emotional states are transmissible, bad feelings travel faster. During Covid, teenagers – mainly girls – began presenting to doctors with a potpourri of rare psychiatric symptoms and self-diagnoses. Take Aidan, from Calgary, who erupted in spasms, 'whistles and whoops' while walking into the house one afternoon. Thousands of other teens – all of whom had been watching videos on TikTok of peers claiming to have Tourette's syndrome – began to display similar symptoms around the same time. As paediatric neurologists worked their way through the barrage of cases, a new syndrome was coined: 'TikTok Tics'. Concurrently, many teenage girls also developed atypical symptoms of eating disorders, autism and identity disturbances related to dissociative identity disorder and multiple personality disorder, as the world of 'plurals' (disconnected, alternate selves within a person) became popular on social media. Heavier users of TikTok were found to be prone to a host of psychiatric and pseudopsychiatric symptoms and self-diagnosis of various mental conditions.

Targeting the vulnerabilities of young people, influencers on social media also passed around tips and tricks for those flirting with an eating disorder or self-harm. Young teenage girls would be served 'thinspo', or recommendations for how to restrict calories and skip meals. Girls who sought membership in communities of the depressed and the anxious would pick up detailed instructions for how to cut themselves, how much medicine to take to overdose successfully, or how to tie a foolproof noose.

By 2025, symptoms and illness identities and behaviours travelled freely through social media, with the help of curated content, relatable memes and the extremely online habits of the digital natives. Indeed, self-diagnosis became the rule rather than the exception for youth seeking mental health services, and came to be a defining feature of Gen Z.

Social Media: Traumatiser

I am deeply grateful to have come of age before social media. When I first got Facebook (or if I'm honest, was it Friendster?), I had the classic FOMO experience: I saw that a friend of mine had hung out with another friend of mine and I wasn't invited! I recognised that was a totally normal thing – for two people I know to hang out without me – but I really didn't like seeing evidence of it. I remember thinking, *Why do I have to know this?*

By the time of my first social media exposure, I was already a fairly well-adjusted adult, yet I still lost several minutes of my life being upset over something totally unremarkable. After this initial bad experience, I was able to walk away: social media wasn't for me, and I dropped it.

A girl coming of age today doesn't feel like she has that option – social media is an unavoidable part of her reality. And social media harms girls every day.

It's an old story that girls and women are hypnotised to believe the most important thing is their body and appearance, that purchasing the right products is the path to happiness, that in order to be their 'best self', they need to spend lots of time and money on their looks. It's a more recent story that they believe this is also the path to empowerment. Girls in the nineties inhaled the first message – and a bit of the second one – from the pages of *Seventeen*. One couldn't escape the message that there were things to be, and not to be.

I'm not the first to observe that social media celebrates the highest achievers in looks, popularity, love and talent – and consoles the rest with tips for self-improvement. Just like the glossy women's magazines of the seventies, eighties and nineties, but available 24/7, social media also has built-in addictive technology powered by billionaires that knows your every want, plus a selfie camera – and your whole class watching.

Yes, phones keep girls on their toes in old and new ways. Becoming a young woman is now a spectator sport. What's more: phones provide a constant stream of labels, catchphrases, hashtags – things you can be, should be or shouldn't be. It's important to be body-positive . . . but pressure on looks has only increased with a culture that trades in photos and videos. If you're lucky, you might be a tastemaker and an influencer . . . but dear God, don't be thirsty. You should buy the right backpack, sneakers and scrunchies . . . but at all costs, avoid being basic. Do everything in your power to be physically attractive . . . but check your pretty privilege.

In general, girls of this generation take #MeToo as bedrock, and might critique the problematic male gaze at the kitchen table. But social media has compelled so many of them, in equal measure, to feel that posting bikini videos on TikTok is a necessary part of life. The expectation of opportunity and power has seemed to blossom alongside a profound need to be desired and approved in a way that feels obviously regressive. Whereas in past decades the contradictions a girl had to navigate were relatively simple – maybe you could be pretty *and* smart, or cheerful *and* angst-ridden – nowadays the data points are orders of magnitude more numerous, and more contradictory. It's enough to drive any girl crazy.

There are indeed real mental health consequences. It's now research-driven common knowledge that the more time girls spend using social media, the less likely they are to feel confident and the more likely they are to be depressed, with a steep increase after one to two hours a day. Social comparison causes dissatisfaction with oneself, and so any girl on social media is walking around feeling uneasy in her own skin pretty much all the time. In one major study, 80 per cent of teenage girls said that they compared themselves to others online, and, of those, 90 per cent said they rated themselves as 'worse' or 'much worse' than the others they saw. Conversely, studies show that decreasing social media use dramatically improves symptoms of depression and loneliness. Psychologist Jean Twenge has found that for girls in particular, social media use is a more powerful risk factor for depression than binge drinking, early sexual activity, marijuana use, hard drug use, school suspension or lack of exercise.

The mental health harms from social media are not limited to comparison quicksand. Smartphones have also made the social world more treacherous, with relational aggression and cyberbullying surging in girls. On social media, relationships are meaner, more superficial and more fleeting. Not happy with someone? Block her. Want to get back at someone or let them know you're not a fan? Unfriend. Relationships are easy come, easy ghost. And just as people can vanish from your phone, they can pop up unexpectedly, haunting you in pictures on other people's pages. There's no possibility of letting go or moving on. You have to see your ex's face every time you check your email and every time your phone offers you, unbidden, a musical montage of what you were doing on this day two years ago.

I had a patient who told me about a friend breakup with someone at a different high school. I said, 'Well, at least you won't have to see her every day.' She looked at me like, *What are you talking about?*

Teens will be the first to tell you that social media is ruining their mental health but feel unable to stop themselves. A Pew Research survey found that 48 per cent of teens say that social media harms the mental health of people their age.

Finally, social media injures girls by providing fertile ground for sexual abuse. Image-based sexual abuse (IBSA), aka 'revenge porn', has made slut-shaming a living nightmare for many young women. In these situations, privately exchanged photographs are widely distributed – to a broader text chain, to the whole school or just posted online for anyone to see – without permission from the subject. In some cases, images have been stolen by hackers, who then threaten to distribute a girl's nude photos to her classmates and family unless she supplies the hackers with even more explicit ones. In other cases, 'deep fakes' have been circulated, causing trauma on par with other IBSA. Ninety per cent of the victims of IBSA are women, and given the degree of exposure, the infinite reach of the internet, and the immortality of images online, the experience has been described as 'life-ruining'.

In 2024, the US Surgeon General finally called for a warning label on social media platforms, officially deeming them a source of harm to the mental health of teenagers. In 2026, the UK government proposed a ban on social media for under-sixteens, following the example set by Australia.

Social Media: Your Psychiatrist

'Are you hurting?' says the cute guy in the video. He has a scruffy haircut and wears a checked button-down. He sits hunched caringly towards the camera. The vibe is somewhere between sensitive teacher – the kind who plays in a band on the weekends – and dream boyfriend. He looks you right in the eyes, as much as that's possible on TikTok. 'If you are hurting, you have trauma.'

How could you not click on the bold red block letters, advertising 'The Trauma Test'. Fun! And once he starts talking, you're hooked. After all, he's a Licensed Professional Counsellor (LPC). And that eye contact is just hypnotising. *You're hurting. It means you have trauma.* 'And don't you ever let someone tell you that you don't.'

'Do you avoid or fear certain situations?' asks a professional female voice talking you through a diagram in the next video. 'Are you unable to control your emotions at times?' *Yes. YES! I do! That's me!* 'You might have high-functioning PTSD.'

'Often stressed, yet productive? Ruminate on negative thoughts?' High-functioning OCD.

'Low self-esteem means your nervous system is dysregulated,' says a middle-aged therapist in a turtleneck. With thick grey hair and tasteful makeup, she's giving *kind auntie.*

'It's okay to cut toxic family members out of your life,' says a tall man at a podium. 'Blood is not thicker than your mental health.'

Maybe you don't think it's *that* bad. You're not, like, fully mentally ill. But something feels off these days. Life shouldn't be this hard. Maybe you're just *neurodivergent?*

Here's a game to help you find out. 'Hold up ten fingers,' suggest countless therapists, life coaches and 'wellness entrepreneurs' on TikTok. Now put a finger down if any of the following is true for you: Do you plan conversations in your head? Are you both introverted and extroverted? Do you ask lots of follow-up questions? Do you have an interest in personality types? Do you talk out loud to work through your ideas? Do you write in half-cursive, half-print? Do you sleep on your side? Do you have the ability to focus and unfocus your eyes? Have you ever had an existential crisis?

We've come a long way from classic or boho, Ravenclaw or Hufflepuff.

Maybe you're not the type who's taken in by experts or searching for a diagnosis. Maybe you're just looking for company in your own pain.

If that's the case, you'll be captivated by the young woman crying as the words scroll across her face: *When you just can't do it anymore.*

Next video: POV of someone peering onto subway tracks. In the comments, suicidal people posting the dates they plan to kill themselves.

Next video: snapshots of a boy, with a countdown to the moment he died by suicide. The last image is a picture of his grave.

Not all the mental health content on the internet is that grim. You might find a 'mental health advocate' wearing hospital scrubs, an 'autism expert' with sharp glasses who *actually has autism,* or one of the million girls just like you, making fun of themselves, dishing on what they learned in their therapy sessions. 'I'm going to tell you something today, and I really want you to take this in.'

Lots of their advice is vaguely correct; some is even spot-on. 'This goes out to all my girlies with the big feels: *Fear is memory of pain.*'

But a girl can get overwhelmed doomscrolling through the litany of pseudotherapeutic advice dispensed by young women seated cross-legged on their beds, self-styled experts in some field of psychic struggle that happens to correspond to *exactly* what is wrong with you.

In fact, young people are sick of drinking from this fire hose. They are craving a way to sort the good information from the rest. Unfortunately, the more curious you are about mental health, the more inundated with content you'll be and the more paralysed you're likely to become. And if you weren't in the market for mental health advice, just searching what's on your mind – normal stuff for a teenage girl, like 'issue with friend' or 'body image' or 'stress' – will prompt the algorithm to peg you as a target for mental 'wellness' content. You'll see more, and more, and more. Soon, days when you weren't even thinking about 'issue with friend' or 'body image' or 'stress' will find you flashed back to an old painful state of mind – when maybe all you wanted was to watch someone restock their fridge or rate the texture of a new slime.

The Rise of the Medical Model

If the internet and social media are responsible for the widespread distribution of psychiatric labels, the field of psychiatry itself is responsible for having created them in the first place. This is not a crime, of course. But it does have its own story: a discrete period of time when a profession that was primarily humanistic and patient-centred metamorphosed into one that was more regulated, more mechanised – and more reductive.

Before 1980, the prevailing wisdom about mental health was

psychoanalytic: to understand a person, you needed to know about their inborn temperament, early experience, attachment relationships and coping mechanisms. You needed to spend time with them, to learn what it was like to be in their unique presence. If someone was unhappy, you had to learn what conflicts burdened them, what pain or trauma they had experienced. The path to healing was therapy that encouraged bountiful expression and reflection. Healing meant not only recovering from symptoms but finding meaning and purpose in life.

That was fine for a subset of doctors and patients. But many others – policymakers, insurance companies and patients themselves – were getting, well . . . impatient. It all took too long, the results were too fuzzy and many people could not access care. Plus, new medicines (the SSRIs) were being developed that might solve people's problems faster and more affordably.

But first, the field needed a rebrand. So in 1980, the *DSM* received a complete overhaul. Instead of the mushy, heavy language of neurosis, there would be nice, clean checklists of symptoms. Known as 'operationalised criteria', these eliminated any mention of psychological causes. Whereas the *DSM-I* had listed some diagnoses as 'reactions', now whatever you might be reacting to no longer mattered. The doctor didn't need to know anything about your childhood; they just had to look at the list, tick off your symptoms, and make a diagnosis. If you met the criteria, then you had the disease. These lists evolved through a few more editions of the *DSM,* but essentially held stable as the criteria psychiatrists like me use today.

There were positive effects of these changes. Medicines indeed provided a cheaper, faster and easier way for people to feel better. Primary care doctors could offer an SSRI to anyone who seemed unhappy. Psychiatric help could suddenly reach a wider range of patients, including the many people who did not have access to a therapist.

Therapy underwent a dramatic transformation, shifting emphasis from an individual's subjective experience to objective signs and symptoms. While psychoanalysis had been described as an archaeological process, *excavating* important memories and digging into the mind for answers, the new metaphors were about *optimising:* tweaking and correcting glitches in the *computer* that was the human brain. Cognitive behaviour therapy (CBT), which embodies these principles, became the treatment of choice, alongside medications. Designed to be focused and efficient, CBT was easier to study and support with the metrics familiar to evidence-based medicine.

Also arriving on the scene was 'health literacy,' the notion that people should have access to medical knowledge themselves, not just be recipients of expert advice from doctors. A patient was not just a patient, but a consumer and a partner in decision-making. Enter: the internet, and now a person could go on WebMD to learn about what ailed them. Mental illness awareness grew, and stigma began to decline.

Managed care pushed psychiatry further towards the medical model. American insurance companies were happy to pay for medications instead of therapy, and grew more stringent about which visits they would reimburse and which diagnoses they considered worthy of treatment. Visits shortened from forty-five-minute therapy sessions to ten-minute medication check-ins. A patient's time spent with a doctor decreased to nearly nothing.

Leading American psychiatrist authors have bemoaned the decline of the doctor-patient relationship. 'In an earlier era,' says Daniel Carlat, 'we would dig. We would ask pointed questions. We wouldn't let the patient off the hook until we had figured out what made him or her *tick*.' However, the new model replaced this with 'the illusion that we understand our patients when all we are doing is assigning them labels.'*

* Psychiatrist and professor Daniel Siegel, founder of the field of interpersonal neurobiology, expresses a similar sentiment: 'The sad thing that I saw with my trainees was as a physician if you were then given a label for someone, like let's say this person is depressed,

This is where things stood around the turn of the millennium, when I started my own training. I remember the first day of my psychiatry rotation in medical school. There we all were, in the conference room – doctors, nurses, social workers – surrounding a platter of stale bagels from the night before and running the list of who had been admitted to the hospital. As the chatter among the staff quieted, I waited for the wisdom to spill forth. How do you heal a human soul?

Instead, I heard this: 'She's a fourteen-year-old with chronic OCD and recurrent depression, refractory to two SSRIs, now with an exacerbation of suicidality,' the list began. 'He's a twenty-one-year-old man with bipolar disorder, recently decompensated in the setting of multiple personal, financial and academic stressors.' The cases went on: the meds they were taking, the symptoms that prompted the recent admission.

My brain began to flatline.

This really bothered me. Who *were* these people? And how did knowing this information set me up to make a therapeutic connection with them?

This training did point me towards the right medicines that could reduce these patients' symptoms. It helped me know whether the person was in imminent danger of dying and needed the protection of a hospital to stay alive, in the literal sense.

The medical model taught me that symptoms cluster together in predictable ways. It helped me envision the brain pathways and neurochemicals that are involved in these processes. It sharpened my ability to distinguish 'sick' from 'not sick'. And of course, it facilitated conversations with my patients about what they were experiencing.

or this one has schizophrenia, or this one has autism, whatever, and you said this is a brain disorder . . . you would stop actually knowing the client.'

Those conversations can be really helpful – including psychologically and socially. The medical model allows a person to position herself apart from – and against – her symptoms, which can, to a point, feel empowering. It helps people explain their problems to others; it legitimises and destigmatises mental illnesses. In its expansion, the medical model has brought relief to millions of people who may have never considered themselves psychiatric patients deserving of help, or who would never have been able to access it.

Medical categories can also help us understand ourselves and one another more deeply. If you learn, for example, that a person has autism, that might help you feel more patient as they struggle through a schedule change. Paradoxically, objectifying mental illness includes a call for subjectivity: look at how the world is *for you,* and *for me*!

However. While it gives with one hand, the medical model takes away with the other, offering a shortcut that can interfere with more substantial healing and growth. Imagine if Violet and I had never uncovered the mistrust she carried through the world, or if Chloe and I had just focused on managing ADHD.

The problem, then, is not that the medical model is wrong. The problem is that *we have overvalued it and relied upon it too much.* It has vacantly proliferated to the exclusion of fuller and more accurate representations of ourselves. As a result, we now see generations of young women whose identities suffer from reductionism and fear of what their emotions mean.

The Expansion of Diagnoses

A condition is considered 'overdiagnosed' when it is attributed too uncritically to too many people. Turning to the medical model, psychiatry made overdiagnosis easy. Take, for example, the case of major depressive disorder. Before 1980, there had been no such entity, but for the new *DSM,* authors gathered the vague symptoms of various neuroses into one big 'objective' category. The next edition went a step further, conflating mild with serious depression, and 'exogenous depression' (a reaction to external events) with 'endogenous depression' (from within). From that point on, psychiatrists would lump many different kinds of experiences together as 'major depressive disorder', which, in turn, became easy to diagnose.

Although nobody wants to be depressed or anything like it, admission into the 'major depressive disorder' category conferred certain advantages in the US. It was a necessary prerequisite for receiving the increasingly popular antidepressant medications. Furthermore, insurance companies required every psychiatric patient to receive a medical diagnosis, and some diagnoses were more reimbursable than others. A patient with 'adjustment disorder with depressed mood' might not be reimbursed for their visit, but someone with 'major depressive disorder' would be. This encouraged the doctor-patient team to reach for more serious-sounding labels.

Categories that offer a benefit have a way of expanding. As philosopher Ian Hacking describes, psychiatric categories are particularly porous and stretchy, given their dependence on the changing tides of culture. In his essay 'Making Up People', he calls this phenomenon 'the looping effect'. For example, he writes: 'Before 1975, high-functioning autism was not a way to be a person . . . People didn't experience themselves in this way, they didn't interact with their friends, their families, their employers, their counsellors, in the way they do now.' Once a new 'type' of person becomes widely accepted, more people push into the category and identify with its label.

Australian psychologist Nick Haslam developed the related notion of 'concept creep', describing how harm-related psychological concepts like 'abuse, bullying, trauma, mental disorder, addiction and prejudice' expand both 'horizontally', capturing different presentations, and also 'vertically', absorbing less severe forms of the same presentation. Haslam argues that over time, these expansions have made humans more sensitive to various types of harm, which has both costs (e.g., preoccupation with risk) and benefits (e.g., intolerance of injustice) to society.

Depression diagnoses exploded between the 1980s and Y2K, and continue to rise among young people. Some have argued that the shocking statistics about teen mental health that are still making headlines may actually be misleading – a result of a process called 'prevalence inflation'. Popularised by British psychologist Lucy Foulkes, this term means that the statistics are not as dramatic as they seem, because those data may be influenced by forces other than a real increase in disease. According to Foulkes, prevalence inflation occurs through improved recognition of genuine mental illness (a good thing) combined with 'overinterpretation' (a problematic thing).

Prevalence inflation, notable especially in young women, relies on emotional contagion. According to Foulkes, it follows a typical pattern. Increased public discussion of mental illness leads people to notice and privilege symptoms that may be ordinary or normal; knowledge of others with mental health conditions leads young women to see signs of illness in themselves. Then they find support for their suspected condition in online communities, and the condition escalates from a possible nothing to a definite something.

Expanding individual diagnoses also made it easier for people to accumulate several at a time, known as 'comorbidities'.* Carlat describes a moment where he realised that over time, he had diagnosed the same patient with ADHD, depression and five distinct anxiety disorders. 'With Lorraine,' he writes, 'I had fallen into the trap of what I call "DSM-think", in which I spent too much time trying to fit her into categories and too little time trying to understand her as a person.'

* The majority of people with mental illness have comorbidities. For example, 82 per cent of people with schizophrenia have symptoms of other disorders. Similarly, 80 per cent of patients with depression suffer from at least one other mental disorder, commonly anxiety, alcohol use disorders or personality disorders.

The Costs of Illness Identities

Indeed, research has shown that psychiatric labels have a way of reifying themselves. This means that the more we talk about them, the more definitive – and determining – they feel.

Moreover, psychiatric diagnoses are poor sources of identity because they are not always the solid entities that many people believe them to be. They can change and overlap with one another, and in children and adolescents, they change more than they stay the same. Interestingly, this is especially true in girls.

Despite this fact, psychiatric diagnoses tend to stick to a person's sense of self. In *Pathological: The True Story of Six Misdiagnoses,* writer and psychiatric patient Sarah Fay describes her Kafkaesque journey through the mental health system and its impact on her:

> Yes, I was told – with certainty, one after another – I had anorexia, major depressive disorder (MDD), anxiety disorder, attention deficit hyperactivity disorder (ADHD), obsessive-compulsive disorder (OCD), bipolar disorder . . . Each diagnosis was a self-fulfilling prophecy. The sicker I believed myself to be, the more evidence I found confirming I was sick. The more evidence I had, the more certain I became. The more certain I became, the more willing I was to undergo treatments. The more treatments I underwent, the sicker I believed myself to be.

Patients like Fay find themselves in this confusion because psychiatric diagnoses create an illusion of concreteness that does not always align with the life of the mind. These categories are *representations* of mental phenomena rather than naturally occurring 'things'. As one senior psychiatrist told a focus group on the subject, 'A finger pointing at the moon is different than the moon itself.'

This concreteness – also known as 'neuroessentialism' – can lead people to believe they are more stuck in their diagnoses than they are. If 'this is just how you're wired', a person does not have much agency: their condition just *is*. If a girl blames her unhappiness on a naturally occurring fault in her own brain, the powerful psychological and social sources of her discomfort are minimised, demoted to 'triggers' or 'stressors' activating a preexisting condition.

Above all, when taken on as identities, psychiatric diagnoses can actually make people feel worse – and get worse. Those who hold anxiety disorders as central to their sense of self believe they are less capable than others with the same symptoms who don't label themselves with a disorder. People with depression have been shown to feel more hopeless and pessimistic if they think of their symptoms as a medical condition, especially if they believe it is caused by a 'chemical imbalance'.

Finally, neuroessentialism can have harmful effects on society. Locating pathology in the brain of an individual can let bad actors in the world off the hook. For example, when pathological gambling was made into a diagnosis, no one was happier than the casino owners. When we look at the 'girl-destroying culture', now amplified by social media, we can blame its victims: their suffering is because of the anxiety, depression, neurodivergence and PMDD that exist in their bodies and brains – not because any company has decided to mine their misery for profit.

I think about my own patients, whose sense of self-worth is still forming. Violet, Chloe, Hazel, Kaia . . . each of them is having such a hard time finding her voice and agency, dealing with an age-old internalised misogyny and confusing cultural expectations. Given the long and powerful history of misogyny in our culture, which contributed to patriarchal notions within medicine and psychiatry, girls like my patients are at risk of living diminished lives. Female identity has always been refracted through the gaze of the powerful, and split at its root. We have been fragmented and fractured down to the molecules that make us who we are. Therefore, anything that reduces the female self should be treated with some caution.

In leading with psychiatric labels online, young women are unintentionally facilitating the objectification process like never before. And when we as medical professionals or caregivers allow girls to believe they are sick and crazy when they may not be, we impede their progress towards equality. We replace the real power that comes with believing in the rationality of one's reactions and emotions with the false power conferred by illnesses: a sense of deficiency and an entitlement to care – rather than respect.

And so, strange bedfellows that they are, social media and the medical establishment worked together to produce a 'new' kind of girl who is really a timeless female archetype, rebranded with a post-feminist self-consciousness and a dubious claim to self-empowerment. It's the girl who hides her suffering while dressing up in it. The girl who believes there is something wrong with her. The girl who seamlessly, if not happily, takes on the role of the patient: *I'm the problem: It's me.*

PART TWO
What I'm Hearing

4

Anxiety Girlies

> Indeed, it is not at all unusual for a girl to say to me, 'I have anxiety,' as if she were describing a grave and permanent congenital defect.
>
> **Lisa Damour,**
> *Under Pressure: Confronting the Epidemic of Stress and Anxiety in Girls*

> It just seems like, you agree to have a certain personality or something. For no reason. Just to make things easier for everyone. But when you think about it, I mean, how do you know if it's even you?
>
> **Angela,**
> *My So-Called-Life*, Season 1, Episode 1, 'Pilot'

Sleepless

Becca sits sideways in my chair, swinging her legs over the arm, like a kid. She has such an easy manner, you would never suspect this fourteen-year-old was uncomfortable inside. Except that she's rubbing her eyes.

'You look tired,' I say. 'Were you up late?'

'I fell asleep on FaceTime with my friend Layla. She blocked this guy, so we were on Instagram seeing if he was tagged in any photos, and then it got late.'

This is the second time I'm meeting Becca. She's here because she seems more stressed-out than she's been in the past, according to her parents. Becca started high school last fall, and while she's doing fine academically and has friends and a boyfriend, her parents confided to me that they think she spends too much time on her phone and that some of her friends seem 'kind of negative'. I'm wondering if they were talking about Layla.

I ask Becca more about her social life.

'Well, um . . .' Becca looks at the ceiling. 'I guess I have like different friends. I mainly hang out with my friend Daisy and with my boyfriend, Noah. And then there's my friend Layla who's kind of in a different group. My parents aren't huge fans of hers.'

'Oh, why is that?'

'I don't know, I guess they think she has a lot of insecurities, like family stuff, body image stuff. Her parents are getting divorced, so we talk about that.'

I nod. 'Sounds like you and Layla are close.'

'Very,' she says. 'She's the best to talk to when you're stressed-out, you know? She really understands when I'm feeling like that.'

'Oh, you were feeling stressed-out yesterday?'

'Yeah.' She looks out the window. 'I just have anxiety.'

Having Anxiety

In the past several years, clinical diagnoses of anxiety have increased to unprecedented rates, especially in teenage girls. Abundant research has demonstrated that girls experience higher rates of anxiety than boys after the onset of puberty. But clinically speaking, anxiety is only considered pathological if it does not suit the circumstances that bring it about. Reports of rising anxiety still leave open the question: are increased symptoms a product of more disease, or do they indicate a natural reaction to stressful circumstances, overwhelming pressure and conflicting expectations?

Whether the rise in anxiety diagnoses reflects actual disorders or not, I've observed girls refer to anxiety almost universally as something they 'have'.

This language has struck me, because it is different from how girls describe other feelings. One would not 'have' anger, sadness or fear; one would 'feel' them. The language 'to have' implies a condition – something wrong with a person. As Lisa Damour notes, the way it's used also suggests permanence. Anxiety, in this sense, is not described as a passing state ('I'm hav*ing* anxiety' would be totally different) – but rather apologised for as an unfortunate, yet defining feature of the self.

The other notable thing about the phrasing 'I have anxiety' is that it is vague and impersonal, seemingly unrelated to what the girl thinks or feels. It's just kind of *there*. A person who says 'I have anxiety' is both owning and disowning the problem at the same time. It invokes what writer Leslie Jamison calls the 'post-wounded voice, a stance of numbness . . . that implies pain without claiming it'.

Technically, everybody 'has anxiety'. Anxiety is a necessary and adaptive mechanism, alerting humans to the presence of danger, and motivating us to do our best. Therefore, it would be very bad if you didn't 'have' anxiety. It's like 'having' temperature or blood pressure.

Normal anxiety (like temperature and blood pressure) rises and falls in reaction to internal and external events. It is different from fear, which is a response to an *outside* threat. You could 'fear' bad things happening, like being followed on the street, or having your classmates judge you, or finding out your parents are getting divorced.

Anxiety is more complex. It is a response to both external and *internal* dangers. For example, one is not simply 'afraid' of a test; one is *anxious* about a test. A test triggers a broader network of hopes, memories, thoughts, feelings, relationships and notions of one's identity and self-esteem. It's natural to feel anxious before a big test for all of these reasons. The same could be said of going to a party. It's not just fear of a specific thing happening, but a broader anticipation of conflicting pressures and priorities. Similarly, it's natural to feel anxious before a difficult conversation with an important person.

Some people naturally 'run anxious'. One in five people is born with a temperament style called 'behavioural inhibition' that leads to shyness and stress in the many social situations that everyday life demands. While these individuals are more prone to developing clinically significant anxiety, more than half of them do not. Parental behaviour makes a big difference. A child is more likely to develop clinical anxiety if she has parents who express lots of anxiety, who are controlling and authoritarian, or who are overly accommodating in an effort to reduce the child's distress. Other temperamental styles, such as the 'highly sensitive person' (HSP), can also lead to increased, but not necessarily pathological, experiences of anxiety.

A sensitive child can also become a more anxious person in the course of ordinary relations, depending on her environment and experiences.

Let's say you are four years old. Mom is feeling grumpy after a long day and is setting a plate of salmon and peas down in front of you for dinner. You really don't like salmon and peas, but you also hate seeing disappointment or irritation on your mom's face, so you experience a sense of internal disturbance. There's a part of you that wants to object to the dinner: *How could she give you something so disgusting?* Maybe you've even told her before that you hate salmon and peas. *How could she forget?* But another part of you fears the consequences of these feelings, or feels bad for feeling them in the first place. So what do you experience? Anxiety. Now let's say you come from a family where everyone is very sensitive or has strong feelings: the 'salmon and peas' sorts of moments might happen many times a day; you might become someone who keeps a great deal inside in order to get the very best out of your caregivers, whom you need so badly as a kid. What do you experience, then? A *lot* of anxiety.

Anxiety is a physical experience. An anxious state includes uncomfortable body sensations ranging from muscle tension, shortness of breath and a fast heartbeat to stomachaches and headaches, and even to experiences deep in the nervous system like vision changes, blurring of thoughts, and dissociation. These experiences drive people further away from their anxiety-producing feelings, perpetuating a vicious cycle. When it comes to anxiety, the body does not just keep the score: it also plays the game.

Even when anxiety is normal and useful, it can feel incredibly uncomfortable. So when we feel anxious, we must regulate ourselves. Some of this regulation is physical: we discharge it by moving around, fidgeting, breathing deeply, etc. When anxiety is unregulated, it can be unbearable. Anyone who has had a panic attack would agree, and in cases of severe depression, anxiety is often what drives people to suicide.

Our brains are busy regulating anxiety all the time, and do a lot of this work before the anxiety ever hits full consciousness. It happens through automatic defence mechanisms that keep anxious feelings in check. Some defences work well and others don't, but the mind is always searching for them. One common defence mechanism is worrying. A worrier's thoughts spin round and round, trying to exert control over the anxiety, which, in turn, tries to alert the brain to an ongoing danger. Often, worrying and other defence mechanisms epically fail. We obsess, ruminate, blame ourselves, try to please people – and wind up feeling more anxious more often. Faulty defence mechanisms can make anxiety worse.

Still, the frequent or even intense experience of anxiety does not necessarily constitute a disorder.

What Is an Anxiety Disorder?

According to the *DSM,* anxiety disorders are clusters of symptoms. A *DSM* diagnosis requires experiencing enough symptoms over enough time, in addition to the presence of distress or disruption to one's life from the anxiety. Examples of anxiety disorders include panic disorder, generalised anxiety disorder, social anxiety disorder and specific phobias. Treatments for anxiety disorders include various types of psychotherapy and sometimes medication, or a combination of the two.

But the *DSM* is merely descriptive. It does not offer much guidance about how much anxiety is appropriate in a given context, nor does it take into account underlying causes or cultural standards and expectations. Therefore, the label of 'anxiety disorder' can be applied easily, leading individuals to believe erroneously that there is something wrong with their brains.

An anxiety disorder label can sometimes be extremely helpful, both personally and interpersonally. It can help correct misconceptions (*Oh, he's not rude, he just has social anxiety*) and can also help a person recognise their anxiety, which is the first step in regulating it.

Overreliance on anxiety as an identity, however, can be harmful. Although anxiety disorders can be validating and can provide relief, research also shows that *labelling anxiety as an illness can actually make anxiety worse*. As I mentioned earlier, people who hold anxiety disorders as central to their identity believe they are less capable and can become more fearful and avoidant compared to others with the same symptoms who don't label it as a disorder or an identity. Indeed, in recent years anxiety diagnoses have been generating more requests for academic accommodations, such as not having to attend class or be called on by a professor. But avoidance behaviour can often make a person's anxiety symptoms worse. In this way, anxiety illness identities can become self-fulfilling prophecies.

Moreover, whether one has an anxiety disorder or not, the emergence of anxiety is always a reaction to some felt danger. In other words, it's always *about something*.

I'm wondering what it's about for Becca.

Social Purgatory

'So I guess I've still been stressed this week. Layla and I had a long talk last night about it until my parents made me go to bed.'

'Sounds like a good conversation.'

'Yeah, it was. I love her.'

'What were you guys talking about?'

'Oh, just annoying social stuff. Layla has anxiety too, so I can talk to her. She also has some body image issues. She's not fat or anything, but I don't know, we were talking about this girl from her camp who posts a lot on Instagram – she has a *lot* of followers because she's pansexual, right? But she's also like really pretty, but also super skinny, so we were just talking about how she's so anorexic and it's annoying.'

I take this in. As is often the case in teenage girl parlance, 'anorexic' means 'skinnier than me' or 'a thin person I hate'. I realise I have no idea yet how Becca feels about her own body.

'But anyway, yeah, she has anxiety too, like me, so it's good to talk to her.'

'Becca,' I say, 'you've mentioned having anxiety a few times. Could you tell me more about what you mean?'

'Oh' – Becca bites a cuticle absently – 'just that my wiring seems off somehow.' She takes her finger out and scowls at it. 'Like, nothing is really wrong with my life, so it's just my anxiety that makes me feel bad.' She wipes the finger on her jeans. 'So.'

There's that blasé biologism. *Wiring. Just my anxiety that makes me.* Followed by the supporting statement *Nothing is wrong with my life,* therefore *something must be wrong with me – a random act of genetics.* Which at best is only a piece of the puzzle – and at worst prevents us from looking for the other pieces.

'So,' I say back. I hunt for her eyes.

'Well, no, just like I don't know why I'd be anxious.'

'So you've been feeling anxious lately?'

'Yeah, kind of.' She looks at me like I might be dumb.

'Like more anxious than usual?'

'Yeah, I guess?' Finally, the sidelong glance. Maybe my provocation is engaging her. I'm trying to get her to see that anxiety is a *state,* not necessarily a defect – and sometimes a great source of information. We'll see.

'Okay, interesting.' I lean forward, as if she's showing me a rare tropical skin rash. I want her to join me in this detective work. 'Is there a time when you noticed that state coming on, that anxious feeling?'

'Yeah, for sure – that's why I called Layla last night.'

'Huh.' A clue! 'What was making you anxious last night?'

Becca cracks her neck side to side. 'I don't know, it's just my friend Daisy . . . I was hanging out with her yesterday – me and her and Noah. Daisy just stresses me out, I don't know.'

I learn that Becca and Noah have been going out for a few months, and Daisy is a close mutual friend of theirs.

'Just the other day when we were at my house, like usual. And she was just going on and on about this guy who likes her and she doesn't know how to tell him she's not interested, and Noah was like so obsessed with helping her. It was like, *Am I here?* Daisy is a drama person. She will get over this. Tomorrow it will be something else. I mean, can we all just *chill*?'

'Hmm.'

'So I don't know. Noah seemed fine. Layla says I'm having anxiety, so she's helping me deal with it.'

I'm struck by her *questions: 'Am I here?'* 'Can we all just *chill*?' It will be necessary to call her attention to what's in those questions and help her turn them from questions to statements about how she feels. And feel all the anxiety that comes with that, and listen to the feeling underneath. But we're not there yet.

Where we are is at the beginning of a therapeutic relationship, and we can use her anxiety as a road map. When she experiences anxiety not just out in the world, but right here in our sessions, it will show us that we are close to the underlying feeling causing it. The dots have not been connected yet, but they are starting to show up on the map.

'I don't know, I feel like it's fine,' Becca says. 'I mean, everyone is annoying. I'm sure I'm annoying, too.'

Becca is turning away from the signal. She's generalising, being vague, mildly attacking herself. It's like she read the textbook on how to manifest anxiety as a teenage girl.

I'm suspecting she is blowing this off because she feels stuck, so I try to find out if I'm right. I learn that Daisy is 'tricky' and can be hard to talk to, especially about anything Daisy might be doing wrong. A conflict could damage the friendship. And the friendship is part of a group that includes Becca's boyfriend; having a conflict that involves him might not go well either. Becca doesn't have the security to rock the boat. And jumping ship does not feel like an option.

I need backstory. 'Becca, tell me more about you and Daisy and Noah – all of that.'

'Well, Daisy and I have known each other since our moms met in a baby music class or something, but now we're in school together for the first time. And Daisy and Noah are good friends from their middle school – they're kind of, I don't know, like popular, I guess. So then he and I started going out and she was just, like, automatically our other friend and now since school ended we just mostly hang out at my house because Daisy and her mom have a small apartment and my parents work a lot. Daisy is obsessed with how we have this, like, raised area off my kitchen with benches and a TV and she's always like, *your house is so amazing* and stuff.'

'And what's it like, when you're just hanging out, the three of you?'

'I don't know. We're mostly on our phones or watching TV. Daisy and Noah both like smoking so we do that sometimes, but not a lot – I don't really like weed. But Daisy has this whole thing about how weed and Spindrift is the perfect combination and we have a mini fridge just with Spindrift because my mom likes it.'

Sounds like Daisy calls a lot of the shots.

'And what about Noah? Tell me more about him.'

'He's a cutie. I don't know . . . he's tall. He likes the Mets. He's a very friendly person. My parents like him because he's like polite, or whatever.'

'And do you like him?'

'Yeah. He's like, very *boy,* you know?' She blushes a little. 'Like, simple.'

I'm picturing nice smile, bro-ey good manners.

'And what's his relationship like with Daisy?'

'Honestly I think he would take a bullet for her. It's kind of annoying, just how they're like so close. He always says she's like a "brother" to him.' (She does air quotes around the word 'brother.') 'But he's also always hugging her and punching her and stuff. Whatever,' she sighs. 'It's just how they are.'

Just then, Becca's phone dings in her bag. She takes it out and looks at it.

'Ugh, see, this is what I'm talking about.'

It's customary to ask patients to put their phones aside during therapy sessions. With teenage girls, however, I find it useful sometimes to see the girl and the phone in action. 'What's going on?'

'It's Daisy. Hold on a sec.' She frowns and scrolls.

'May I ask what's happening?'

'Here.' She holds up the text for me to read. I lean forward, squinting to see: '*Hey hot stuff, I dragged ur bf to sephora and now he smells like vanilla mist- meet us here when u r done. Hope you're working out all your shit, you fucking psycho.*'

'See?' she says. She takes a heavy sigh.

'Yes, I think I'm getting a picture.' Daisy seems confident, and flirty. I get the sense that even though she's known her forever, Becca is a bit intimidated by her. I'm guessing Daisy is a pretty girl (the kind of girl who could drag a guy who's not her boyfriend to Sephora, who could get him to accept being sprayed with perfume). I'm picturing Becca feeling compelled to do a lot of laughing along.

'It's fine. She just gives me anxiety. It's stupid.'

Becca doesn't strike me as someone who could come up with a good zinger in response. Maybe like '*Yeah, my therapist has a good idea about someone who could help you with your personality*' – or something.

Instead, I say: 'Becca, we're almost out of time, but I can see it's uncomfortable to think about the ways Daisy can be, as you say, "tricky". Maybe one thing we can note is that your anxiety has to do with some feelings you might have when she is being annoying.'

Becca nods slowly. I can't tell if she's totally with me or not.

Yes, Becca's main people are limited, it seems. Kids in high school are often not mature enough to be everything the other people in high school need them to be. And they are stuck with one another! I see why it's worth it for Becca to stay up late having these FaceTime sessions with Layla. And I wonder how we can loosen things up for her, just a little.

'Whatever. It is what it is.' She smiles and shrugs. 'It's okay, there are a lot of us out there. I'm just an Anxiety Girlie.'

And now I have my homework assignment.

The Girlies

On my TikTok feed, a young woman chats with me as she puts on her makeup. It feels like I am sitting inside the mirror. She dispenses advice to me, to us, her audience, the 'Anxiety Girlies': 'Other people do not think about you as much as you think they do.' The advice scrolls across the screen like subtitles. Now she's dabbing some dots of concealer on her cheeks, smoothing them out expertly with a contour brush. 'Just try to remember that.'

The next video appears. Another cheerful 'Anxiety Girlie' who sits in the passenger seat of a car and is about to brave her performance review at work. She 'just wanted to share' with us that her new Rare Beauty aromatherapy pen does wonders for her anxiety. She uncaps the pen (also referred to as a 'girlie'), dabs her inner wrists, and takes a deep, cleansing inhale. Like a chant, the Girlies say: 'We're Anxiety Girlies: *Of course* we're going to read the label. We're Anxiety Girlies: *Of course* we think everyone is mad at us. We're Anxiety Girlies: *Of course* we don't go anywhere without our emotional support water bottle.' Next, I see several videos recommending that as an 'Anxiety Girlie', I should feel fine about fidgeting with my jewellery and can even purchase some 'worry rings' sensuously unboxed in the video: 'Look, they can spin!'

After that, the videos get darker. Several girls film their stress hives; others bitterly mock those who try to tell them 'everybody feels this way'; girls confess they have merely been 'cosplaying secure attachment'. There's a whole other montage of videos by girls who twirl their hair dreamily to music while words scroll across their faces clapping back at the Anxiety Girlies for making light of mental anguish: 'I have such bad OCD I have actual scars from picking my skin'.

My head is spinning with reactions. Even today, I'm still struck by how the most public forum hosts the most private issues. I know that's how it works. The relative anonymity and lack of context make people feel safe. But what's the vibe, exactly, of the Anxiety Girlies? Is anxiety being depicted as something normal (cute, even) to trade tips and hacks about – or a serious disease?

Seems to be all of the above. The Anxiety Girlies of the internet appear to love their label. In this dreamworld, anxiety is something to be, in equal parts, disclosed and performed, normalised and pathologised, and even romanticised. But do these Girlies feel they can maintain such a loving relationship with their vulnerabilities IRL?

And what to make of the word 'Girlie'? The prettification of female pain for public consumption is, we know, nothing new.

To help organise my thoughts, I read some articles online about Girlies – anxious and otherwise – including one called 'We're All Girlies Online . . . It's Not That Deep'. My favourite quote is: 'The fact that literally anyone from your dad to your best friend can be girlies is the main part of its allure.'

I love the idea that dads can be Anxiety Girlies. There's so much humour and intelligence in this notion, precisely because the whole point of Anxiety Girlies is that anxiety is feminised. The word 'Girlie' also conjures a hearty sisterhood – one that offers so much humanity and compassion, it may even have some left over for boys.

So what's the verdict on Anxiety Girlies?

When I'm confused about girl culture, I go on Etsy. I search for 'anxiety girlie' and find many T-shirts saying things like 'Probably Anxious' or 'Anxious AF' or 'Anxiety Girlies Wear Pink'. I find a T-shirt that really charms me. It features a fluffy mouse who could have wandered straight out of a Little Golden Book, accompanied by text reading ‘small and anxious’.

Modern-day nuances notwithstanding, these young women are sending a gendered message out into the world. It says: *anxiety-so-big-it-defines-you* is a routine female (or feminine) experience, and one that makes girls want to be little again – perhaps because they need a special kind of comfort.

When little girls get hurt, they are likely to receive coddling and hugs (whereas boys are taught to push through). Parents, especially fathers, have been found to be more nurturing and attentive to little girls when they show ‘submissive’ emotions like sadness and anxiety. The ‘little girl’ part of teenagers and young women turns out to be something many wish to reclaim.

‘Just a Little Girl’ has been a popular meme on social media. It is used on TikTok, often in videos with the 1995 Gwen Stefani song ‘Just a Girl’ playing in the background, showing young women in a variety of emotional situations. One girl is struggling to park a car, another to zip an overstuffed suitcase. They seem to be asking for a bit of help or encouragement, or at least a knowing smile. Other ‘just little girls’ are found luxuriating in classically feminine pleasures, like putting on lip gloss while seeming to beg the viewer’s pardon to indulge. And then there are videos documenting raw pain. A young woman is curled up crying, staring red-eyed at the camera as the text scrolls by: ‘I’m just a girl who wants to be loved.’

All of these link girliness to vulnerability – a kind that these women must feel is not fully accepted as they get older.

The Just a Little Girl meme is part of an effort among young women to make girlhood something you don’t have to leave behind, but something you can take with you. This movement flowed through the early 2020s, the ‘Year of the Girl’ (2023), and into the years that followed. The ‘Year of the Girl’ featured Taylor Swift’s Eras Tour and the *Barbie* movie. Several other girl-related memes went viral during this time, including Girl Dinner, a collection of snacks from the fridge, and Girl Math, a system of calculations that defied logic and justified gendered guilty pleasures, like shopping. In one video, a pretty teenager tries to explain girl math to her dad. He patiently tolerates this, with an amused smile that says 'this makes no sense, but I love you'. It seems like that's largely the point of girl math: allowing yourself to have some silly priorities, aware on some level that, as a girl, those are the priorities the patriarchy wants you to have. And therein lies its power.

Girls today are growing up post-feminist and post-wounded. An Anxiety Girlie gets to have her pain without claiming it. She's not Rubenesque and burdened (and burdensome) like a woman. She still gets to be breezy and cute. She can still have fun, while getting some TLC. In a generation where girls have taken on so much responsibility, 'Just a Girl's are making an important statement: just as 'boys will be boys', girls want a pass from having to girlboss 24/7.

Still, I'm haunted by the videos posted by really distressed Anxiety Girlies, who are saying quite clearly that the flattening of this category – 'anxiety' – has harmed them. It's not all about aromatherapy pens when you're picking at your skin until you get an infection. An ironic storybook mouse doesn't make herself bleed. How is a girl with moderate anxiety supposed to know which of these groups she belongs to?

One thing that does concern me about this trend is that anxiety seems to be understood as a thing that just *happens to you*. If anxiety is something you 'have' rather than something you experience for a reason, then it's your identity but still not *really* you. That may free you to talk about it socially, without judgement, like a seasonal allergy or a migraine, but the person whose opinions and feelings generated the anxiety has lost her place in the story. The person who 'has' anxiety is an object, not a subject.

This is the opposite of what we aim for in therapy, which is to help people make friends with their anxiety and treat it as a valuable part of themselves connected to feelings that matter. It may be excessive for the situation, but it's usually not senseless. It's not weakness or defect, but an internal message that has not fully computed. Our job is to 'make it make sense', as the kids say. That's how people get better.

The Teenage Girl Brain

This week my supervision group has to meet on Zoom because Zach isn't feeling well.

'I'm starting with my camera off because I'm still putting my makeup on,' says the green box with a big *E* for Eloise.

Zach is lying on the couch, looking swollen and making various silent facial expressions.

'Zach, you're muted,' Eloise says.

'What I was saying is thanks for meeting remotely today.' He takes a tissue and blows his nose.

Eloise and I offer sympathies and unsolicited advice, and then I start.

'So I have this new patient, Becca. She's fourteen, freshman in high school, feeling stressed-out and anxious. Stays up at night co-ruminating with her friend about social stuff. She's like, "I just have anxiety."'

'I know,' Eloise says, 'they all say that nowadays.'

Zach and I nod.

Eloise turns on her camera. She is clutching her forehead over thick black glasses. Her lipstick is freshly applied. 'I mean, there's certainly plenty to be anxious about at that age. Do you think she has an actual anxiety disorder?'

'I wouldn't give her an official diagnosis based on what she's said so far. She's a high-functioning kid. I get the sense she keeps it all inside.'

'I find myself handing out anxiety disorder diagnoses to so many of my teenage girl patients,' Zach says. 'I think clinical anxiety is truly on the rise. It's almost like the teenage girl brain is just a walking anxiety disorder.'

'They did such a good job of showing all the brain stuff in that movie – what was it called?'

'*Inside Out 2?*' I say.

'That's the one,' Eloise says. 'Where Anxiety is just a character that takes control of the brain. Do you doctors agree they did a good job reflecting the neurobiology?'

'Yes.' I sit up tall, eager for the three of us to put our heads together about neuroscience, psychoanalysis, culture and the daily realities of clinical practice. These are my favourite moments.

I recap for my colleagues how the teenage brain is more sensitive to threat than the adult brain, and how in early adolescence, girls are more vulnerable to anxiety than boys.

One reason for this is the timing of the development of the amygdala, a structure involved in fear processing. The amygdala is a kind of anxiety relay centre in the brain. When it gets input suggesting a danger, it triggers the fight-or-flight response, telling the body's stress system (the hypothalamic-pituitary-adrenal, or HPA, axis) to release stress hormones: adrenaline and cortisol. During adolescence, the amygdala undergoes significant development. It matures in parallel with puberty, which happens in girls on average eighteen months earlier than in boys. The onslaught of oestrogen during puberty also potentiates the stress response system, which may explain why the HPA axis (featuring the 'stress hormone' cortisol) is more reactive in teens than in adults and especially in females.

'It's not just the amygdala, though,' Zach says, moving on to the other major brain area relevant to this discussion: the frontal lobe, the last part of the brain to develop. Adolescents are filled with thoughts and feelings and impulses, but as a result of incomplete frontal lobe development, they lack a full set of self-regulation skills.

The teenage brain contains a great deal of content, but not nearly enough organisation and connectivity to make sense of it. Compared to adults, teenagers have more grey matter (neurons) and less white matter (high-efficiency myelin pathways). This means that teenage brains are highly active but not integrated. In particular, the rational, 'thinking' parts of the brain cannot yet 'talk' to the deeper regions that are busy freaking out.

'Okay, but here's my question,' I say. 'If anxiety is such a natural experience for the teenage brain, why at this moment in human history do so many teenage girls and young women go through life saying, *I have anxiety*? Is there actually more illness or does everyone just see the whole anxiety spectrum as illness?'

Zach rolls his eyes. 'I think it's a genuine increase in illness. From all sorts of places – social media and also the fact that they use the phones to co-ruminate about their mental suffering all the time, which makes it worse. You saw it – "Anxiety Girlies", or whatever.'

I'm quiet as I think about how to respond. Co-ruminating is when two people fixate on a problem, going around and around without finding a solution. Indeed, girls who ruminate are more prone to anxiety and depression. As one researcher said, 'They kind of get together and make things a little bit worse for each other.'

'Rumination is a poor coping mechanism,' Zach adds.

But it also has its benefits.

'I think it's more complicated than that, Zach,' I finally say. 'To me, rumination is an attempt at mastery. It's how we solve complex problems: going over the nuances millions of times. You wouldn't be so quick to pathologise if they were two physicists labouring day and night to come up with a scientific breakthrough.'

'And that *closeness,*' Eloise says. 'The deepest friendships are built on gossip and vulnerability.'

'I couldn't disagree more,' Zach says. 'It's not vulnerability; it's dwelling.'

'I don't know,' says Eloise. 'I think neuroticism is underrated.'

Neurosis 101

When we say 'neurotic' today, we usually mean a person who is moody, prone to negative emotions like anxiety, sadness, anger, guilt and shame. Neurotic people are inclined to expect the worst and dwell on their own faults.

But that's not always what the term has meant. 'Neurosis' originated with Freud as a broad label for any psychological disorder. He famously said the goal of treatment was to transform 'neurotic misery into common unhappiness'. The word 'neurosis' used to be part of the *DSM*. But in 1980, it was replaced mostly by depressive and anxiety disorders. Eventually 'neurotic' came to mean what it does today: someone who has a personality that's kind of depressive, kind of anxious – not someone who is extremely mentally ill.

Neuroticism is one of the 'Big Five' personality traits (openness, conscientiousness, extraversion, agreeableness and neuroticism – aka OCEAN), something that's considered at least partially inborn, closely related to having an anxious temperament. It's one of two major personality traits, along with agreeableness, that's been found to be higher in females.

Psychodynamic therapists put a finer point on it. To us, 'neurotic' has a very precise technical meaning. The short version is that it means 'not that sick'.*

Still, neuroticism gets a bad rap – as do the young women who display it.

---

* The idea of what 'neurotic' meant was operationalised by psychoanalysts into 'levels of personality organisation' based on several aspects of a person's mind: their sense of identity cohesion, the quality of their relationships, their ability to 'test reality' or see the difference between external facts and what's just in their head. It also takes into account the predominant types of defences a person uses: whether they are mostly 'repression-based' (healthier) like intellectualisation, sublimation, altruism and humour, or 'splitting-based' (less healthy) like projection, idealisation and devaluation, or projective identification (a way that people project things into you that you feel, like when you feel really weird around a person but don't know why). Whether a defence is healthier or less healthy can sometimes be assessed through countertransference.

This stratification all came about to help therapists figure out who got better from 'talk therapy' and who didn't, and who was served best by which approach.

Tend and Befriend

'Strong minds discuss ideas, average minds discuss events, weak minds discuss people.' Originally spoken by the historian Henry Thomas Buckle and recorded in writer Charles Stewart's 1901 autobiography, this assertion has travelled through the centuries and has been frequently repeated (often spuriously attributing it to Eleanor Roosevelt). It captures a widely held belief that devalues the kinds of issues that occupy girls like Becca and Layla. If concern for the nuances of social life were something the world did not denigrate, a relentless focus on them might not be so readily considered a mental problem – or a sign of inferiority.

On the contrary, there is value in this kind of co-rumination. Feminist psychologist Phyllis Chesler observed that these conversations develop a vital system of social connection and attunement. Current research supports this take. Girls attach more importance than boys to their friendships starting in childhood, and have a more powerful 'affiliative need' that intensifies during puberty. Girls are stronger in empathy and faster developing language, so when life is tough, 'girls discuss while boys distract'. And girls who co-ruminate have closer friendships.

It won't surprise anyone that those who co-ruminate are also more likely to develop clinical anxiety and depression. Interestingly, teenage girls may even prioritise social intimacy over a certain kind of sanity. This serves the main psychological task of adolescence: identity formation. Teenagers, especially girls, define themselves largely through the eyes of others. Their brains show heightened reactivity to the social world, including the emotional circuits involved in sizing one another up. Anxiety-ridden as it may be, it's a process that ultimately helps you figure out the kind of person you are.

Interestingly, the teenage girl's fraught relational system may even have a way of soothing itself. Stress is classically thought to produce a 'fight or flight' response, but in women, it has also been found to trigger a 'tend and befriend' response, mediated by oxytocin, the 'love hormone'. It stands to reason that these mutual caring practices provide a kind of treatment to the anxious brains of girls and their friends.

Some experts more generously call these thoughts and conversations 'ruminative *coping*'. It's likely that this perplexing habit of teenage girls is actually useful. I wonder if I would view Becca's anxiety differently if the *DSM* had been written by women.

Are You Saying I Should Have a Fight with Her?

Layla, then, is an extremely important resource for Becca. She gives her the closeness that comes with co-rumination, and an outlet for the discomfort, the 'Anxiety Girlie' in herself that she can't bring to (and is largely induced by) her primary social life with Daisy and Noah. The trouble is, Layla cannot be her therapist; the co-rumination has an endless quality because given the state of their adolescent brains, it's truly the half blind leading the half blind.

When Becca comes back, I'm excited to share my research about the Anxiety Girlies.

'I spent some time with the Anxiety Girlies!'

Becca blushes.

'I think they have a lot to offer. It seems like between them, and Layla, and everything with Daisy and Noah right now, you're trying to put together a lot of things about who you are.'

She nods.

'But here's the thing with anxiety that I didn't see scrolling through the Anxiety Girlie reels. When you feel anxious, that's not just a thing about you, a thing that comes and goes, or something you "have".The thing with anxiety is, it tells you something. It's meaningful.'

'What do you mean?'

'Well, can you think of a time this week when you felt anxious?'

Becca's eyes widen. 'Yes.'

She tells me about another 'annoying' moment with Daisy and Noah. The usual.

'So, Becca,' I say. 'Daisy was being annoying, right?'

'Yeah.'

I see Becca's face and neck start to flush. Her breathing is getting a little bit tight.

'Do you notice you're feeling anxious in your body right now?'

She is able to observe the tightness in her breathing. 'And a little in my stomach.' Her face scrunches.

We spend a few minutes practising how she can regulate this anxiety when it arises, by observing herself this way, and by recognising what brought it on.

Then I push her a step further.

'So, Becca, we saw how your body reacts with anxiety when you think about this annoyed feeling you had, right?'

'Yes . . . ?' There is caution in her voice.

'So now I'm wondering if instead of feeling anxious you can just let yourself feel the annoyance. In your body.'

She flushes a darker shade.

'But . . . are you saying I should have a fight with Daisy?'

'No.' I get this question all the time. 'On the contrary. I'm saying you need an additional best friend.'

'Huh?'

'Did you see how we were able to go from this notion that anxiety just happens to you, to the fact that anxiety comes on when you have certain feelings?'

'Yes.'

'And how when you slowed down and paid extra attention to the anxiety in your body, you could actually decrease the anxiety you were feeling – so you have some control over it, right?'

'Okay . . . yeah.'

'So that's kind of like having another friend – a perfect best friend – someone who's sitting there with you all the time. Like, an inner Layla, in addition to the real Layla.'

'Uh-huh . . .'

'And someone who thinks you are the most important, most fascinating human being who ever lived. She's obsessed with you.'

'Sounds like an annoying best friend.'

I laugh because she's so right. 'Okay . . . so let's give her some balancing qualities. She also knows *all* of your faults. She does not think you are perfect – far from it. She just thinks you are really cool. Is that better?'

'Sure.'

I stay silent for a moment to let this sink in. Becca's broad smile gradually softens. I lower my tone to match.

'And she thinks your anxiety is a sign of the truth – like you have a special ability to *know* things.'

She's got her eyes closed now.

'She's fascinated by your every move. So when you get that tightness in your breathing, or a feeling in your stomach, she's like: *Wait: Everybody be quiet! Becca's stomach is telling us something*. She's scanning your body, waiting . . . like an obsessed bird-watcher.'

Becca opens her eyes. 'And what's the wisdom I have, then? That I feel annoyed?'

'Yes! But here's the hard part: how about letting yourself *just have that feeling*?'

'But I don't understand – what am I supposed to do? If I'm not going to have a fight with Daisy, what's the point of getting annoyed?'

'You already are annoyed.'

'Okay, true, but what am I supposed to do with that? Just *feel* it?'

'Yup. Just let yourself feel it.'

'And don't say anything?'

'Don't discharge the feeling. Just see what happens if you keep your feeling in mind.'

I can tell Becca is a bit confused. She'll have to play around with this IRL. I'll see her again next week.

The week goes by quickly, and it's our last session before Becca leaves for summer vacation – and she's beaming. She describes the scene from the night before: the three friends lounging in her elevated kitchen area, heady on hormones and Spindrift and weed, amid the giggles and the cuddling and palling around.

'So Daisy is going on and on about how she thinks she's fat, how she thinks she should get a tattoo on her shoulder, how she doesn't know which bikini to bring on vacation and she keeps asking Noah what he thinks . . . and I finally did that best friend thing and realised I was getting annoyed. So I said something.'

'What did you say?' I'm so proud of her already.

She sits forward, handing this to me carefully, like it's a giant glass vase. 'I was like: "Daisy, you have thirty more seconds of talking about your problems, and then it's my turn."'

5

Too Much

NELL:
that's funny
my family says stuff like that about me all the time
like my mom says it to my aunt on the phone like I
can't hear, she's like
'Nell's just a lot'
'Nell is so dramatic these days'
'Nell is too much for me right now'
I dunno like
I think it's just
when people say stuff like that
they always kinda mean the same thing
you know?
like what they really mean is just
'Nell's a girl'

Kimberly Belflower,
John Proctor Is the Villain

The Queen of Quantities

A few years ago, I noticed that many of my patients were obsessed with Taylor Swift. I needed an education, fast. Diving into that world and attending the Eras Tour, research project gave way to fever dream. On a sparkling May evening at MetLife Stadium, I happened upon a sublime and awe-inspiring display of female solidarity, a pop-up megachurch devoted to the emotional gospel of young women.

Taylor said it all in the opening moment of her Eras Tour. After a marathon of anticipation – the hype, the price, the frenetic assembly of outfits and bracelets – we fans stood on our tiptoes in the springtime air, gaping as the giant analogue clock counted down. And then, onstage, bloomed a dreamy, billowing procession. Out of the haze, she rose on a platform, a statue sparkling in a silver bodysuit. Microphone in hand, she began. The song was 'Miss Americana & the Heartbreak Prince', and the masses were coaxed into a nearly religious chanting, heaving, delivered, as Taylor finally greeted the audience:

'Oh hey,' she said.

It was Taylor's classic one-two punch: she's a lot, then not. Now a superstar; now just your friend, waving in the hall. And what does she sing about? A boy who has devastatingly moved on, while she is stuck remembering it 'All Too Well'; a partner whom she strives to impress, only to watch him 'Tolerate It'; a day in the future when she finds herself less compelling than the latest starlet. This Tortured Poet who redefined celebrity is just like you: pretty convinced she is, or has been, or will eventually be, nothing special.

You might be someone who's spent decades obsessed with Taylor and knows way more about her than I do. You might be someone who likes her music but is totally sick of hearing about her. You might see her as a feminist icon. You might see her as an icon of white feminism only. You might not be a fan.

But most would agree that Taylor embodies a dizzying paradox. On the one hand, with a voice clean and youthful, lyrics nuanced but direct, she has a persona that conjures the ordinary girl – one that millions of young women relate to. Many feel that she speaks to them privately, gets them as only a close friend could. And yet on the other hand, Taylor is a master strategist and unparalleled capitalist success, endlessly and deliberately cultivating and reinventing herself. Some consider her positively diabolical. Taylor has been so good at playing the game, she basically broke the game.

Through her cultish, yet deeply mainstream vibe, Taylor gives girls permission to feel *a lot* about things viewed (by many) as *little,* like crushes, grudges and friend drama. For example, a five-and-a-half-minute 'All Too Well' didn't quite say it; we needed a ten-minute version to capture the size of the feelings. She sanctifies these everyday pains with the light of her attention, freely expressing the miseries and joys of a certain kind of girlhood to which many of my patients relate.

But it's also more than that. Taylor's iconography of excess and her ever-expanding volume of material embody a muchness that excites teenage girls. This demographic often feels they contain multitudes they cannot express – in part out of a fear of being 'too much'. This is part of Taylor's therapeutic charm: she's someone who is quite 'a lot'. In fact, nobody is more. She's both obsessively self-conscious and unapologetic about it, hailing those who are 'much too much to handle'. Her fraught 'a lot'-ness appears to be both deliberate and unavoidable, both articulated and embodied.

Taylor gives language to an anxiety that lies at the centre of the teenage girl experience. In her songs and in the clinical space alike, young women describe navigating a dangerously narrow channel, attempting to squeeze between two condemning self-narratives: they are either 'too much' or 'not enough'. For the young woman who speaks about being 'a lot', this overflow of self correlates not only to an excess of feeling, but an excess of desire, of presence and of expression. She responds by objectifying herself, becoming both the measurer and the measured. Often, she finds her full self is both falling short – and fundamentally not allowed.

You'll See

'Are you talking about this with a therapist?' says her friend, gently; says the frat boy she's sleeping with, trepidatiously; says her mother, tenderly. This is the instant they leave her. Everybody leaves her – sometimes by backing out of the conversation, sometimes for good. But I won't know this for a while.

'She's a handful,' Sloane's mother tells me, on that first phone call when I explain the admin and the ground rules: that I will keep Sloane's confidentiality, but welcome parents to share any of their own observations or concerns. 'Anyway,' she says. 'You'll see.'

Sloane has found me on her own, through the university counselling centre. She is a freshman in college, a musical theatre major. She steps into my office, broad smile and excellent posture, carrying the heavy aroma of a botanical garden. She tosses a cascade of honey-brown curls over the strap of a long beige sundress. In her gold sandals and delicate ankle bracelet, Sloane's got Greek Goddess energy.

The first thing she does is go crazy over my dog. Drops to the floor and starts vigorously scratching him and wailing: she always wanted a dog *so much,* but her mom was allergic. She pauses briefly in sadness, like a car at a stop sign; then she resumes emoting over my dog, this time by inhaling his head.

Should I sit down on the floor with her, I wonder, like I do with child patients? I'm guessing she would find it cold of me to venture across the room to my therapist armchair. I pause and wait, resting a knee on the tufted sofa.

'That smell! Is he a Bernedoodle?'

Sloane hugs my dog tightly and rocks him side to side. He hangs limp in her arms, a survivor of years of manhandling by children, well practised in radical acceptance.

'Cavapoo.'

'Awww! I LOVE him!'

He is now sitting on the floor leaning against her, panting at me with a dopey smile while she scratches behind his ears.

For a second, I worry what the therapists down the hall will make of all this noise.

'Looks like you made a friend,' I say.

The intensity Sloane gives off already has me wondering if she warrants a psychiatric diagnosis. I've got to make sure that she is not currently on drugs like cocaine, that she isn't bipolar and manic, that she isn't in any kind of danger. On the other hand, maybe she is just a passionate person. I wonder why she thinks she's here.

Sloane clutches my dog with both hands on his muzzle, like she's about to give him a deep, passionate kiss. 'I love you,' she solemnly declares, and then shifts off the ground into a chair.

Her body is calm; her speech is not fast; I am able to interrupt her. She does not appear to be manic, or on drugs.

'Tell me about what brings you in,' I say.

'Well, just basically for my mental health. You know, for self-care, and to get my ADHD meds.' She cocks her head to the side. 'You can prescribe medications, right?'

'Yes, I can. But tell me about why you are taking medicine.'

'Well, I've had ADHD since middle school.'

I take a little history.

It was seventh grade when she got the ADHD diagnosis. She did fine in school but had some trouble concentrating, and she was having a 'difficult year socially'. But saying someone is 'having a difficult year socially' in seventh grade doesn't tell me much. It's like saying someone was 'having a difficult year financially' during the Great Depression.

Sloane tells me her group of friends shut her out that year. 'It was hard for me to stay focused in conversations – we found out it was an ADHD thing.'

This feels like only part of a story.

'Did the medicines help?'

'Definitely. I take my meds every day.'

We chat about what she's tried, and she feels her ADHD is under control.

'And how would you say you're doing now?'

'Great!' she screams.

I feel compelled to match her energy. 'Amazing!' We are both beaming, for some reason.

She goes on to tell me about her awesome roommate ('I think she was like a *big deal* child actress in Korea'); the perfect match with her academic advisor ('Do you believe in synchrony?'); and even what she had for lunch yesterday ('I mean, *finally,* real New York pizza!').

Our time is up. After I close the door behind her, I stand in the silence. What just happened?

Our second session is another hyperthymic lovefest. This time, Sloane blows in from barre class, her hair in a tight bun, her olive skin dewily aglow. I learn that her parents are 'the most incredible people'. Sloane's dad, a doctor at the VA in North Carolina, where she grew up, is 'the funniest man alive'. Her mother, who runs a web design business from their home, is 'a queen . . . a genius'. I hear about how everything in Sloane's childhood has been 'perfect'. How she is 'blessed' and, yes, 'a passionate person'. Near the end, I nudge her back towards the question of what she would like to work on in therapy, at which she scowls: she is 'not sure'. She resumes her celebratory monologue, which is starting to sound like an Oscars acceptance speech: the 'true closeness' she shares with her friends, the 'most inspiring' classes she is taking, the thrills of exploring the culinary delights and the nightlife and vintage clothing stores of New York City.

I'm left feeling that if I bring up anything about problems – even referencing her earlier comment about 'mental health' – I'd be the world's biggest party pooper. But if she won't go there, I'm not sure how I can help her.

This is one of those moments when countertransference is an important thing to listen to. Mine is: *I'm walking on eggshells with this person.* I have a distinct sense that she's always on the verge of being totally unreachable. I put together that feeling with how she is talking about her parents. Sloane is displaying *idealisation,* a defence mechanism that can indicate deeper problems, depending on a person's age and how often their mind functions that way. On the other side of idealisation is always total *devaluation,* which could come out at me, others in Sloane's life, or towards Sloane herself. I don't feel totally safe in the conversation, and she must not, either. I take a tentative step closer to her.

'Sloane, that's all so good for me to know. I'm wondering, though, what it is you'd like my help with.'

She grows quiet and looks at the floor. We spend the last two minutes in silence.

'See you next time,' I say softly, holding the door open.

Eggshells

'Is Your Team Struggling?' inquires a *Forbes* headline. 'Their Dysregulation May Impact Your Performance.' 'Signs You Need to Rebalance Your Nervous System,' says *Vogue*. 'Oversensitive and Overreactive?' asks *The Guardian*. 'What is Nervous System Dysregulation and How Can it be Resolved?'

'Dysregulation' is a clinical term that has gained increasing attention over the past several decades. Someone is 'dysregulated' if their emotions are outsized for the situation, causing them to feel ungrounded and behave irrationally. Toddlers, by nature, are 'dysregulated'; it's a parent's job to help them calm down, soothe them when they're hurt, and soften disappointments by offering perspective: 'No, we can't have ice cream *now,* but we can have it *later.*' If you are a dysregulated person, it means you have trouble coming back to centre, trouble grounding yourself. Dysregulation can also describe severe anxiety states and difficulties common on the autism spectrum, such as poor frustration tolerance and a tendency towards sensory overstimulation.

Although mental health professionals have long used this term to describe certain patients, 'dysregulation' didn't become a buzzword until the early 1990s amid the emergence of dialectical behaviour therapy (DBT). DBT was principally designed to treat disorders involving dramatic mood swings and erratic, self-destructive behaviour – bipolar disorder* and borderline personality disorder† – and

* Bipolar disorder is a mood condition where periods of depression alternate with episodes of mania – a high-energy and sometimes dangerous state.

† Borderline personality disorder is a condition of chronic emotional instability, trouble maintaining relationships and a weak sense of self.

DBT practitioners often focus on 'emotional regulation'. Dysregulation then broadened into a nearly household term as it became linked with 'trauma'. The nervous systems of people who have experienced trauma can become dysregulated, so as professionals and the wider culture increasingly placed trauma at the centre of mental health narratives, 'dysregulation' came along for the ride.

But as with many psychiatric concepts that have been absorbed into therapy culture, 'dysregulation' has now stretched well beyond its meaning, especially on social media. For example, a popular TikTok video highlights 'weird behaviours you think are normal (but are actually nervous system red flags).' These include 'feeling uncomfortable when someone stands too close in a line'; 'randomly getting a burst of energy at night but knowing you'll regret staying up late'; 'feeling like the wrong pen ruins the entire vibe of your notes'; and 'feeling guilty when you leave a small shop without buying anything'.

When we use 'dysregulation' to describe feeling on edge after a poor night of sleep or a tense day at work, we have crossed into over-pathologising. And yet, the concept is now so prevalent that according to a national survey, Gen Z's top goal in life is to achieve a 'calm nervous system'. Its popularisation has, alas, led us to pathologise the experience and expression of any strong feeling. Or even any mild-to-moderate feeling. Possibly any feeling at all.

And so, when it pops up in my mind as I'm thinking about Sloane, I cringe for a moment. I resist the impulse to supply her with a term – even if it's correct – that I know will be so misconstrued the more she Googles it. Yet this phenomenon seems to describe Sloane accurately, so we will have to find a way to talk about it. Sloane attributes many of her problems to ADHD, and it is true that ADHD is increasingly being recognised as a 'regulatory' disorder, resulting in poor impulse control and trouble with 'executive functions' such as inhibition and modulation. In other words, ADHD is quickly becoming yet another 'dysregulation' problem.

But, thinking about how I feel around her, ADHD-type

dysregulation does not seem to fully capture what's going on with Sloane. Usually, talking to a person with ADHD does not produce that 'walking on eggshells' feeling. I need to follow that feeling and see where it leads.

A Lot

At our third session, Sloane walks right past my dog, sits down, flings her tote bag to the floor, and starts bawling.

'I don't know what this is doing to me,' she heaves, searching for a tissue. She stares at the ceiling and dabs at a tear. 'I don't know who I am anymore.' Her accusing eyes find mine.

What is going to happen now?

She looks away again and puts the tissue to her face. She is crying softly.

'I'm sorry, Sloane. I'm not totally clear what you mean – can you help me understand?'

She swipes the tissue across her eye and puts her feet on the floor, holding my gaze at last. 'I don't know if this is good for me, working on myself.'

'What do you mean?'

'Like . . . if we are finding things about me to *work on,* it means that things are *wrong,* and that's what I've been told my whole life – that I'm *a lot.* That I'm *too much.*' There's the devaluation.

This is the problem she is here to work on. She is telling me – and showing me – right now. Maybe our task is coming into focus. But only if she recognises it as *her* problem – not simply the result of everyone else (including me) being too critical, too judgemental, just not getting her.

I pause and proceed carefully. 'Sloane . . . you should only work on yourself if *you* want to,' I say with soft authority.

'But I do! I know I need to! I just feel like if we are "working" on me, we are agreeing with all the haters who say I'm too much.'

Sloane spills forth with stories about how she never felt like she fitted in with her parents. Her dad was sweet but passive and somewhat distant; he tended to go along with her mom, who really ran the show. Sloane's mother was an extremely organised person, very focused on 'doing things a certain way'. Etiquette was a big deal. The dinner table was a microscope, and Sloane, the specimen: *Don't take so much food; don't talk so much; don't be so 'dramatic'*. But there was a pressure inside Sloane: the stories of who said what to whom that day in school needed to tumble all the way out, in full colour. Otherwise, what was the point of anything? As she recounts these memories to me, I imagine her mother was trying, in an ordinary parental way, to teach Sloane social skills. Of course, it's polite to take it down a few notches. It *is* necessary to make room for others.

Suddenly I'm right there with her. This exuberant kid at the dinner table, brimming with stories, so hungry for a kind of connection, shot down hundreds, thousands of times by parents who were probably, understandably, annoyed.

My thoughts return to her diagnosis. Sloane's extreme sensitivity to judgement could be a function of rejection-sensitive dysphoria (RSD), a syndrome associated with ADHD. Kids who get diagnosed with ADHD are often bursting at the seams – and constantly being chastised, glared at and punished. Then, their brains have a way of magnifying those criticisms tenfold.

Our session is over, and Sloane is about to stand up, but she takes an extra moment. 'Once I got the ADHD diagnosis, my parents were so much nicer to me – especially my mom,' she says.

All of this makes sense, and yet I still feel like there's more to this case. This last comment, however, brings me a step closer to what we are missing.

That evening, I find myself thinking about Sloane's mom – a person I won't ever meet. I'm pained picturing this mother, who didn't know what to do with her daughter, and who must have felt so much shame, not being able to control this unruly child. Moms come under attack for everything their children do, and I've had so many mothers break down in my office describing how that feels. When your kid is the one who doesn't totally fit, you don't fit, either.

Sloane and her parents all relied on the ADHD diagnosis to hold a space for 'that part of Sloane's personality we can't stand'. It was a way to kill off that part, labelling it as sick, not bad – but in either case, making sure it goes away.

What would it have meant to try accepting Sloane exactly the way she was? Standing up for her when she talked too much or showed too much emotion? Deciding not to care what people thought? It would be easy to pass judgement, to imagine that is what a 'good parent' would do. But is that even true? It's also part of parenting to help your child adjust to the social world. Like so many parents, this mother had a hard job.

Sloane has given me a window into why she puts me (and presumably others) on edge. It's not just that she may have ADHD, an impulsive nature or 'big feelings'. She does not feel safe around me. In fact, her dysregulation itself likely has something to do with a fear of being authentic with other people. I have a hunch her 'too much' behaviours are not just fuelled by temperamental impulsivity, but by a deep insecurity, a terror of being unlovable. She needs constant reminders that she is good, and she seeks those out in her beaming superpositivity, her extra-glamorous appearance, the dramatic expression of her anguish. These are behavioural manifestations of inner terror that she is not lovable, not enough.

The thing is, Sloane herself does not see it that way – not yet. And so far, I do not see any sign that she is ready to look closely at the way her mind operates. She speaks of 'mental health', but I'm not sure what she means. Nor do I understand how she wants to improve or 'optimise' it. That's because she doesn't know either.

Our first task, therefore, is to help Sloane feel more comfortable with me. Brains are 'anticipation machines,' and Sloane anticipates rejection from others; this process will not be easy. I'm going to have to be a steady, non-rejecting person, no matter how she is acting or how frustrated I am. And eventually, I'm also going to have to help her – slowly, very slowly – look at how she's behaving with me, what she imagines I'm thinking about her, what she feels she needs to do to earn my approval. But in order for her to step back and examine this behaviour, she will have to feel at least a tiny bit lovable in here, first. It's a funny paradox: she'll have to feel like 'enough' before she can address how she feels like 'not enough'. My acceptance of her will pave the way for her acceptance of herself.

The Eye of the Beholder

We all come into the world as 'too much'. It's the job of parents and caregivers, at the start, to do the regulating for us. When our hunger is too much, our caregivers feed us; when our exhaustion is too much, they help us fall asleep. Parents have their own personalities, and they will respond in distinct ways to a baby depending on who they are. How much is 'too much', from the very beginning of a baby's life, is a relational question.

The challenge of learning self-regulation varies widely, as babies are inherently different from one another. I've never met a parent who disagrees. 'Oh yes, Stan was Stan from Day One,' they'll say. Doctors and laypeople alike call this concept 'temperament'.

What does it mean to have a 'good' temperament? That answer largely depends on the match between caregiver and child. What's obnoxious to one parent is delightful to the next. What's cosy to one parent might be dull to another. A 'handful' is defined by the hands doing the holding.

This concept is so important, I'm giving it its own line. It's called 'goodness of fit'.

When the fit between parent and child is good enough, parents can tune in to the needs of their child, and can signal to the child that they are good enough and will get what they need. When the fit is off, children often grow up with what we call 'attachment' problems, of which dysregulation is a leading symptom. When attunement between parent and child is really, really bad – let's say, because a parent is severely depressed, or drunk all the time, or abusive in big or small ways – we call that 'attachment trauma'.

Too-muchness can come from basic temperament features like having high impulsivity or strong emotions. But the behaviours that lead all of us to call a person 'a lot' – some of which Sloane displays, like being loud, extreme and performative – are often defence mechanisms or mediocre coping skills. These are usually driven by anxiety, by fear of not being loved or accepted.

I see this sometimes with patients whose mothers were very depressed for significant portions of their early life. Any normal baby wants her mother to be happy, to meet her with positive energy. If a mother is severely depressed, that gives the baby a special challenge. When she's a few months old and learns how to smile, she might teach herself to smile more often or more broadly than she would want to otherwise, in order to get a smile back. If she just exists in her natural state, she won't get a lot of smiles from her depressed mother. She'll feel in some preverbal, inchoate way that she is falling short, that she may not be important or lovable.

That's just one of a million ways a child can compensate for feeling like not enough by being a bit too much.

Here's one more way.

Maybe you've heard of 'splitting'? It is an *unconscious* mental process in which we divide people into all good and all bad. Since it's unconscious, we are not aware we are doing it. When a kid is under stress, splitting can serve a vital function: protecting the good in one's view of a loved one, or in oneself. Children are neurologically incapable of appreciating certain complexities, and they think in terms of good guys and bad guys. That applies to parents, too: when Dad is being nice, he's a good guy; when you're in trouble, he's as evil as any Disney villain. (I'll discuss this process in more detail later in the book.)

That's all fine when you're five. When you're eighteen, you're supposed to be able to see a more nuanced picture. But if you grew up in a house where parents were volatile, where there was frequent strife, addiction, turmoil or abuse, you might have to rely on splitting for a bit longer – maybe a lot longer. Sometimes the dark forces are just too poisonous to integrate with all the rest: you have to keep them separate. A kid's most vital relational need is to preserve an idea of 'good' parents at whatever cost. When your mind needs to protect your sanity through splitting, your daily emotional experience becomes one of absolutes, a chequerboard of black and white. When you're in one square, you feel exhilarated; when you move to another, everything comes crashing down. That's dysregulation.

I don't know much about Sloane's childhood or family yet. I wonder what the mental health of her parents was like, what the energy was in the house, and how they responded to Sloane. Any child who feels like too much in the microsociety of their home will be haunted by a sense of shame.

And then, there's the impact of the broader culture. Women live in fear of being considered 'a lot', which is not so different from 'hysterical'. Sloane probably sensed from an early age, like all girls do, that being 'too much' will make you an outcast.

Too Fat, Too Slutty, Too Loud

> A weeping woman is a monster. So too is a fat woman, a horny woman, a woman shrieking with laughter. . . . After bellowing like a barn animal in orgasm, hoovering a plate of mashed potatoes, or spraying out spit in the heat of expostulation, we've flinched in self-scorn – *ugh, that was so gross. I* am so gross.

So begins Rachel Vorona Cote's *Too Much: How Victorian Constraints Still Bind Women Today.* 'In the broadest terms,' she writes, 'mental illness is too muchness with a diagnosis.'

What we mean when we call a woman 'a lot' is that we don't like her, and that there is something wrong with her. Her excesses drive us away: she is selfish, she is tone-deaf. She needs too much; takes too much; fails to 'read the room'. Her feelings and desires are too big, and the expression of them, which she either can't or won't control, takes up too much space.

'A lot' (or 'too much') is something deeper and less sympathetic than being a 'hot mess', but just as gendered. While a man who is a lot might be accused of bellicosity, grandstanding or egotism, a woman who is a lot is needy and self-absorbed – hysterical, inappropriate, bossy, slutty, loud, aggressive, abrasive, shrill, dramatic, hormonal and moody. For a man, 'a lot'-ness is an engaging feature: he'd be an entertaining guest at the party; a woman who is 'a lot' is someone we quietly don't invite.

Being 'a lot' is, of course, a relative term: a girl is 'a lot' only in an environment that deems her so. I have another patient in my practice, a young woman whose boyfriend finds her to be 'too much' socially – she is the type of person who likes a raucous dinner party with delicious cocktails and turns on dance music at 11:00 pm; she is too driven, too hungry for adventure, too bothered by current events. Her boyfriend is a reserved fellow, so for him, she's just 'too much' – a label that may end the relationship. She could try to tone it down around him – indeed, it's lousy for a partner to feel boring or insufficient. But she does not really want to be different: she *is* 'a lot', and yet when I reflected this back to her in a therapy session, she took it as a rejection.

There are so many ways for a girl to be too much.

Classic children's literature teaches these lessons through plucky heroines who colour outside the lines: the Matildas and Harriet the Spies. These are cautionary tales: athough these characters ultimately prevail, you don't fully want to *be* them. They spend considerable time alone or in trouble. Even *Frozen* sends a mixed message, featuring

Elsa, who has a 'too much' problem she learns to manage. But Elsa is skinny, wealthy and altruistic – she's a cartoon Disney princess. Is a normal girl just as safe to 'Let It Go'?

Older too-much girls get themselves into lots more trouble. After puberty, the stakes of excess are higher, the messes hotter, the train wrecks more catastrophic. The public loves to watch an unbridled young woman get what she deserves. Whether it's the disintegration of a pop star into catfights and rehab or the unravelling of a basic bitch on reality TV, gawking at young women's 'a lot'-ness is a pet pastime for Americans.

An endless stream of female characters, artists and celebrities hold too-muchness as both their cardinal sin and their favourite topic. I think of Reese Witherspoon's character in *Election,* shunned for her shameful display of adolescent pride, ambition and sexuality. More recently, singer Kacey Musgraves has highlighted the double binds of female lust – being either 'a whore', or 'a bore'. Pop star Olivia Rodrigo sings about how she learned to stop eating birthday cake, and to stifle her feelings – now, she 'scream[s] inside to deal with it'. Rapper Megan Thee Stallion describes the stress caused by living in fear of being called 'rude' for being self-protective, and 'a ho' for being confident about her body. And actress, writer and producer Mindy Kaling puts a comedic twist on the trope, from *The Office*'s Kelly Kapoor to *Never Have I Ever*'s Devi, whose angry side is so 'too much' that it earns its own persona in the voice of tennis hothead John McEnroe. In 2025, actress and writer/director Lena Dunham released a Netflix series entitled, literally, *Too Much.*

Difficult

In Victorian times, the girl who fascinated and aggravated doctors with her 'a lot'-ness was called a hysteric. Hysteria is no longer an official psychiatric diagnosis. Instead, we hear lots of talk about anxiety, depression, ADHD. But there are other diagnoses people don't tend to advertise about themselves. Chief among them are the personality disorders. These are extremely common: nearly 10 per cent of human beings in high-income countries have one. Borderline personality disorder affects almost *one quarter* of psychiatric outpatients. And yet, this is still one of the most stigmatised diagnoses in medicine. Criteria include impulsivity, extreme sensitivity to rejection and emotional dysregulation. Because they have a reputation for being 'difficult', these patients are often thought of – even by doctors in hospitals – as patients to avoid. As a result, they often receive worse medical care.

If you're a woman, you are almost four times more likely to receive a borderline diagnosis than a man. Men who display similar features often end up being classified as narcissists – which is no picnic, but indeed, it's more socially acceptable to be a narcissistic man than a borderline woman. For example, narcissistic men tend to be world leaders.

In summary: I have seen both men and women worry about not being enough, but I have seen mostly girls and women worry about being too much.

I am wondering if, ultimately, borderline personality disorder is the diagnosis that best fits Sloane. As they say online, 'big if true': For obvious reasons, borderline personality disorder is not a diagnosis I would make lightly. It's controversial whether any person – especially a young person – benefits from a personality disorder diagnosis. If the world has grown more accommodating to diagnoses like ADHD and depression, it has barely budged on personality disorders. So many people warrant them, but how many people do you know who go around saying 'I have borderline personality disorder'? Exactly.

Furthermore, the literature is unsettled about whether personality disorders can be identified in adolescence with good predictive validity. After all, in order to properly make a personality disorder diagnosis, a pattern must be *enduring,* and the adolescent brain is in a great deal of flux. While this provides reason to be cautious applying these labels to teens, clinicians are also responding to a cultural push towards early identification and treatment. Of course, there are clear cases where the label is necessary – for example, if a patient has engaged in repeated and dangerous self-harm or suicidal behaviour and has been hospitalised several times. But in most cases, clinicians give this label with a heavy heart.

I do not see a value in discussing a personality disorder diagnosis with Sloane – at least not for a long while. Her executive function, social judgement and self-regulation are still developing. Still, I am curious if I should orient her treatment more in the direction one would take for borderline personality disorder, if only to prevent it from developing. One of the most popular treatments today is dialectical behaviour therapy (DBT), which combines concrete, user-friendly, cognitive behaviour techniques with mindfulness training, and focuses on the patient acquiring 'skills' for self-regulation. Maybe we could incorporate some of those?

Skills Culture

Hard pass from Sloane. 'Please, God. Please, no.'

'Okay,' I laugh. 'No skills.'

I wonder where Sloane's opinion is coming from. She has no direct experience with DBT, although she probably has no idea how much popular culture has been influenced by its concepts and its language.

Part of the shift within mental health at the end of the twentieth century towards short-term, behaviourally focused alternatives to the open-ended talk therapies, DBT has been lauded especially for its efficacy in reducing self-harming behaviours. Unsurprisingly, this modality serves a young, primarily female clientele.

Our mass focus on *mindfulness* was in large part introduced by DBT, which added concepts from Zen Buddhism to the Western framework of cognitive behaviour therapy (CBT). And despite the focus on *skills* in earlier behaviour therapies like CBT, it was DBT that really put *self-regulation* skills on the map.

Perhaps your holiday haul this year included some essential oils that you use to feel calm. DBT would include that in the 'distress tolerance' skill set that relies on using the five senses. If you're in a bad mood and choose to help yourself by watching a funny movie, that's an old trick. But thinking of it as a decision to 'use distraction' frames your choice as a clinical strategy or therapeutic tool. Perhaps your friend has urged you towards 'radical acceptance' to deal with the mushy mac and cheese in the cafeteria. Again, that's a skill from the DBT collection. Ever felt *invalidated*? That's a DBT term, too.

Many parents come to me asking if I can 'give' their child 'skills'. What I have found is that people only benefit from skills if they want them. And even when they learn specific skills, most of the help skills offer comes in the moment when a person realises 'Wait, I can use a skill right now,' which requires a great deal of personal motivation and self-awareness. It's like hitting the brakes on a high-speed train, making the decision to come to a screeching halt. That – in itself – is the big skill. When a person is not motivated from within, skills training often backfires.

So why is Sloane opposed?

'I don't love the idea that I'm supposed to *control* myself. My mom was in town over the weekend and we went out for dinner and the whole time she was like, "*You're talking so* loud*, Sloane, are you taking your meds?*"'

Sloane is correct that there is something Victorian about our current skills culture. The language of controlling one's emotions – even the language of 'regulation' – privileges calm and balance. Like CBT, it descends from the ancient Greek philosophy of Stoicism, which held that the 'passions' were malevolent forces to be suppressed. Like all therapies, DBT channels a set of values: steady is better than unsteady, peace is better than chaos, and accessing a 'wise mind' where one can think and feel is better than an 'emotion mind' where one is gripped by strong feeling. Zen-infused wellness culture plus the patriarchy drives a powerful message asking women to please *chill*. Skills therapies function as a kind of 'soft police', putting hot-blooded people, intense people – especially girls – at a disadvantage, and possibly robbing our culture, to some degree, of passion.

And yet, dysregulated states make it tough to get things done in this world (recall *Forbes*'s cautionary tale of the dysregulated team), and they can make you a difficult person to be around. There is nothing wrong with 'big feelings' – they are a powerful source of information and strength. But there's a difference between how you feel and how you express yourself. Adolescence is when most of this gets sorted out.

Now I'm beginning to understand Sloane's resistance to working on herself. She feels like she's fighting a war all the time, but she's not sure what the fight is about. From my perspective, it is, in part, a war on female emotionality, carried out on many battlefields, including her home and now, my office. In this war, Sloane fights the idea of being controlled. She is terrified of being called hysterical, too dramatic, too much. She feels anxious all the time, anticipating these criticisms. Her anxiety flares whenever she feels a big feeling or an impulse coming on, because she knows she's likely to go too far. But at the same time, anxiety leads her to use the maladaptive defence mechanisms she's come to know so well: splitting, being performative, being volatile and defiant. In other words, her anxiety about being too much makes her . . . even more.

I hope Sloane and I can work together towards a ceasefire in which the negative message of *control* could be replaced with a genuine desire, on her part, for *regulation*. I know she must have that desire on some level, but first we have to lower her anxiety and ensuing defences.

It's been a few months, and Sloane and I have talked about this and that but we have still not established any clear therapeutic goals. As I settle into my chair to wait for Sloane one day, I notice I am tense. I realise I'm preparing myself for the experience of being in the room with Sloane – that *eggshells* feeling.

The office is bright with the glare from midday cloud cover. There is a soft knock, and I get up to let Sloane in.

She takes a seat carefully. 'There's something I'm not sure I'm ready to talk about.' Today Sloane's voice is quiet and shaky. She looks at me.

'Hmm. Would you like me to help you find a way to talk about it?'

'Okay, fine, I'll talk about it.' Sloane clears her throat.

I can't tell if she's going to sit up tall and give me another grand performance. Therapy works in mysterious ways. We spend a lot of time laying groundwork, building rapport and trust, and figuring out what our shared goals are. It's so hard to predict when something important is about to happen. But my sense is, this is one of those moments.

Sloane tells me her parents used to fight. It was late at night, when she was in bed. She would hear them screaming at each other.

Did they scream at her? No. Was it physical? She didn't think so. Maybe a few times she heard her father punch a wall. She mostly heard her mother yelling. And doors slamming.

What were they fighting about? Well, she didn't know for sure, but like all kids, she thought it might have something to do with her.

They fought so much, Sloane worried they would get a divorce. But it was clear she shouldn't ask about their problems. The days that followed a big blowout, her dad would be at the hospital even later than usual; her mother would be irritable and preoccupied. This went on for most of her childhood. Her dad even moved out for a few months during her sophomore year.

Sloane's response? Like most children, she held herself accountable for the problem. If she could just be better, maybe they would be happy. She tried to fix it: *Be entertaining and delightful. Do great in your voice lessons, dance lessons, school plays. Definitely don't eat too much!* She tried to fill the house with the strong perfume of vitality and achievements so that no one could smell the marriage rotting.

But in the process, Sloane cut herself off from her insides, from being aware of how anxious she is all the time, and how she copes with that anxiety using methods that drive people away. If she keeps going uninterrupted, she is indeed the kind of person who could develop a personality disorder. And although Sloane sees herself as a 'passionate' person, those 'big feelings' will be much more useful to her if she can calmly and confidently access them. My hope is that we can help Sloane see how hard she is working just to feel okay, and how *that* has become her biggest problem.

It's Complicated

Although trauma belongs to whoever claims it, I am cautious about giving my patients trauma diagnoses. The term has already been so diluted. Nor do I wish to make people more upset about their lives than they are, or put any ideas in their heads about what has happened to them. Furthermore, Sloane's was not necessarily the kind of trauma one could call the authorities about: she was not in physical danger; her basic needs were met; her parents loved her and did not abuse her. It was just night after night of shaking in her Elsa pyjamas, followed by day after day of eerie silence and aloneness.

Recently a new diagnosis has been added to the *International Classification of Diseases,* the *ICD-11*. Although it's not in the *DSM,* complex post-traumatic stress disorder (c-PTSD) describes a PTSD-like condition that results from years of repeated trauma, producing disturbances of emotion regulation, self and relationships. It overlaps considerably with borderline personality disorder, which can also develop in relation to traumatic early experiences. But the two conditions are different, and one of the reasons psychiatrist Judith

Herman identified c-PTSD in the 1990s was to provide a label for common trauma symptoms without the stigma.

I think back to where we began, talking about the possible role of ADHD. Sloane definitely has the ADHD-style temperament. One might even say she 'has ADHD'; she certainly meets the criteria. So how is this related to her trauma? There are really two stories one could tell.

One story puts her ADHD at the centre: she came into the world with a disorder, ADHD. That disorder made her *too much*. In response to that, her parents were critical and unavailable to help her process tensions in the home, causing complex trauma.

The other story goes like this: Sloane's temperament was not pathological. It may have been quirky, or different from her parents', or not what they would have preferred – but it was only *too much* in relation to them. On top of that, things were tense in her household, and she reacted by shutting down her authentic emotions. The temperamental mismatch plus the added family discord led her to develop problems with self-regulation that look a lot like ADHD. This story puts the focus on *interaction* and *experience,* not on an essential defect in the girl.

For some, the difference between these stories may be merely academic. After all, ADHD meds would help control her impulsivity either way. But I happen to think for my patient – the rebuilding of her self-esteem, the reduction of her anxiety, and ultimately, her interest in developing the ability to self-regulate – the difference is extremely important.

So that is why I like *adding* c-PTSD to her diagnosis – yes, adding another psychiatric diagnosis! Unlike ADHD, which describes a problem in her *wiring,* c-PTSD adds the relevance of her *experience*.* My hope is that if she can start thinking about her too-muchness as

* Because of its emphasis on negative experiences rooted in the culture, some have called trauma the 'only acceptable diagnosis for women clients'.

having some relationship to her life as she has lived it, Sloane can develop greater compassion for herself and an openness to real work in therapy. It's not just a new label; it's a marker that might help us find the trail.

When she gets the trauma diagnosis, Sloane looks grateful – gleeful, reborn.

'But what about my ADHD?' she says. 'Don't I still have that?'

I assure her that we don't need to reject the idea that she has ADHD. She is one of the many too-much girls for whom that diagnosis has described something true about her temperament and also served as an important transitional object. So we can take it with us – but now, at least, we're getting somewhere.

6

Not Enough

You're too much, and not enough. You'll never belong anywhere.

Zoey,
K-Pop Demon Hunters

Perfectionism is internalised oppression.

Gloria Steinem

Best Friend Necklace

A best friend necklace is a metal heart, divided into two halves with a jagged break down the middle. Each half has a matching jewel – a plastic ruby, emerald or sapphire. Like a diamond ring, it's an amulet: everyone knows that you have a special person, and that person finds you to be enough.

My own best friend necklace exchange with – let's call her 'Gretta' – in fourth grade was possibly the most romantic event of my life. Gretta had a direct line to the absurd or the delightfully weird in any situation. Unlike a lot of the kids who were more popular and probably better adjusted than either of us, Gretta was willing to get privately psycho with you at any moment. When your zany idea met hers in midair, the giggles hit so deep that someone was going to pee their pants. She had a giant tabby cat named Dorito that she carried around like a baby, who happily moulded himself to her. She had a pile of stuffed animals who had personalities and distinct voices, and when they talked to you it felt rude not to respond in kind.

We went to school in a former apartment building, and kids took the stairs between floors. On each landing there was a garbage can painted in a unique design; one was just plain white. One day, for some reason, this struck us. We each broke from our places in the line and stopped in amazement before it, allowing our classmates to thunder past on their descent, shouts echoing, sneakers squeaking as kids tried to see how many steps they could jump. We locked eyes and, like those Muppet aliens on *Sesame Street* who land on earth and puzzle in wonder over a telephone, we began to utter words to each other. '*Blaaand*,' she said, in one of the stuffed animal voices. 'It's a *blaaand* garbage *caaan*,' I added, in the same voice. We had seen truth. From then on, every time we passed by, we paid respects, stroking the garbage can discreetly and chanting its name: the *blaaand* garbage *caaan*.

You can imagine the heartbreak when I found out one day, after school at Gretta's house slurping our Fudgsicles that tasted like her mom's freezer, that I was not her one and only. She broke it to me, tentatively, guiltily: she also had a best friend necklace with Erica B.

'You're still my best friend also,' she exhorted, shiftily, as I sat there dying. She might as well have just thrown me in the blaaand garbage caaan. It was obvious: I wasn't enough.

Looking back, I should have simply accepted this and moved on, maybe found my own bonus best friend. But my fourth-grade heart was an extremist. Is there any other kind of heart?

Stressed

'I think I have test anxiety,' Eliza says after she's settled in for our first appointment. She's wearing rolled sweatpants with her school logo and a ribbed tank top. She has silky black hair and a face full of freckles.

What I know so far is this: Eliza is part of a group of smart girls in the tenth grade at a school that is known citywide as a ruthless place where hedge fund managers and A-list celebrities send their kids to compete for spots at the top colleges – and everything else. She's got plenty of friends and is on the cheerleading team. Her parents sent her to talk to me because she seems 'stressed'.

'Tell me more.'

'Well, I don't know . . . I just get nervous before tests, even when I know I've studied, and it's a problem because sometimes I get really panicked and my mind will go blank. And then I have to take deep breaths to even keep going, and I'm worried I'm going to run out of time. There are *tons* of posts on TikTok about this. I think something is wrong with me.'

My chest tightens just listening to these opening remarks.

Outside, it is dark and raining. A warm light glows from the parlour floor of an old townhouse. Late rush hour makes its steady noises: the swish of a taxi; the bark of a big dog; a tired mother calling 'Lucas: *Come. On.*'

I can feel the damp air on my face, starting to blow the rain in through the open window; I stand up and push it shut. In the sudden quiet, Eliza and I are much more alone with her problem.

She says she's stressed about a big end-of-year math test.

'I've gone over the homeworks. I've made review sheets and flash cards. But every time I sit down to take a practice test, I just freeze.'

Eliza always feels like she is going to fail but ends up doing well. Still, no amount of reassurance from parents, friends or teachers brings her comfort. Each time she has to perform, she has a mini breakdown.

'Why is this test so important?' I ask.

'Because my GPA has to be above a ninety-five. Everyone has good grades in my school and if I don't keep it there, I won't stand out.'

'Stand out to whom?'

'Colleges, I guess?'

'Oh,' I say, playing dumb. 'What's important to you about college?'

She looks at me like perhaps her parents should have selected a psychiatrist from Planet Earth. 'Um . . . getting into a good one?'

'Hmm.' I pause. 'Why?' I wonder if anyone has ever asked her this before.

She takes the question seriously. 'I don't know . . . just because.

There's this day after early decisions come back when everyone wears the sweatshirt of where they got in . . . it's just kind of a thing my school has.'

Eliza is correct that one test could change her standing: a disappointing score could stick her with a totally different list of schools.

'I just don't want that look people give you when you get in somewhere not that great. Of like, pity . . . but they're trying to hide it. Ugh! Cringe.'

What's on the Test?

'Test anxiety' is not a medical diagnosis, but many people get anxious around test-taking, and many girls come to me reporting it as a quasi-medical condition for which there might be a medication or some other quick fix. Indeed, the experience of anxiety often includes physical and psychological symptoms, and social media abounds with hacks, tips and suggestions – all of which can be somewhat useful.

Girls believe what they are afraid of is performing poorly on the test. But 'test anxiety' is a symptom of a larger epidemic of perfectionism that is growing in young people. Perfectionism refers to a personality trait, established in childhood and consolidated in adolescence, in which a person sets high standards and strives for a flawless performance. She lives in constant danger of making mistakes, which she will view as failures. Her self-esteem is like a bucket with holes in the bottom: it keeps needing to be refilled.

Perfectionism is not always a negative force. 'Self-oriented perfectionism' refers to being driven from within, striving to be one's best – and it can generate motivation and positive self-esteem. 'Socially prescribed perfectionism' is when one is striving to appease others, and it tends to lead to psychological distress.

Girls more than boys are showing this distress. About fifteen years ago, the United Kingdom started to see a sharp rise in girls reporting the need to be perfect: a 165 per cent bump from 2011 to 2016. In the

United States, a 2023 study found that 79 per cent of girls report they are going to 'explode with pressure' coming from all sides.

'Not-enoughness' is seeded in girls at an early age and blooms at puberty.

Let's say you're a fourteen-year-old girl on an average day in America.

You'll wake up when it's still dark out and look at your phone.

You'll spend the next hour or so in the bathroom trying to feel okay about your body, face, hair and clothes. The truckload of products influencers have recommended that are spilling out of the cabinet just don't seem to make you look good enough.

That's because the pressure to manage your physical appearance is higher than ever in human history. No amount of discussion, awareness, outrage or education has changed the basic fact that you feel objectified, objectify yourself and your friends, and live in a constant state of falling short. Yes, 'body positivity' is cool, but please – that's not real life.

Speaking of your body, you have Gym first thing, which is rough because you have your period. Like for most girls, that makes physical activity pretty unappealing: you feel bloated and self-conscious.

You make it through (thankfully this unit is Volleyball, which is fun) and you hear that same group of boys as always, walking out of the locker room, comparing muscles and talking openly about one another's hairy balls.

As you walk to class, you wonder if your butt looks good in your jeans. Would you be considered a 7 – at least, 'for your school'? If you tried harder, could a good glow-up bring you to an 8?

You sit down in second period; you reapply your lip balm and take your binder out. It suddenly hits you that you are *so tired*. Like other girls, you sleep less than the boys your age. That's partly because also like other girls, you are more stressed than the boys about school – especially tests. Case in point: because you were second-guessing yourself so much on your last mathematics exam, you ran out of time on one question. Anyway, you have another mathematics test tomorrow; remember to save time to study.

But here you are in History, and you are keenly aware that trying too hard has never been less cool. As the research shows, your generation prizes effortless perfection. And, as nobody will stop reminding you, it's harder than ever to get into university – but if you make it look like you care, you've already lost. There are names for that kind of person: a 'try-hard', a 'pick me girl'. You don't want to be one of those.

Lunch is either the best or the worst part of your day – depends on the day, and depends on what happens. Biologically, your brain is focused on one thing above all: how you are perceived socially.

After piano, you come home and flop on your pile of Squishmallows with a heavy sigh, scrolling on Instagram. There is your brother having *so* much fun in university. There is your camp friend huddled happily in a group photo with her school friends in Connecticut. You, on the other hand, have *so* much homework, and scrolling has already eaten up forty minutes. Maybe if you manage to put that phone down and grind out at least an hour, then you can finally dig yourself out from the last test. And if you do better this time, maybe your parents will actually stop looking at you like you're the literal devil every time you tell your sister to please get out of your room – which you feel bad about anyway because as they say, '*She just wants to be close to you*' – and maybe if you do really, really well on this test they will even consider removing your screen limits on weeknights like Mandy's parents, who are reasonable.

Oh shit, it's Phoebe's dance recital tonight – can you go? And Ava is texting you again to help with her love drama. But the math. You are experiencing what the experts call 'role overload'. You pick up your phone for the 498th time today, and have the distinct feeling again that most people have better lives than you. Even though you actually really like that picture you posted from your friend's birthday party last weekend and it got a lot of likes. But you haven't had anything good since then and plus, you didn't get tagged in the photo someone else posted who was there, and you wonder if that means what you think it does.

The envy itself makes you feel bad: after all, likable girls are supposed to be happy for other people. Feeling threatened is a sign that you're insecure, that you care too much, that you're not *chill* – and that your worst fear is coming true: you do, in fact, kind of suck.

Your parents remind you of the hazards of social media all the time, but you know even more than they do how destructive your phone is. *Of course* social media makes you feel worse about yourself, but the idea of removing the phone from your life would be as absurd as cutting off the hand that holds it.

Back to the math test. What's at stake, really? Just as the majority of girls (89 per cent) say, it's not the grades, school, friendships or family that's the problem, but the 'pressure to fit into specific roles or stereotypes', which somehow does relate to math.

You're used to being the apple of your dad's eye; a 'role model' to your little sister; a confidante to your mom.

Let's face it: you've cared so much about grown-ups thinking highly of you for as long as you can remember – maybe it was ever since you were six, and Ida's mommy said you were 'a good sharer'. And Miss Emily said you and Eden were always 'sitting so nicely with your hands up'. You loved going to Ida's house – her mom made cloud slime – and you never wanted to disappoint Miss Emily or any of the other teachers who have seen you as a 'great kid' ever since.

Honestly, you wish everybody would shut up about your perfectionism: maybe it's the thing that's been keeping you going all along.

And yet, you feel lousy all the time, constantly aware of the painful gap between who you are and who you want to be – a problem psychologists call 'cognitive dissonance'. Some of your peers deal with this through procrastination, avoiding those tasks that might reveal their flaws. But you do the opposite: desperately and shamefully, you strive. Sure, you're a bit depressed; of course, you're anxious all the time; and yes, on the bad days, vague thoughts of suicide darken your mind.

Sometimes you wonder if something is wrong with you – that you 'have anxiety', perhaps. After all, as a female, you're used to making 'internal attributions' about whatever goes wrong. (As Rachel Simmons notes, when guys don't get the job, they blame the economy; when girls don't get the job, we blame that *stupid thing we said*.)

Now it's 11:00 pm and you still haven't finished studying. You're starting to freak out – about getting tired, about getting a bad grade. But not just that – what you're afraid of is something so deep and so pervasive, it's hard to name.

Parts Work

'Is test anxiety the same as performance anxiety?' Eliza says, tucking a lock of hair behind her ear. 'A friend of mine does debate and I think she takes something before the tournaments.'

Today, Eliza is not interested in my thoughts about the unreasonable demands on female existence. Today, I have to meet her where she is, which means trying to figure out how to feel better about this big test.

I start off practical. If this approach doesn't work, we will get more psychological – more therapy-ish.

The first thing I'd recommend is studying, but I know she's doing that. Test-taking strategies? This kid time-blocks, circles key words, grabs the easy points first – she's a master. Relaxation techniques? She has every app, has been to every yoga class, could teach a graduate seminar on box breathing.

What else? Well, another thing for tests is to get aggressive. Stop letting it beat her down and decide to beat *it,* instead. I think of the way a ski instructor once taught me to approach a field of moguls: you have to get angry. If you're not mad, you can't get through them – each one will throw you back. The only winning position is forward, the only winning attitude: kill.

But none of this does it for Eliza: the pressure is still too overwhelming. She just cares about that score too damn much. Her nervous system is out of control, preparing for a battering, not for skiing down a bumpy trail or . . . taking a math test. The only way to beat the system is to care less about the outcome. But how can you get someone to care less?

I try giving her some grown-up perspective. That where you go to college does not determine your success in life.

A weak smile, as her mind takes a hard pass.

I try updating her beliefs to meet the reality of the current environment: 'I happen to know where you go to college matters a lot less than it used to. Everyone is up against the same impossible standards. People don't assume a pedigree means everything. The workforce of the future looks different . . .'

As I ramble, she manages a polite cough: *You haven't met my family, or my friends.*

I try offering something that worked for me at her age. When I was applying to college, I tried to visualise a good life for myself at any of the schools on my list. At my last-choice school, which dorm was cute? In which corner of the library could I envision myself encamping? There would be deep conversations, dance parties and cookies at midnight, no matter what.

She clears her throat: *See above.*

I try getting her to check the facts: do you know any examples of people you admire who didn't go to a fancy college?

Now she shifts around in the chair. *I said, See above, lady.*

I even try stepping out of my role as therapist: 'You can trust me – I've been part of the medical school admissions process!'

She rubs her eyes, takes a big stretch and returns to my gaze, blinking at me like a flashing light: *Yeah, but I'm not going to medical school.*

We are at a standstill. It's time to change course.

'So, Eliza, what you're saying is there's a big part of you that cares very much about getting over a ninety-five on this test. Right?'

'Yes.'

'Would it be okay for me to talk to that part?'

A sidelong glance. 'Okay . . .'

'Great. So, part who cares very much about Eliza getting over a ninety-five on this test: what did you say your name was, again?'

She giggles. 'Huh?'

'Your name. The name for that part of Eliza I'm talking to.'

'Oh, um' – her eyes search around – 'the test anxiety part?'

'Great. So nice to meet you, Test Anxiety Part.'

More giggles, her brown eyes brightening. 'Nice to meet you too.'

'So, I see that you've been busy lately doing a lot of important work for Eliza. Could you tell me a bit about the job you do for her?'

'Okay . . .' She's playing along now. 'Well, I need to make sure Eliza does really well on her tests like this upcoming math test so she can get into a good college . . . I need to make sure she studies a lot and doesn't get off track.'

'Hmm. And what would getting off track mean for Eliza?'

'I guess it just would mean she doesn't end up at a good place.'

'Like a good college?'

'Yeah.'

'I see. It's very important to you that Eliza be successful.'

'Yes.'

I'm tempted to start challenging this part's beliefs – What does it mean to be successful? What makes a college 'good'? – but this part is nowhere near ready to be disrupted. We have only just met.

'So, Test Anxiety Part, may I ask how long you've been in your role?'

'Oh wow . . . a long time.'

'How old was Eliza when you began working for her? When did she start to require your help?'

Eliza thinks hard about this.

'That part – I mean *I* – was definitely there when Eliza was in middle school. And probably before that, too.'

'When did the job officially begin?'

Eliza gets quiet and sinks into herself. 'Like probably when I – when Eliza – was really little.'

Inner Critic

Perfectionism, the concept, has undergone various rounds of public scrutiny. A few decades ago, it was considered a legitimate 'flaw' – the only one, really – to confess in a job interview. But everyone eventually saw this for the humblebrag it was and 'my worst flaw is perfectionism' became a dull joke.

More recently, therapy culture seems to want us to fight against our perfectionism.

If you google 'inner critic', you'll find plenty to read.

There are books and articles, TikToks and infographics galore teaching how to quiet, silence, dethrone, tame or break free of your inner critic.

Thousands of therapists and aspirational therapists on social media have thoughts about this. If you need merch or supplies, the inner critic journals you can buy on Amazon practically outnumber kinds of Tupperware. Etsy will offer you mugs, T-shirts and lighted signs that tell your inner critic to fuck off.

But the problem with talking back to the inner critic is it won't work until the inner critic feels understood as a protector with good intentions. You have to develop a collaborative relationship with the inner critic before it will listen to you, much less accept your 'talking back'.

Everyone has an inner critic to some extent, but inner critics behave differently from one person to the next. Some inner critics are tyrants; others are cooperative prime ministers. So what makes a person's mind more likely to foster an authoritarian regime?

Bad experiences in childhood can produce a harsh inner critic and the perfectionism it demands. Children who had to deal with more than their fair share of stress or responsibility at a young age pull themselves together in various ways. One way is developing parts of themselves that try to protect them the way a parent would. The only problem is, those parts can't be more mature than the child herself, so they are often rigid, concrete or blunt in their opinions and guidance. These parts often behave like bossy, childish grown-ups. Sometimes they stick around for a lifetime, never maturing from the age when they were originally called into action.

A person's temperament can contribute to the rise of an inner tyrant. As discussed earlier, temperament is the biological basis for personality, and includes how strong one's feelings are naturally and how quickly the feelings come and go. The effects of temperament can be amplified by experience. Kids who have bad things happen to them may feel more anger and sadness, and if their emotions are naturally strong, they become overwhelmed and turn to perfectionism as a way to cope.

Certain social environments lend themselves to the development of inner critics or bullies. The pressures of high-achieving families or schools and communities that are restrictive or judgemental due to religious or political values can often take hold in a person's mind.

Sometimes early success in childhood can create perfectionism by setting the bar too high. Kids who are known at a young age for their natural gifts of intelligence or talent can get the message that they must keep it up. If they see themselves as playing a special role in their family or community, they may grow fearful of what would happen if they stopped.

Children with inherent neurodiversity or learning issues, medical problems or parents with any of the above can develop an early sense of difference and shame. They often try to compensate by becoming superperformers in areas where they can succeed.

So what is causing the perfectionism that plagues Eliza?

This Other Weird Thing

Eliza and I meet on Zoom this time since she had a late practice and lots of homework.

She's sitting against the headboard of her bed. Behind her there's wall décor: a poster of the Dallas Cowboys Cheerleaders; a framed picture of a preschool-ish Eliza sitting on a beach towel, arms wrapped around her little sister; a small, crocheted tapestry with the word 'Breathe'; a smattering of glow-in-the-dark stars crawling up towards the ceiling.

Eliza sits cross-legged on her bed, wet hair in a high bun.

'Hi there,' I begin.

'Hey,' she says.

'How's it going?' I ask.

'Good,' she says, smiling obediently. She is waiting for me to direct her.

I catch the beginning of a countertransference reaction in myself: an ever so slight frustration with her people-pleasing, waiting to follow the rules. For this to be a good session, I've got to shift her out of that mode.

'Eliza, as we start off, I'm wondering what stayed with you from our session last week.'

'Hmm . . .'

I can see her searching for the 'right' answer. My way of asking didn't quite do the trick.

'Actually, let me put it this way: what was interesting or useful to you from our last conversation?'

She takes a deep breath. Her head nods as her focus shifts from my expectations to her own experience.

'I thought it was good to think of the test anxiety as a "test anxiety part". That was really helpful. It somehow makes the whole thing feel a little . . . smaller.'

'That's great.'

'But ever since then I've been noticing all these other parts of me that kind of like . . .' – her eyes dart to the side a few times – 'hang on.' She walks away from the Zoom and I hear her fiddle with the door. She comes back and takes an even deeper breath. 'Sorry, I was just making sure the door was closed.'

This is going to be good.

She starts off again, sotto voce. 'I guess I was just thinking about how there's some other stuff, too.'

'Okay.' I lean in closer and realise I'm matching her whisper.

'Well . . . I'm kind of in a weird thing about food. I looked it up and I think I might have bulimia, or binge eating disorder. I think there's a medicine for that, right?'

'Hmm. Tell me more about what's happening?'

'Well, it's like . . . I've been tracking my food in an app for a long time, but everybody does that. I mean, my friends are all just kind of obsessed with eating healthy. And I definitely don't skip meals or starve myself like some of them, so I don't think it's anorexia.'

I rest my chin on my hand. 'Mm-hmm?'

'But I kind of have this other weird thing where like, I don't know, it's hard to describe.'

'Just try.'

'Well, sometimes like if I've had a hard day, before I start my homework, I'll run down to the store and get candy.'

'Okay.' I shrug.

My first thoughts are the commonsense ones. Well, of course she's feeling deprived; she's collapsing. Her body needs the pleasure that comes with crunchy candy shells and melty milk chocolate. Nobody can be 'good' all the time. Maybe it's healthy? Maybe we just need to talk about bringing more balance into her diet, into her life.

But common sense turns out to be misleading. When I start babbling back at her about the human need for enjoyment, she looks down.

'Yeah, but the thing is, it's not just like a little candy. It's usually like one of those share-size M&M's, or a Kit Kat. And I'll just house the whole thing.'

Okay, so I have to figure out if she's bulimic. I ask about throwing up or going nuts at the gym to compensate. She says she doesn't do those things, and I believe her.

'Also,' she adds, 'it's not pleasurable. At all.'

This is taking a turn.

'I mean, I don't enjoy the M&M's. I don't even taste them – I just chew and swallow them as fast as I can, and I feel horrible from start to finish. It's all just pain.'

What we realise after talking some more is that Eliza experiences these small binges as something more like self-punishment, or self-harm. She's doing the bidding of an inner tyrant.

Recognising this behaviour as self-punishment helps Eliza. Over the next few weeks, her binges decrease.

But they don't go away. We sprinkle in a little more focused behavioural work: whenever she feels the urge to buy candy, she is to sit in a special chair in her room, a glider rocker from when she was a baby, with faded spit-up stains and a threadbare muslin throw covering them. She is to stay there for a few minutes, observing the urge and how it feels in her body, observing how she is talking to herself, examining the self-harming impulse at its core – and waiting for it to pass.

After a few weeks of practising this, Eliza's binges stop.

Mean Coach

It's spring. There's a soft, floral breeze filling the air near my window. Eliza comes in wearing a navy pleated dress and Converse. She looks older.

'You know, I think I'm very critical of myself,' she says, opening our session.

It's great when patients pick up right where we left off. It means they've been engaged in the therapy throughout the week, and they've arrived ready to work. This catches me slightly off guard; I put my phone on vibrate and place it face down on my side table. 'Tell me more,' I say.

'It's like, I've noticed, sitting in that glider, that I kind of hate myself a lot of the time.'

I take this opportunity to jump right back in. 'Eliza, can I talk to the self-hating part?'

She smiles; by now she knows the drill. 'Sure.'

'So, Self-Hating Part, I see you've come to therapy with Eliza today. Glad to have you here.'

She laughs. I urge her to stay in character. 'In fact, to help us stay with this part, can we get a visual? Like does this part have a look? Is there a certain way it talks?'

She shifts her body and face around. 'I guess it's kind of like a mean lady.'

'Oh really? Like what kind of mean lady?'

'Kind of like this coach I had a few years ago who used to yell at us a lot.'

'Interesting. And what does she sound like, this Mean Coach Part, when she talks to you?'

Eliza scrunches up her face. 'Kind of nasal, and sharp, like No! That wasn't it! Do you want to make regionals or not!'

Okay, great. 'So, Mean Coach, thanks again for joining us today. I hear you've been spending a lot of time with Eliza lately.'

Eliza scrunches her face all mean again. 'Yeah.'

'And, Mean Coach, you've been working pretty hard for her, haven't you?'

'Yeah, I have.'

'And are you the one who's telling her to go eat the candy?'

'Yeah.' Scrunching, squinting.

'Could you tell me what your mission is there, for Eliza?'

'Well, I just think she needs to suffer. I know she'll feel bad if she eats that candy.'

I pause for a moment. 'Why does she need to suffer?'

'Well, you don't know Eliza.' She looks down. 'She's not always the greatest person.'

'What do you mean?' I say softly.

'She just thinks . . . things she shouldn't.'

'Huh.' I look at her. Her eyes are still on her toes. 'Like what?'

'Like . . . about her friends.'

Eliza looks up at me, her face returning to normal. 'Like the other day, just before the candy thing happened, it was a really hard practice. I was feeling kind of off. And my friend on the team, Juniper, who's actually become one of my best friends this year – she's a really good cheerleader – the captains were all giving her high fives and stuff because she got the routine really fast. I don't know, she's just good that way. She's probably going to get captain next year. And I know I'm supposed to be happy for her – I mean, we're literally on the same team. And like, so what? She had a good day and I had an off day. But I wasn't. I wasn't happy about it. I didn't even say good job. I just felt like shit.'

'Oh,' I say quietly. And whisper: 'Eliza, can I talk to the Mean Coach again?'

'Sure.' She makes her voice nasal and scrunches. 'Hi.'

'Hi there. So Eliza was just giving me some really important information about what happened that day before the candy episode. Was this what you were talking about? Like when you said Eliza wasn't the greatest person?'

'Yes, exactly. She was jealous, and she shouldn't be.'

'Oh, what are you worried could happen if Eliza were jealous?'

'She's not going to have any friends or be a success in life. Jealousy is bad, and she should be embarrassed about it. Plus, Eliza should be grateful for everything she has. A lot of people have worse lives.'

'I see, so you're out for Eliza's best interests – for her to have a successful life and lots of support? You want her to be the best but also have all the camaraderie and not fail on the relationship front. Which probably makes you be extra hard on her all around, right?'

'Yes,' Mean Coach sighs like an exhausted parent, 'I just want her to be okay.'

'I see that.' Finally, Mean Coach and I are making friends.

'Now, Mean Coach, how long have you had these wants for Eliza? How long have you been there, protecting her?'

A pause. 'I guess since she was little.'

'Like how little?'

'Oh, like around seven, eight?'

'Aha. And, Mean Coach Part, have you ever met Test Anxiety Part?'

'Oh yeah, I know her. She works for me.'

'Oh okay, interesting. And when Eliza was seven or eight, what was going on that you needed her there?'

'Oh, I don't know, I just wanted to make sure she didn't mess up.'

'Was she showing signs of messing up?'

'No, not like, outright. I just wanted to make sure she kept things going well.'

'Okay, that's helpful to know. What was going well for Eliza?'

'Lots of things.'

Eliza breaks from Mean Coach and looks at me again. 'I'm just remembering stuff – er – is it okay if I talk to you as just me?'

'Yes, of course.'

'It's funny, that was such a good time in my life.'

'What was good about then?'

'Just like, my parents were always so proud of me.'

'That's so lovely. Does anything specific pop to mind?'

'Yeah, just like every time I brought home a drawing or a poem or something from school, they would be so happy and put it on the fridge.' Eliza's eyes smile. 'They were always just telling me I was amazing.'

'Sounds like a nice feeling.'

'Yeah.' Eliza is quiet for a moment. 'But also, it was – and I don't remember too many details – but kind of a stressful time for my family. We were moving apartments; my dad got a new job. I mean, I think things were fine – it's the apartment we still live in and it was bigger than where we lived before. But I don't know, maybe my mom was kind of stressed? I don't remember much except one time I think I asked her if we were poor or rich and she was like "*rich, but Daddy has to work very hard*". And I think I was kind of scared that we would lose all our money. I don't know why.'

Wow, I think to myself, so many kids take on family burdens and make them bigger and heavier in their own minds. It's almost an occupational hazard of childhood.

'And that's when I started being more body conscious, too,' she goes on.

'Oh?'

'Yeah . . . it's weird. I was never, like, fat or anything, but I think I just started worrying about eating dessert and stuff. My mom was very health conscious, too.'

Eliza suddenly looks at me in protest. 'She never said anything bad about my weight, though. She just . . . I don't know. She drinks a lot of green smoothies.'

The Intergenerational Transmission of Not-Enoughness

'Can we talk about this young woman I've been seeing?' I say in group supervision. 'Unless you guys have anything burning?'

'Sure,' says Eloise, looking at Zach, 'go ahead.'

'So this sixteen-year-old girl comes in with some anxiety about tests, kind of typical private school girl perfectionism, body stuff, people-pleasing. Kind of a cool kid at her school, spotless academic record, friends. On her cheerleading team.'

Zach grooves along with his head like he's seen this movie before. Eloise leans in closer.

'Yeah, well, we've been dealing with some harsh inner critic, inner bully type issues. She's taken well to parts work and her defences are loosening.'

'Great,' Eloise says.

I go on. 'She has this one really interesting symptom I thought was going to be the tip of the iceberg of an eating disorder but turns out was something more like self-harm.'

'Huh,' says Zach, sitting back.

'So we did some talking to the part that thinks she's bad, that wants her to suffer, and it brought her back to around age seven or eight when her dad changed jobs, family was kind of moving up in the world, bought a bigger apartment, she vaguely remembers Mom seemed kind of stressed-out about money.'

'First world problems,' says Zach with a smirk.

Eloise turns to him, batting her eyelashes: 'We don't judge, Zach.'

'And she got back to this memory of just feeling really good at stuff. Her mom being really happy with whatever she would bring home from school – pictures, poems, whatever. She's a talented kid.'

'*The trauma! The trauma!*' Zach pretends to stab himself in the heart and falls off the chair.

'Ha ha, but seriously,' I say.

'It's true, Zach,' says Eloise. 'I think I see where this is going.'

'Where's it going?' says Zach. 'Do you think it's all the pressure from the parents – *Drama of the Gifted Child* kind of thing?'

We pause to consider this.

'Like I always say,' he adds. 'Praise effort, not intelligence.'

'Zach, everyone says that,' says Eloise.

'And plus these parents have read every parenting book,' I add. 'I'm sure they did plenty of praising her effort.'

'Although,' Zach says, 'I did just read that girls are more likely to credit their effort when things go well and never think it's just because they're smart.'

'I know.' I kick the stained antique ottoman out in front of me and cross my feet on top of it with a sigh. 'It's tough to argue that being wonderful in the eyes of their parents is the trauma of someone's life. I mean, Jesus, if that's true, as a parent, you truly can't win.'

'Well,' says Eloise, 'not everything is parenting.'

'Funny,' I say, 'that's where I was going with this. Like, this mother . . . she's been kind of weird from the beginning about money with me.'

My peers look at me expectantly.

'Like when we were first setting up the treatment and talking about fees and everything, she asked me how low I could slide, how many sessions it would be total – the kind of things people inquire about when they're stretching financially.'

'Do they need sliding scale?' says Eloise.

'Well, that's the thing, is that they don't. At least not from what I can tell. Dad in finance; three kids in private school; house in the Hamptons; "fire and ice" spring breaks,' I say, with the air quotes.

Zach raises his eyebrows. 'Fire and ice?'

'Snowmass to St Barts,' I clarify.

Eloise emerges from a deep thought. 'You know, people can feel poor no matter how much money they have. Remember on *Succession* how Tom tells Greg that the worst thing to be is the guy with five million dollars? The little guy at the big table?'

'Yes, and speaking of five million dollars, isn't that what like *all* of *White Lotus* is about? That people feel this bottomless sense of need, and that the more money they have the stronger the need and the less happy they are?'

Zach leans back and folds his hands together. 'All anyone wants to do is watch rich people be miserable.'

'Nothing better than a little schadenfreude,' Eloise says.

'Well, yes,' I say, 'but in this case I think it's more than that. This mother seems to have a thing about money, from who knows where, but whatever it is, it must make this kid feel a sense of not-enoughness that she can't quite put her finger on. And there's stuff around food, too. I don't think the mom ever said or did anything wrong in terms of food or made my patient feel bad about her body directly – she was just telling me her mom drinks a lot of green smoothies.

'I feel like money is at the root of so much of this not-enoughness. I mean, money is not a thing. It's a symbol, a stand-in, a signifier, whatever – but it's also a currency for something.'

'Yes, money is a currency,' Zach says, smirking.

'Thank you, Zach. No, but I mean a currency for the exchange of not-enoughness. People feel poor, and insecure, and like someone else is more loved than they are, and it all gets talked about in financial terms. In little comments. You know?'

'Totally,' says Eloise.

'My parents were totally fucked up about money,' Zach says.

'Mine, too,' says Eloise.

We sit there silently for a moment.

'And the food thing is important,' Eloise says. 'Come to think of it, my family was equally fucked up about food. My parents used to make outright fat jokes.'

'Right,' I add. 'Parents are so much more careful these days, but the fear still gets across, you know?'

'It's like if people's emotional problems used to all be about sex and how fucked up their parents were about sex, now it's all about money,' Zach says. I see the money issues are more salient to him than the food issues.

'Right.' I sit forward. 'I always think about this line from my training years: "Everything is about sex except sex, which is about aggression."'

'Yes,' says Eloise. 'Money is about sex.'

Zach rolls his eyes. 'You mean the Freudian stuff? Is that all this is? Penis-measuring for us guys? Penis envy for you ladies?'

'Yes, Zach,' Eloise says. 'Penis envy is timeless.'

'*Iconic,*' I add.

Then Eloise and I are quiet. I'm wondering if it's true that women feel fundamentally incomplete, and men feel fundamentally like they have to prove their sufficiency, and if these girls who are told to go out and be everything and get everything are just the ultimate victims of some psychosexual clusterfuck of jealousy and shame that we've all turned to capitalism to resolve for us?

'But it's not just that, right?' I say. 'That basic feeling of not-enoughness – it's so in the human condition. Isn't the experience of hunger – to go back to the food thing – isn't that what drives us from the moment we are born?'

'Everything is about desire,' Eloise says.

'Right – about getting enough until we are satisfied, until we are full.' I sit with this and then recall the eating dimension of Eliza's case. A girl who feels not enough and then stuffs herself. Whose mom is clearly concerned with amounts of money and amounts of food, and whose friends are obsessed with those things, too.

'You know,' I say, 'the trigger for my patient's most recent binge was actually a moment where she felt jealous of one of her friends who killed it in a cheerleading practice and got a lot of attention. Then my patient felt bad about being jealous and thought that was the worst thing in the world and deserved this . . . punishment thing she does with bingeing.'

Eliza is in a bad cycle of not-enoughness and too-muchness – stuffing herself with food to fill an emptiness, while also trying to numb her too-much feelings, and abusing herself for those, as well.

'Interestingly,' Zach pipes up, 'I was reading something recently about teenagers being biologically programmed to experience more intense jealousy but also to be more panicked by their jealous feelings. Which would, in turn, lead them to turn those feelings against themselves, since those feelings are socially unacceptable.'

'So you'd see this all as normal?' I say.

Eloise shakes her head. 'Sensitivity to social rules, yes; but this kid is self-harming. Sounds like she has a massive superego problem you caught just in time.'

Psychodynamic therapists locate the problem of inner critics, inner tyrants, inner forgivers, etc., in the 'superego', the part of the brain with the 'shoulds' and the judgements. Freud said patients with problems based in the superego were the hardest to treat, in part because they are often very attached to their nasty superegos, which can be helpful in producing excellent work products and earning external rewards. The superego also helps us get along in the tougher social moments: they move us to be gracious when we receive ghastly gifts, and to refrain from taking food for our own plate before everyone else is sitting down. But an unbridled superego – an inner tyrant – tends to produce a lifetime of psychological torture.

'To go back to the money stuff,' I say. 'She's got this "Mean Coach" in her mind, but the Mean Coach is weirdly getting instructions from some part of her mother that feels deficient.'

Eloise nods. 'You know how we speak of intergenerational transmission of trauma? It's kind of like that.'

'But not necessarily trauma,' I say. 'We don't know enough to say, in this case. But we can say for sure Eliza has a case of the Intergenerational Transmission of Not-Enoughness.'

'Let's add that one to the *DSM*,' Eloise laughs.

Zach leans his elbows on his knees and looks at us. 'But, to what extent is this a parenting issue?'

They both turn towards me.

'Doctor?' Eloise says.

'Well, yes. I'm getting there,' I say. 'As Eloise said, it's not all about parenting – as in, the activity. Maybe in this case it's just as much the culture – the water she's swimming in. But she's more vulnerable to the culture than some, because of messages she took in at a young age based on who her parents are and what they feel. Her mom seems to have this feeling of insufficiency – likely more than some parents. Eliza, sensitive kid that she is, picks this up. And, talented kid that she is, becomes aware of the power she holds to make her mom happy.'

'To "fill her bucket", as they tell my kids in their kindergarten,' Zach adds.

'Right,' I say. 'But she recognises the mom's bucket has holes in it. It's easy enough for her to keep filling it, so she keeps doing that, and gets addicted to that good feeling – partly driven by pleasure, partly by a not-quite-conscious fear of whatever her mom is uneasy about.'

'And you'll never know exactly where that dis-ease comes from in the mom,' Eloise says.

'It's not a disease; it's a dis-ease,' Zach says, beaming.

'Right. That's what it is. A sense of not-enoughness gets passed through the generations, especially from mothers to daughters. That feels really right.'

'Or at least . . .' Zach is on a roll. 'Close enough.'

This Is Water

It can take a lot of work for a young woman to feel like enough. But this work is doable.

One way is to do what Eliza did: go to therapy. She and I have come a long way since her original hypothesis that she 'had' a disease called test anxiety; that she 'had' a disease called binge eating disorder; that she would possibly need medications for these conditions. Or even, that she had a different kind of ailment: 'being a perfectionist'. All of these framings located the lesion deep in her brain and self. In this narrative, these were her own personal defects.

We found a vulnerability in her – the 'Mean Coach' – that was collaborating with forces in the shadows of her family history, as well as in the culture, to make her feel bad all the time. Once she named it and isolated it and, above all, helped understand and appreciate what it was trying to do for her, the Mean Coach was finally able to consider retiring. One day, she even told me, with a new confidence, like a glow-up from within, that it was 'time to hire a New Coach'.

Therapy is not the only way to put some distance between girls and their sense of not-enoughness. We can help them see that feeling not good enough is the rocket fuel of capitalism, and that girls and young women have always been its most vulnerable targets.

How are we feeling when we impulse-buy a thirty-five-dollar hair mask on Amazon?

We want to look better, and to have a sensory experience: to play with cool textured stuff that smells good and makes us feel pampered.

But why do we need that kind of fun, in that moment, on a dreary Tuesday evening while we're probably avoiding doing something else less pleasant? Maybe the impulse is directly related to the product, like we're unhappy with how frizzy our hair is – or maybe it's just a general sense of malaise. How much of that malaise is a vague sense of not-enoughness? If we felt we were cool enough, maybe we wouldn't spend a small fortune on the concert T-shirt to prove we were there. If we felt happy with our bodies, our energy and how our day was going, maybe we wouldn't impulsively splurge on yet another Hydro Flask because it has pretty colours and because maybe that will somehow make us go to the gym more.

We can help girls push back on consumer culture.

When a girl feels pressure to buy things, she can play the 'What's Not Enough' game, herself: *What's not good enough about me or my life that I'm buying this?*

Once you start playing the What's Not Enough game, you see the not-enoughness everywhere. It's like shining a black light in a dive bar bathroom: it's gross. If Eliza got in this habit, she would note how her little sister, who yesterday was making slime and digging in the dirt, overnight became a sales rep lecturing, with shocking corporate polish, on the benefits of hyaluronic acid. And on the singular importance of the Brandy Melville dress that comes in one and only one style: short, strappy and bodycon. And on the need for a body to go with it. She might help her little sister get hooked on the What's Not Enough game, too.

The What's Not Enough game is perhaps most helpful in the digital world. Most girls, like Eliza, are not willing to give up their social media. But just like with consumer culture, it's possible to put space between a girl and her screen world.

A girl can make choices about what she will and will not use social media for. As Rachel Simmons suggests, she can decide to use social media but refuse to do so in order to prove herself to others – to compete or to show off. Instead, she can use it (though not without some consequences) to say something about herself, what she cares about, stands for. She can use it to connect with people and entities that are bigger than her, and that speak to her values.

But perhaps the most profound thing we can do for girls is to show them what it feels like to *be enough.*

We need to circulate visions of what 'enough' looks like. Psychology has leaked some very useful ideas to the public. In 1953, Donald Winnicott, a British paediatrician, coined the notion of the 'Good-Enough Mother'. The best mother is not a perfect mother, but one who is 'good enough' – who gradually introduces frustration and her own imperfection into the child's experience.

Being a good enough mother is not a guarantee that your child will be completely free of mental health issues. Eliza's mother, for example, wound up putting some of her own internal pressures on her daughter. As is the case for all 'Good-Enough' parents, her insecurities had an effect on her parenting. Of course, we should all do our best to protect our children from our own psychological struggles. But here is the paradox: Eliza's mother would have the best chance of helping Eliza if she saw herself as starting from a place of Good Enough. For one thing, it would be great for her perfectionistic daughter to see a mother who models acceptance of her own imperfections. Importantly, acceptance does not mean unwillingness to change or improve. In fact, it's the opposite. (Acceptance also does not mean that time in a fight when you say, 'Well, I'm sorry I'm not perfect!') None of us can really go on, much less improve, unless we feel good enough. So, 'good enough' is a great therapeutic or personal goal no matter how close to – or far from – perfect you may be.

While it's widely accepted nowadays that some frustration is good for child development, young women have yet to see a real value in their so-called flaws. To the extent that there is a value, it mostly has to do with making oneself more likable, more relatable, less of a threat. Why did I love my best friend Gretta so much? Can I go so far as to say it was her imperfections? Can we get to a point where girls and teenagers and young women can view their imperfections – and one another's – as inherently valuable? Can we go so far as to say that it is precisely our imperfections that channel our authenticity? It's not a perfect rule to live by: after all, not all imperfections are charming. But some are.

In my business, we know that the antidote to envy, to feeling insufficient, is gratitude. Gratitude journals do help people feel better. Thanks to therapy culture, you can pick one up at almost any stationery store. But while gratitude can be encouraged, nudges to 'count your blessings' or 'look on the bright side' are often just annoying, unless your problem has been deeply appreciated first.

Sometimes a parent can say a wonderful thing that stays with a child forever. Over the years, I've heard a few good ones. One father said to his daughter, 'You know, I had to work for years to learn that thing you do naturally.' One mother says to her daughters, 'I love you every single minute of every single day.' One grandfather said to a patient of mine, knowingly, when she came home from a party: 'So, were you smart enough, charming enough and beautiful enough?' She didn't feel like she was any of those things, but the fact that he knew to ask – well, that really moved her.

When I was little, I asked my mother if I was pretty. She could easily just have said yes, but instead she told me a story about a beloved babysitter of mine, who asked her own mother, 'Mommy, are you pretty?' when she was little. And my babysitter's mother said, as retold by my own mother with a confident head toss: 'You know, I'm pretty *enough*.' Just hearing that 'enough' was an option took decades of pressure off me.

7

The Curious Case of the Bitch and the Narcissist

> These girls aren't wounded so much as post-wounded . . . aware that 'woundedness' is overdone and overrated. . . . The post-wounded posture is claustrophobic. It's full of jadedness, aching gone implicit, sarcasm quick-on-the-heels of anything that might look like self-pity.
>
> **Leslie Jamison,**
> *The Empathy Exams*

> Sometimes being a bitch is all a woman has to hang on to.
>
> ***Dolores Claiborne***

Watch Out

'I was a bit of a bully in high school,' Skylar, twenty-four, tells me dryly in our first meeting as she sits back in the chair, adjusting her tailored black work dress. 'Yesterday I was a heinous banshee to this guy at work,' she mentions offhand later in that session. 'Watch out,' she includes with something just shy of a twinkle, 'I can be a real bitch when I want to be.'

At first, I am almost scared of Skylar.

She tells me in our initial session that if she isn't happy with me, she will probably say mean things, ruthless things. She's got shoulder-length blond hair, pointy features and a good job in human resources. She recently moved in with her fiancé, Geoff, who works in private equity. The ring is distracting. At least four carats, cushion cut.

Skylar is ambivalent about being in therapy in the first place.

Maybe her life is *fine,* she blinks, as if I've pestered her into making this appointment. Maybe she just needs to, sigh, do more yoga. Be more *grateful* for what she has, she says bitterly. Maybe this therapy will be *bullshit.*

Skylar is here, though, because she is not that happy. 'I know I sound like a spoiled brat, because my life is pretty close to perfect.' She goes on to describe the luxury rental in the West Village, dinners at Buddakan and Sugarfish, share houses in the Hamptons.

She's unhappy because Geoff works all the time – and hates his job. He comes home late, grunts at her and heads up to his 'man cave'. The recreation hours do not bring them together, either. Often she'll wake up on a weekend morning and he'll have left for a day at the golf course without any notice. She feels like his last priority. The other night she got up for a glass of water. There he was, at 2:00 am, in boxers and undershirt in the glow of a laptop, grinding away at a report. She walked in and tried to rub his shoulders, but he just swatted her away and said, 'Go get your beauty sleep.'

Skylar and Geoff do have things in common. They both come from divorced parents and grew up without a lot of money compared to people in their communities. It was clear from their first Hinge date that they were similarly excited by the idea of a sexy, swanky New York City life that was more fun than the turkey casseroles and creaky old houses and trips to TJ Maxx they had grown up with, in small towns several states apart. They both love the ocean and want two kids.

They have been engaged for six months, but 'it's gotten pretty bad in the last few weeks,' she tells me. 'He only thinks about himself.'

I ask for an example.

'Well, like he has some weird money issues. A few days ago I bought a thing of really fancy olive oil – like it cost almost ninety dollars. I had it in a restaurant and I was like, *What is this?* It literally tastes like fresh-cut grass. It's insane. Anyway, I know it was kind of a splurge, but he got all huffy and was like "*I'm not made of money, you know,*" as if, by the way, I don't also have a job, and plus then he'll go and spend *thousands* of dollars on a top-of-the-line sound system for his car because that's important to *him*.'

I take this in. 'So, how did you handle that?'

'I said nothing, like usual. I just kind of stood there, stunned, and then said I would return it.'

This surprises me.

'And then last night he left the toilet seat up and I totally lost it and told him he's a narcissistic piece of shit and I don't want to marry him. I guess I have an anger management problem.'

I think for a moment about what I've just learned. Skylar is someone who buries her feelings, avoids confrontation and then lashes out. But sometimes lashing out is caused by anxiety; I mention this to Skylar.

'That's interesting. I never think of myself as that anxious, compared to some of my friends. I'm more the ice queen.'

This reminds me that I had been wanting to know more about her life as a high school bully.

'Yeah, I don't know, it was just typical stuff. I played the game, looking people up and down, making them feel insecure. I could always dish it back to guys and they always thought that was kind of hot, so I just kept doing it. I guess the bitch thing just kind of worked for me.'

She seems rather relaxed telling me about her past – not like a person in crisis. I realise I have not yet understood whether she wants help improving the relationship or breaking the engagement.

'Oh yeah anyway, the next morning after I crashed out at Geoff I just apologised for being such a bitch.'

'Got it,' I say. Apparently that was the end of their discussion.

Skylar goes on to tell me about what a huge bitch people think she is at work, too – and how she probably deserves it. She delivers snarky one-liners to the assistant who double-booked the conference room; she snaps at the intern who forgot to press send on the email; she slams the door after chastising the asshole who neglected to include her in an important client call.

One day when I'm feeling brave as she postures around her nastiness, I invite her to show me her bitchy side. What kinds of thoughts are brewing right here, right now? I want to show her I can take it, that whatever vicious attacks she can muster will not break me or turn me against the project of helping her.

Skylar seems taken aback by this. She shifts in her chair and tries to bring it: 'Well, I think I'd start with the fact that you're drinking from a jar of Vaseline.'

I hadn't been expecting to laugh, and it almost sends my sip of water spraying across the room. She's so right! My water bottle is lemon yellow, with a royal blue cap and a straw. 'I picked out those colours because I thought they looked beachy!' I say.

I sit back and take a sip of my Vaseline.

She's the first to call it out: this confrontation isn't working, she says, because she's not mad at me. To bring the full bitch, she has to feel it.

As the months pass, I wait for her to try to hurt me, to make me feel ashamed. I notice I'm taking steps to protect myself. I remember to wear lipstick and earrings to our sessions. I fully recognise this is a countertransference reaction: if I'm feeling like shame is a risk, that must have something to do with Skylar and that feeling.

In any case, the dreaded moment never happens, and I find myself lowering my guard. Skylar is warmhearted and hilarious. I have a suspicion she might secretly be a nice person.

'Where are you taking your family for vacation?' she asks one day. With many patients, I dutifully hold neutrality, at the risk of sacrificing a smidge of warmth: *Oh, what are your thoughts about that?* Not with this bitch.

'Disney World,' I say.

'Jesus Christ' is her response. 'Can't you bring them to Copenhagen, or something? Please? I don't want your children to be stupid. You can blame me.'

Another time, she shows me a photo of herself at peak awkward stage – so different from the expertly put-together person sitting here now. She says she'll text it to friends when they are having a hard day. It strikes me how thoughtful that is.

All-American Bitch

Through the ages, women have been trying to find a place to put their aggressive feelings. Often, a girl will deal by calling herself a bitch – or even acting like one.

Beginning in the fourteenth century, 'bitch' was deployed as a pure insult, a way of morally degrading a woman who displayed aggression. And it's still that way, but complicated by one fact: men love bitches. Viciousness has conferred sex appeal and social power from Homer's Sirens to TikTok's Southern sorority girls. Feminists recognised this dynamic as highly problematic for women, but despite their insight and the broadened cultural conversation, by the 1980s and '90s, pop culture seemed only *more* fixated on the trope of the mean girl. Fascination with the clique in *Heathers* grew up into fascination with the bossy career bitches of *Melrose Place*. In 1998, Elizabeth Wurtzel, mental health whisperer of the teenage girl, dropped a Ritalin-addled manifesto on the topic. Two things seemed to be happening: bitches remained objects (as ever), but now girls also called themselves 'bitches' as a form of empowerment. A female badass would henceforth be known as a *Bad Bitch*.

In the new millennium, the sun finally began to set on the actual mean girl. The anti-bullying movement took hold in schools along with increasing cries for social justice and kindness to victimised youth. Those who would have been shoved in a locker in 1985 for their sexuality, family structure, religion, body type or passion for coding were increasingly humanised. The millennials, raised on the gospel of *Mean Girls* (2004), driven by a growing concern with emotional health, and propelled by #girlboss rocket fuel, assumed control of the narrative: Queen Bees took their curtain call with the series finale of *Gossip Girl* – or so it seemed.

The Official Message had changed: it was no longer cool for a girl to be mean. And yet.

The Hidden Curriculum

It's summer, and a lot of my patients are out of town. With a free hour midmorning, I step out into the heavy New York City air. A dad chases after a child scootering down the sidewalk. Two college girls in their pyjamas are having breakfast at the Mexican place.

It's too early for another iced coffee, so I wander into the nail salon. I stand still in the air-conditioning and breathe in the aroma of hand cream and nail polish remover. There it is: the wall of pinks and reds in every gradation, each with its own colourful name, a backlit altar in the church of feminine precision. This is where some of us go to ask the big questions: What moment in the season is it? Is it time for the linen whites of deepest summer? Or are we still heralding the sunshine months in watermelon and tomato?

I flip over a few of the bottles to see what the shades are called:

Sugar Daddy. Hi Maintenance. Centrepiece of Attention.

The culture of 'pampering', a mode of relaxation designed to optimise one's feminine appeal, includes an invitation – a nudge, even – to be entitled and difficult, aggressive, greedy and selfish. Even though we are taught not to be that way, this attitude still somehow makes us sexy.

Freud's thoughts on this topic seem to endure. In 1914, he wrote that men are attracted to women who are selfish and vain. The research on this has been mixed, but evidence shows that the 'dark triad' of narcissism, Machiavellianism and psychopathy makes people (of both sexes) more successful on dates – at least in the short term. As depicted in the bestseller *Why Men Love Bitches,* the bitch is a compelling figure: a challenge, someone to tame. She is confident and spontaneous – What will she say next? Who will she choose? Will she ultimately submit?

It's not just boys who are seduced by bitchiness. Girls who display high levels of social aggression tend to be more popular across the board. While it's no longer fashionable to inflict pain on the weak or to relish the subjugation of others, one never achieves social status without a touch of cunning. Ultimately, anyone who survived middle school knows that popularity relies on exclusivity and power. This requires the existence of in-groups and out-groups, and a cold, judgemental girl at the helm to put everyone in their place.

Bitchy behaviour – defined as social aggression through gossip, exclusion and reputation destruction – has reached an all-time high in the social media age. Online, bitchiness equals attention and money, and all of it makes the *Mean Girls* burn book seem as tame as a peek at a Victorian lady's ankle. Today, selfies are savaged on Instagram; hateful comments hide as ephemera on Snapchat; and even without social media platforms, rumours can blast to every classmate's phone in an instant on a WhatsApp group or a simple text chain. In all electronic gathering spaces, fake accounts are created to mask and mock, followed and then unfollowed with intent to harm. And even in real life, girls are crueller than ever. Half of girls say they don't like school because of meanness, drama and competitive attitudes among female peers. Bitchy behaviour still makes trouble on college campuses, among adults, and even in the senior community, as evidenced, amazingly, by a recent article in the magazine for the American Association of Retired Persons (AARP) offering tips to deal with 'Mean Girls'.

For someone like Skylar, I wonder if the increased culture of bitchiness reinforces her own version of what I call 'Girl Self-Defence System', which includes 'bitch' as a valid type of female to be.

The Proto-Bitch

If you look up baby girl names, many of the popular categories are described as 'feisty', 'sassy', or 'fierce'. On the one hand, we romanticise girls who claim a bit of extra power and display disarming flashes of strength. But then, I've noticed, a funny kind of objectification often clouds the picture. I've seen parent after parent – especially fathers – take on this bewildered look, like a man who has been beaten into submission, when talking about his daughter. He will shake his head and say, 'Avery runs our family,' 'Madison's the boss,' or 'Hooh – watch out for Brynn!'

If it's a little girl, she's *a handful*. If it's a tween or a teenager, she's *just-exhausting-but-gee-whiz-what-can-you-do?* In either case, the depiction smacks of an insidious misogyny – all the more so because it is perfectly innocent. Hidden by admiration, awe and sometimes desperation, the message resembles the old knee-slapper: 'Stay away from Deborah when it's that time of the month!' *Women be bitches* is the point. It's both deferential to and dismissive of these domineering, moody females. And yet, describing girls in this way is objectification – and self-objectification – in the making.

Because Avery doesn't *really* run your family – or at least, I hope she doesn't. Madison is the boss of nothing but her own Sylvanian Families (and maybe a hapless toddler sibling); and what exactly will Brynn do if you don't 'watch out'? It's not the same as saying your daughter is a strong person and you value her opinions. It's that she's excessively bossy and is being allowed, semi-ironically, to overpower the family.

There is a widely accepted male stance that loving your daughter or girlfriend or wife means ceding power *unreasonably,* or pretending to, or convincing yourself you have, and affecting a kind of helplessness about it. The same flavour of misogyny is present in many marriages of the older generations: *Mildred is the real boss of this house!* Girls then associate being loved with having this kind of objectified – but not real – power, proven by being able to get what they want when they want it.

For little girls, the word would not yet be 'bitch' but 'brat'. A 'brat' is one of the first things girls are taught to both be and not be.

Let's consider the pout: a facial expression associated with little girls who don't get what they want. This was part of the charm of child actresses like Shirley Temple back in the 1930s, but the look has grown associated with a long line of bratty characters, including *Willy Wonka & the Chocolate Factory*'s Veruca Salt and Michelle Tanner from *Full House.* The look evolved and grew up and eventually; the 'dissociative pout' became the hallmark of the selfie. This trend caused a surge in pout-enhancing lip makeup, including a lip gloss that irritates one's lips until they are swollen to perfection. During the same time span, a 'resting bitch face' was established as something you don't want. So what, exactly, is the right amount of bitchiness to display in your visage? No wonder we look so confused as we contort our faces to pose and post.

Capitalism introduces its bratdom curriculum early in the daily commerce of the little girl. A girl growing up in the early 2000s was presented with Bratz dolls, mini collectible figures with snotty faces who shop and lounge around in plush bathrobes. *Hi Maintenance. Centrepiece of Attention. Sugar Daddy.* When she grows up, these are the notions she will paint on her nails, entitlement she is taught to wear like a pair of big sunglasses. But if she ever makes it to my office, those sunglasses must come off. She will learn that there are *reasons* she's cultivated those parts of herself – that they are doing a job, trying to protect her. Because nobody's true self is a 'brat'.

Cocktails

As I'm waiting for Skylar to arrive for our next appointment, I think about the vision of her that seems to be accepted between her and her fiancé – that she's some kind of spoiled brat. And that maybe he's a narcissist.

I don't quite share this view. I see Skylar as a smart person who works hard, who likes nice things, who has trouble connecting to her feelings and using them as steady guides – and who is convinced she's defective. And as far as Geoff goes – I'm envisioning a man who can be controlling. Maybe even selfish. Also not great at handling feelings. Definitely anxious. But I'm not sure it's 'narcissism'.

For Geoff, perhaps viewing Skylar as a bitch and a princess provides him with a sense of his own purpose – he gets to be the *Sugar Daddy*. By trying to live up to certain gender stereotypes, each forces the other into roles they have grown to resent.

When Skylar arrives, she's in top form.

'I did it again last night. I had had a hard day at work and when he started teasing me about how HR is a "talk-about job" I wound up going off like a vile harpy about everything – how *his* work is a fucking crime ring, how he's just a toxic narcissist and his friends are all sociopaths in a pathetic competition to see who can love-bomb the latest Instasluts and then gaslight them into fake relationships which are basically just barely legalised prostitution. Classy, right? I'm such a good catch. Do you want to marry me?'

I note that 'asshole' seems to have fallen out of fashion. 'Sounds like a productive conversation,' I say.

'Yeah, it was really meaningful. He felt seen; I felt seen. I think our work is done here!'

'It's been a pleasure working with you,' I say with a pained smile. Now it's time to let the deafening silence do the talking.

Skylar is so entertaining, it's a problem. She can tell a tale about her fiancé's misdeeds – or her own – so uproarious that one can forget that this is actually her life. She's aware of it, too. She'll say: 'Shall we just finish this conversation over a few martinis?' Over the next few months, we develop a term for this defence mechanism that keeps us away from the painful realities we are there to work on: 'cocktails'.

I'm guessing Skylar is reflecting on this 'cocktails' moment as she stares out the window for a long while.

'I just don't understand,' she says softly. 'I keep embarrassing myself by being mean, and then we never get to talk about why I was upset in the first place. I just apologise and then all is forgotten.'

'That's a shame.'

'People at work would be shocked to see what a snivelling infant I am in my relationship. It's like, the opposite of my image there.'

'How do they see you at work?'

'Literally, I got feedback last week – when, by the way, I was PMSing like Cruella de Vil – that I needed to be more *approachable*. I guess people have been complaining I'm "too cold" or something. I think I know who it is. It's this troll who is up for a promotion and isn't going to get it because he smells.' She pauses to make a *sorry-not-sorry* face and goes on. 'Anyway, he would *loooovve* to be a fly on the wall in this session, right?'

I see how Skylar's bitchiness keeps reinforcing itself: the acerbic attitude, the tough talk, the self-defeating tantrums and the inevitable writing herself off as the classic unpleasant female. Skylar is not sure what the truth is about her – and no one in her life is asking.

Eventually, we learn where Skylar's avoidance comes from, and in particular, the way she hides from her partner. Skylar's father left when she was an infant and had no ongoing contact with her. Her mother, an assistant professor at the local community college, was intellectually gifted but chronically depressed. They struggled financially. Their house was always messy and uninviting, with piles of books and papers gathering dust on dilapidated old furniture. Skylar longed to be part of a 'normal' family – Mom on the PTA, Dad who coached Little League, taco night. On the inside, Skylar battled a constant sense of shame. But her sassy attitude captivated the alpha boys from a young age, and she leaned on their attention to feel accepted and normal. She rarely ate dinner at home. She gave her mother 'a lot of shit', and 'of all the people I bullied, I was probably the worst to my mom. She always said I have anger issues.'

Anger Issues

These are things I hear all the time: 'Isn't anger bad?' 'I don't want to have a fight with him.' 'Anger is unproductive.' 'My problem is I get mad too often.' And of course, 'It's just PMS.'

For starters, a note on PMS irritability: it's a fact that hormones have a strong influence on our moods. Most menstruating women experience at least one premenstrual symptom per cycle, about 15 per cent have clinically significant distress, and about 5 per cent experience a more severe condition called 'premenstrual dysphoric disorder' (PMDD), which was added to the *DSM* in its fifth edition (2013). Medications like hormonal birth control and SSRIs can be highly effective in reducing mood and anxiety symptoms, but there is some disagreement among experts about whether PMS should be thought of as 'natural'* or pathological, as the name 'syndrome' implies. In either case, irritability is one of the most challenging aspects of the premenstrual experience.

Hormonal fluctuations aside: in our culture we have trouble finding a place for anger. This feeling, more than any other, makes people – especially girls – uncomfortable. Unprocessed anger underlies many people's mental health symptoms. We've seen this play out explicitly with Becca, and it's in the mix with just about everyone else in this book.

So what about when people 'have anger problems' or 'get too mad'? As I discussed with Skylar, these statements often describe someone who feels the need to *discharge* their anger all the time.

* This philosophical difference has treatment implications. If the sensitivity and crankiness of PMS is 'natural', then medicating it may perpetuate a culturally sanctioned disapproval of women. Some even go so far as to say the heightened mood symptoms are valuable, facilitating connection and intimacy. This may serve an evolutionary function to ensure the safety of the product of conception, and to communicate more pointedly with our partners. Those who take this position have advocated for education and supportive measures to help women adapt, adjust and care for themselves differently during this time of the month.

When someone yells and screams, throws things, slams doors and spews invective, those behaviours can be functions of feeling anxious about being angry and needing to get *rid* of the feeling. The problem in that case would be the *anxiety* they feel experiencing anger, not the anger itself.

Anger can also be used defensively, to cover another feeling. (For example, Kaia, my 'chill' patient, gave off a cool kind of anger that was covering up all kinds of vulnerability.) Many 'bitchy' girls use anger as a mask.

While discomfort with anger affects all sorts of people, girls especially spend a lot of energy trying to push it away. 'It's bad to be angry' is a message many girls have absorbed, whether they believe that consciously or not. The stereotypes we have for angry or aggressive females come in two flavours: erotic (as in someone who could be fucked and subdued) or monstrous.

Anger is, in fact, dangerous. Letting it out in the wrong way at the wrong time can hurt or destroy relationships. Anger towards someone who is old, or sick, or traumatised themselves, or simply towards someone who loves you, can be almost impossible to bear.

In a mental health culture that leans so heavily on controlling diseases, and in a world that has always scorned the perturbed female, it's no surprise most women see this feeling as something to silence rather than something to listen to.

But anger is also one of the core elements of human existence, an essential nutrient for the soul. When a person can feel anger – like *really* feel it, *physically,* as a rising heat and energy – it is a power source to plug into, an inkwell for the quill. If we *do nothing but feel it,* it can fuel and embolden us, and can be our best – if imperfect – guide to what's right and wrong in this world. The trick is to let yourself feel the fullness of it without getting too freaked out and acting impulsively.

Bully

Skylar comes to understand more about her feelings, especially her anger, as we work together over the next several months. I've tried to help her feel her feelings during our appointments. I'm encouraged by her ability to recognise when she's angry at a colleague, at a family member, at Geoff. She can acknowledge the feeling, as well as the anxiety and guilt it brings, and she can even feel some heat in her body.

Progress, of course, is never linear in therapy. This work takes place between people feeling real feelings about each other in real time, and when it's working, it gets heated. You can't play with fire without getting burned.

I've been waiting to feel the burn of Skylar's bitchy streak. One day, it finally happens. Skylar comes to her appointment and starts telling me, with a smile on her face and in a cocktails-y tone, that – *Could you believe it? The craziest thing happened* . . . She could have gone on ranting, rather pleasantly, her usual bramble of barbs and all, about how *positively egregious* her behaviour was, how she was a *living nightmare*.

I feel pulled to be an audience for her like so many have been before, laughing at her witticisms while feeling kind of on edge. But I'm beginning to grow impatient with this avoidant behaviour. And I'm also aware that she has a choice to make about her engagement, and while it's not my place to recommend either sticking it out or jumping ship, I'm getting uncomfortable that she hasn't made a decision. She's being passive, declining to take action in either direction. She's just venting, week after week. I imagine on some level she shares my frustration with her apparent lack of progress. I'm nervous about confronting her, but that's silly, right? Isn't that my job?

Later in the session, I decide to address it. 'Skylar,' I say, 'can we pause to take a look at what's going on right now?'

'What do you mean?' She looks suspicious.

'Like, the way you are talking about this' is what I said. 'Here we are at cocktails again. Do you notice you're not looking at your feelings? And that you seem a bit stuck?'

She stiffens. 'Oh really,' she says. And then she lashes out at me. 'Well, I'm sorry you are not better at your job. I'm sorry you have to sit in that dilapidated armchair, day after day, in your *Ugly Betty* glasses, hoping people will change. Maybe if you were halfway competent, people would change faster.'

With that, Skylar gets up and walks out with ten minutes left in our session.

Voilà! The bitchiness has finally been visited upon me. And guess what: it stinks! Despite my years of clinical experience, it still feels lousy when a patient says you suck and walks out of your office. No matter how deeply I know that this is part of the therapeutic process, and even how much of a joke we've made out of our dynamic, when Skylar leaves, the feeling is unmistakable: I've been abandoned at the cocktail bar.

I stare at the empty chair and feel my skin buzzing. Maybe she won't come back, and I'll feel like a failure: if you have one job as a therapist, it's to keep patients coming back until the work is finished. Maybe she will come back and we will work through all of it – her anger, her bitchy way of handling it, what part is a real feeling and what part is defensive, what part is a fair critique of me and what is a projection – or maybe the treatment ends right here.

I go home to lick my wounds, which means calling Eloise.

'I was wondering if you needed an interior decorator. I'm in the market for a new career.' I'm puttering tensely around my living room. I relocate the pile of papers on the dining table to the breakfast bar.

'Oh no,' she says. 'Which patient?'

'You don't know this one. But she hates me.'

'Well, that means you're probably doing something right.'

'No – but like . . . *no*! I totally bungled this session. I should have known not to push her so much – or I should have been able to help her stay calm, or something – and UGH, it's like this *shame* of just being a fully horrible therapist, you know?' I let out a huge sigh and collapse on the sofa. 'Why am I taking this so personally? Whatever. I tried.' I kick my shoes off and pull the dog onto my lap. 'In any case, I'm really good with paint colours!'

A warm, knowing chuckle. Psychotherapist Carl Rogers called this 'unconditional positive regard.' The emotional experience of someone seeming to like me makes me remember to like myself – a little.

'But seriously,' I go on, 'there's nothing like full rejection. You know, being hated.'

'There's that word again!' Eloise says. 'But you know it's not hatred that sent her storming out of that room.'

I consider this. 'People storm out because they're overwhelmed with anxiety.' It's amazing how much knowledge can fly out of one's head when one is in the hot seat. Even if one is a therapist.

'Right.'

'Because they can't face their own angry feelings.'

'Right.'

'And they make conflicts between themselves and others to avoid dealing with the conflict they feel inside.'

'Yes.' I feel myself exhale like a balloon that's been untied. 'I know Skylar doesn't hate me. I know she acts mean and bitchy because she is actually *afraid* of feeling genuine anger at other people like her fiancé and in this situation, me, and she picks fights with people because she can't handle internal conflict. It's easier to make the problem between her and someone else than to think, Gee, I'm frustrated being stuck. And also: Part of me wants one solution, and part of me wants the opposite.'

'Yup.'

'And' – I'm really on a roll now – 'and she called my chair dilapidated. I think she used that exact same word about her mom's house.'

Inner Child

Skylar does come back for her next appointment. She sits down sheepishly.

'I didn't like what you said last week,' she says, holding her voice steady.

A pause.

'But I'm sorry I walked out. I know you were just trying to be helpful.'

'Well,' I say, 'I appreciate that. And I am also sorry that I made you feel like you had to do that.'

I realise there's a key piece missing.

'Come to think of it, how did you feel in here, right before you stormed off?'

Skylar looks at the floor. 'I was mad,' she says softly.

'Yes,' I say, 'that was clear. Do you know what it was that made you so mad?'

'I just felt ashamed. Like you were saying I wasn't making progress.'

There's that word. *Shame*.

In this moment it all starts to come together. Skylar is constantly battling an old sense of shame. That her family was different. That her father was absent. That they didn't have a home she felt proud of.

Usually people's most problematic defence mechanisms are protecting their most painful feelings from early life. Those defences have one mantra: *never again*.

Skylar responded to the shame with an anger she could never identify, even to herself. She was angry at her father for leaving, and at her mother for being too depressed and too poor – unfair as that may be. It never occurred to her that despite their circumstances, she could have expressed a wish that her mother would clean up the house, or get involved a bit more in her school. She felt so guilty being genuinely demanding (even while she was giving her mom 'a lot of shit'). 'After all, she did love me,' Skylar says. Skylar would sweep the feelings away every time. 'My mom just couldn't hear those things,' she adds. 'And my dad wasn't there to help.'

Instead, Skylar developed 'an attitude'. She saved her demandingness for other people. She became defiant and nasty, rather than grounded and assertive. She became very focused on her appearance. She started to believe that having a life that was 'perfect' on the outside would solve her problems.

Now I have an opportunity. 'Skylar, can you find any compassion for the girl who put on that attitude?'

She closes her eyes and sits quietly for a moment. A tear rolls down her cheek. She nods. 'She just wanted so many things to be different.'

We sit for a brief time without speaking, as a wave of sobs tumbles forth. She opens her eyes, all pink and puffy, and looks at me with a new softness in her face.

We haven't quite finished working through what happened. 'Skylar,' I say, 'let's go back to you and me.'

She looks at me cautiously, but nods.

'I think I just didn't want to look at the reality with Geoff. I know I have to decide what I want. I just freaked out and got mad at you instead of facing how hard this is.'

Her nodding grows more confident.

'I know,' I say. 'This is really hard.'

Her whole body relaxes.

By the end of our appointment, Skylar starts to see that lashing out and leaving that session – her bitchy behaviour, if you will – wasn't actually an expression of anger in the way she thought it was, but a moment of panic. She can now recognise that the mean things she said to me pushed away the anxiety she didn't want to face about her relationship.

Over the next few sessions, we return to what's going on with Geoff.

'This week it was our three-year dateversary,' she tells me one day, 'and you know what he does? He buys us an *espresso* maker. Like one of those huge fancy ones that requires like its own apartment. I don't even *drink* espresso.'

Here we go again. The acerbic attitude. The 'cocktails' vibe.

'And I was speechless. I was like, this is *beyond* narcissism. Like, is he literally *on the spectrum*?'

Time to intervene. 'Skylar,' I say, 'tell me about the feeling you're having towards Geoff right now.'

By now, Skylar can see what I'm doing. She can also recognise she needs to stop squeezing her anger through a sarcastic rant – and weaponised therapy speak.

She's ready to try being more honest with herself.

'It's like a white-hot rage,' she says.

'Keep it. Find where it is in your body.'

Her eyes are closed. She is fully engaged. 'It's like a rough heat, rising.'

'Okay,' I say. 'Let that feeling rise. Let it be as big as it needs to be.'

She allows that rough heat to roar through her like a steam engine.

The experience of sitting with that anger is motivating. It's time to talk to Geoff.

It goes okay, not great. Geoff hugs her, says he never realised she doesn't drink espresso. Blames himself for spending too much money on something stupid, anyway. What they really need, he says, is a better accountant.

She's also frustrated by this, of course.

But she is proud of herself for doing something new. For moving past ignoring herself and lashing out and calling names. For behaving like a person she likes better, a person who is mature. Because after all, one can only get married, she says, when one is an adult.

8

Slay-DHD

'Cruel optimism' . . . when you take a really big problem with deep causes in our culture . . . and you offer people, in upbeat language, a simplistic individual solution.

Johann Hari,
Stolen Focus

Humans come in so many different flavours that the categories we've defined potentially fall away. This is not denying the importance and utility of such categories, but it questions their primacy, their fixed qualities, and the ways in which we employ them in intimate conversations and wider cultural contexts.

Jenara Nerenberg,
Divergent Mind

One Simple Thing

Elle sits down and smiles sweetly, almost like she's apologising for taking up my time. Her voice is young and small. For someone in her early twenties, she comports herself more like a timid child.

She's flooded with insecurities at work. She believes she comes off as dumb, or at least not like a very serious person. She procrastinates, although nobody notices because she can 'mask' like a pro. She's often slow responding to people's texts, which makes her feel horrible; it's very important to her to be a good friend. But she's just so tired at the end of the day, overwhelmed by the prospect of grocery shopping – even on Instacart. She's noticed she's easily hurt when friends don't include her in their plans. Is there one simple thing that might explain all of it?

'So,' she says. 'I think it's ADHD . . . right?'

This is a question I hear from almost every patient nowadays. Yesterday alone, I had the same conversation with the businessman who just can't find the motivation to finish that PowerPoint deck; with the girl who talks about herself too much; with the boy who assumes nobody likes him.

Rates of ADHD diagnosis have been climbing since the 1990s, but in recent years, it's young women who have been seeking and acquiring an ADHD label at the fastest rates. This group often self-diagnoses based on information from social media. Among privately insured young women in the US, ADHD prescriptions increased by 344 per cent between 2003 and 2015, and incidence of the diagnosis in young women nearly doubled from 2020 to 2022. Now one in four young adults suspects they have the condition.

What has made ADHD feel like such a fit for so many people, especially young women?

One major inflection point was the pandemic, when people cooped up in their homes struggled to concentrate and also spent more time online. This period saw the rise of for-profit telehealth platforms in the US that dispensed stimulants indiscriminately, exploiting the relaxed regulations during Covid. So, people experienced more symptoms, felt more desperate and had new access to instant medication.

But even before Covid, ADHD diagnoses were skyrocketing. The label offers many advantages: a well-paved path to accommodations at school and work, the expectation of sympathy and grace. Modern life and technology make it harder for people who are disorganised and distractible to succeed. In the right context, people with the ADHD type of brain can be incredibly successful, but our world doesn't provide that context very often. To function in the world as it is, many people need their medicines.

Still, I've found receiving the *diagnosis itself* offers a special kind of relief. Like 'having' anxiety, it comes with a narrative: none of this is your fault, or anyone else's; it's just how your brain was made. The story offers absolution from a life of felt failures and weaknesses, an enduring sense of shame, and a powerful inner critic that's grown louder with every mess you've made. Unlike the other possibilities in its differential diagnosis – learning issues, slow processing speed, nervousness, trauma, personality disorders and even immaturity – ADHD offers a redeemed identity.

Yet there is reason to be concerned about the self-diagnosis epidemic. A 2021 survey showed roughly 90 per cent of people who screened positive on an ADHD questionnaire by the World Health Organisation did not actually have ADHD. Furthermore, social media has proven an unsteady guide: a video on #MentalHealth receives on average more than 13 million views, and yet 52 per cent of the ADHD content on TikTok is misleading – for example, that a sign of ADHD is 'being competitive' and that people with ADHD 'lack dopamine'. Self-diagnosis from misinformation online is so common and so problematic that it has earned its own moniker: 'cyberchondria'.

For anyone, jumping too quickly to this diagnosis poses real risks. Misdiagnosis can put people on a lifelong path of physical or psychological dependence on medicine they may not need, with long-term effects on growth and risks to the cardiovascular system. In 2023, almost four million people age twelve or older misused stimulants.

New research also shows that, just like diagnoses of anxiety and depression, an ADHD diagnosis can provide immediate relief, but it can also take a toll on self-esteem, including one's self-concept and sense of efficacy. In addition, ADHD traits are not always a fixed property of a person and can be situational. For example, one major study found that adolescents experience an improvement in ADHD symptoms when work demands *increase*. The identity, therefore, could be misleading.

Finally, the trend we've been examining of female self-diagnosis is both progressive and regressive, empowering and disempowering, humanising and dehumanising. While this applies to all psychiatric diagnoses, I believe that our mass fixation on ADHD has driven us to a philosophical, clinical and social breaking point.

Something is obviously wrong with the way we, collectively, think about ADHD; fortunately, many smart people are refining the category. While they sort it out, it's easy to collapse into cynicism. A parent really made me think when they recently said: 'If everyone has ADHD, does anyone have ADHD?'

And then, there is the famous advice from Sir William Osler: 'Listen to your patient: he is telling you the diagnosis.' Whether or not the masses of self-diagnosed people 'have ADHD' as we know it, maybe they are telling us something else – about this diagnosis, about all diagnoses, about the way we understand psychiatry's interface with modern personhood and womanhood and girlhood – that we need to hear.

For now, I've got to meet Elle where she is and understand more about her concern.

Elle graduated from college last spring and moved to New York with a bunch of her roommates. She got a good job in consulting, which is going 'okay . . . pretty well, actually', although she's not sure exactly what she wants to do with her life. She's not dating anyone at the moment. 'The guys I meet just don't seem to be looking for anything serious.' I make a note of this.

Where does the ADHD fit in? She tells me more about her work. It's not that she makes a lot of mistakes or anything. She meets her deadlines. Her performance reviews have been 'fine'.

'I guess it's just a procrastination issue,' she says, looking down. 'Sometimes I sit at my desk and go on my phone, and then like thirty minutes have gone by and I realise I still haven't responded to an email.'

'Can you give me an example?'

'Okay, well, there was this client that was asking for a report on something. I'm sorry, this is kind of long and boring.' She giggles.

'It's okay,' I say, smiling. 'Continue.'

A big sigh. 'Well,' she says, suddenly businesslike, 'I just like avoided doing it. I don't know, it just felt kind of overwhelming to respond.'

We explore this a bit more, and I learn that Elle's response required many steps. She had to go and find a draft of the report. She had to make some edits. She had to check a few numbers. Then she had to send it back and also address a few additional questions the client had put in their email.

Before Elle and I leave our first session, I make sure we review the criteria for ADHD. To qualify, she'll need five hyperactive symptoms, five inattentive symptoms, or both.

Like many people, Elle turns out to meet some but not all of the criteria. At this point, I have a philosophical decision to make: I could say we've ruled it out – that she definitely does *not* have ADHD – or I could say those traits still might put her on the ADHD spectrum. Or we could pursue the idea that the procrastinating behaviour has another source. I decide that I need to get to know her better before choosing the course of action.

Our time is almost up for today, but before we end, I offer her the basic suggestion I make for people who procrastinate. I call it 'turning a mountain into a staircase'. What you do is this: when you feel overwhelmed by a task, you write down a list of everything you need to do to complete it, step by step, breaking it down into small parts, then smaller, then absurdly small, like 'search for document on laptop; open document', that sort of thing. The point is to make each step so easy that you can breeze through it. And then the task is no longer this daunting, steep mountain – just a long path of simple steps.

'Thank you,' Elle says, tucking a lock of hair behind her ear. 'That's really helpful.'

It always feels lovely to offer a helpful suggestion to a patient. And there's plenty more where that came from – we could do a whole treatment around helping her with tips and tricks and hacks for becoming more efficient. Plus or minus meds, even. But is that the best kind of help I have to offer her? Is that really what she needs?

Deficit Disorder

'Guess what, you guys, I have another young woman, early twenties, thinks she has ADHD,' I say to my supervision group.

Eloise rolls her eyes.

Zach ignores Eloise and looks at me. 'Yeah, and?'

'Well, you know how frustrating I find this issue.'

'Okay,' he says, 'but as my esteemed colleague I know you can see beyond your own feelings.'

Eloise turns sharply towards him: 'Hey. I don't think it's her own feelings. It's a highly controversial subject.'

I take a tense breath.

Zach lowers his head and looks at me over the top of his glasses. 'Well, why don't we talk about the case.'

And so I tell them what I know about Elle.

'Did you run the criteria?' Zach says.

'Yes.' I sigh. 'Whatever.' I slump down in my chair and stare at the wall.

Zach waves his hand in front of my face. 'Hello? And?'

Why am I pouting?

After a pause, my thoughts begin to line up like schoolchildren. I first encountered the world of ADHD as a medical student in the early 2000s, when all of medicine was stumbling through the wreckage left by managed care. Psychiatry, too. Now we only had a few minutes with a patient – everything was pills and quick fixes. And I didn't like that: that's not why I chose this profession. So much language was changing at that time. It was also when everyone started referring to doctors as *providers*. I was horrified by the reductionism that pervaded medicine. I associated the rise of ADHD with that decline in humanism, and with some of the worst aspects of society:

shortcuts taken by those with privilege, elbowing others out of the way to get accommodations, not to mention teenagers sneaking pills to get high or boost test scores. A culture of entitlement and perfectionism. Pharma money. It was so easy to feel creeped out by all of it.

'Zach, you know how it is,' I say. 'This is the fifth person I've seen this week who thinks she has ADHD. Does anyone *not* think they have this? Is there any problem that still merits any other explanation?'

Eloise jumps on this: 'Sure, but not problems with a magic pill to solve them.'

Zach is silent.

'Exactly,' I say. 'Like, who cares about any other possible explanation, because no matter what the problem is, a stimulant will help you. I mean, who couldn't benefit from a zing of euphoria and productivity?'

Eloise nods righteously. 'Yes. No one wants to go digging in their past for psychological problems when they can opt for a quick fix.'

'Hence the ADHD monoculture,' I add.

Eloise and I gaze at each other appreciatively, but Zach's silence is unsettling.

I take on a more serious tone. 'I mean, it *is* concerning how the justifications for an ADHD diagnosis keep multiplying.'

'Right,' Eloise pipes back up. 'First it was inattention – the most *nonspecific* symptom ever. Then it was hyperactivity – also nonspecific, especially if you've ever met a child. Now this business about rejection sensitivity? I mean, I've never been a fan of being rejected, either. And with the inattention, I don't get it: kids can't focus, but they can hyperfocus?'

Eloise and I are making slightly different points. She thinks the whole construct is misguided. I'd say the category is overloaded and needs to be broken apart. Zach has generally seemed to be more at peace with it.

He finally steps into the brief silence: 'I think the point,' he says quietly, 'is that it's a disorder of attention *regulation*.'

'And thank goodness that narrative is taking over,' I add. 'Part of what's been so frustrating is the name "ADHD", which is cumbersome but also insufficient. It says nothing about emotion, even though emotion dysregulation is such a core feature of the condition.'

'Unless you're a girl,' Zach says, 'in which case you just get a diagnosis of depression or anxiety, because we just assume everything for girls is emotional.'

'It is interesting,' I add, 'that diagnoses of ADHD in girls have grown alongside the view that it's an emotion regulation disorder.'

Eloise looks confused. 'How do you mean?'

I explain that while ADHD can manifest as cognitive or behavioural impulsivity, what I often hear about from my patients is *emotional impulsivity:* going from zero to sixty too quickly. The kid at the birthday party who gets way overexcited and has to go home early. The teenage girl who is too quick to decide her friend 'is a bitch'. (This can look a lot like 'splitting', and the two are easily confused in the absence of a fuller clinical picture.) Rejection-sensitive dysphoria falls into this category as well. Someone who doesn't get the smile they hoped for will jump to the conclusion that it's because the other person hates them.

'That's all fine,' Eloise says. 'But that does sound like every teenage girl.'

Zach is quiet again. What's up with him?

'It's amazing,' I say, pushing through the tension. 'Between the moralism, the judgement about medication, the gender stuff and all of our arguing over the nature and prevalence of this condition – the ADHD issue is practically a microcosm of human bias.'

Indeed, the first narratives about ADHD were purely moralistic. Starting in the 1700s, children – mostly little boys – who were hyperactive or didn't sit and listen were considered 'bad'. An English paediatrician in 1902 described such children as having a defect of 'moral control'. In the 1950s, the condition was reimagined as the hardly more appealing 'minimal brain damage'. At least the narrative was shifting from 'bad' to 'sick', paving the way for slightly greater sympathy – although not much more. An advertisement from the 1970s infamously declared, 'Ritalin: helps "the problem child" become lovable again.'

Unlike the criteria for many other diagnoses, those for ADHD describe children as broken objects – how the child is *behaving,* not what she *experiences*. For example, that she 'fails to give close attention', 'does not seem to listen', and 'often blurts out an answer'. Most other psychiatric disorders describe at least some symptoms from the patient's perspective. For example, the criteria for OCD describe how a person will avoid certain situations or 'endure them with great distress'.

The condition became known as 'attention deficit disorder' in the 1980s, but the attention and hyperactivity components weren't combined until the 1990s, around the same time ADHD was recognised as a disability. The debates that had raged through the decades about whether children were bad, or lazy, or poorly parented, or ill were put to rest as the biological narrative triumphed when highly effective medications arrived and became widely used – and misused.

Naturally, this elicited a new form of social judgement with undercurrents of American Stoicism. As stimulant prescriptions skyrocketed, pockets of society became fearful and judgemental about those who medicated their kids, particularly with addictive controlled substances.

The growing ADHD community nonetheless worked to validate the diagnosis and the use of medications. In my training around the turn of the millennium, at the peak of pharma-backed ADHDemonium, we were taught to ask kids: 'If there was a *magic pill* that could make school easier, would you want to take it?' ADHD was supposedly the *single most treatable diagnosis in medicine*. Taking a stimulant was like *putting on glasses*. I recall an attending physician on a psych ward who would repeat, like a high school kid campaigning for student body president, 'Every child deserves a trial of a stimulant!' Enormous financial support from pharma-sponsored advocacy groups created a world where ADHD was an easy answer, and nothing to be ashamed of.

ADHD's PR campaign, led by a mixed army of distinguished researchers and corporate stakeholders, succeeded. More than any diagnosis in psychiatry, ADHD made a complete turnaround from one of the most stigmatised illnesses to a wildly popular identity.

With this shift, experts began to express concern that the condition was possibly being overlooked in girls. In 2003, the American Psychological Association published an article to this effect, and women began to come forward describing a lifetime of failures and shame, a quieter but no less disruptive inability to focus on tasks and organise their thoughts. They described childhoods spent daydreaming, never marked as afflicted because they didn't bother anyone. Rather, they suffered in silence, masking their struggles and privately feeling deficient. At the same time, those women who had displayed symptoms of hyperactivity, impulsivity and disorganisation in childhood reported experiencing social judgement for violations of feminine norms. Diagnosis in women was found to reduce long-held self-consciousness and improve chronically damaged self-esteem.

As rates of diagnosis have grown exponentially in the past decade, especially in adolescent girls and young women, a debate has emerged about whether more girls are actually developing ADHD, whether they seek mental health treatment disproportionately (referral bias), or whether they are influenced by the wide availability of ADHD content on the internet (information bias) and as a result focus on evidence that confirms what they already suspected (confirmation bias). Whatever the contribution of these various factors, in the past two decades, girls seeking ADHD diagnoses became almost a kind of social movement, and for psychiatrists, giving an ADHD diagnosis to a girl started to feel like an act of social justice. Conversely, withholding the diagnosis from a girl began to feel like an act of social injustice.

The Girl Kind

Elle arrives for her next appointment, put together for work in silk pants and a fitted button-down, carrying the warm smell of hairdryer into my office. She sits down and takes a neat sigh.

I can tell she's looking to me to start. I let the silence hang in the air for another moment to see how she handles the ambiguity.

She smiles. 'So, I wanted to thank you so much for that trick about turning the mountain into a staircase. It's been superhelpful for me, and I've told a bunch of friends about it.'

'I'm glad!' I say.

'And I know I don't meet, like, full criteria for ADHD but I'm just wondering what you think, I mean, if I have a mild case, or if I don't have it, or what?' She's blushing.

Is she anxious because she secretly wants an ADHD diagnosis and is holding back frustration that I haven't given her one? Considering the history of ADHD being missed in girls, if I don't give her one, am I participating in a long-standing gender bias? I read a paper recently about how diagnosis conversations between doctors and patients have become like 'negotiations' in which patients arrive with a particular diagnosis in mind and pressure doctors to confirm it. Is that what's going on here? And if so, are we negotiating something about science, or also about gender equality?

'Well, tell me more about your thoughts or questions.'

'I don't know,' she says, shifting around in the chair. 'I was doing my laundry last night and it took, like, the entire evening. I was folding it and I kept getting sidetracked.'

'Hmm,' I say. Already two views are competing in my mind. *Laundry is boring for everyone!* on the one hand and *Classic ADHD – the 'girl' kind!* on the other. And above all, I don't want to be a doctor who dismisses a young woman's concerns. Is she sheepish because she's expecting me to?

'So I don't know. I mean, I'm kind of meticulous about the way I put away my clothes, but I mostly just keep getting sidetracked. Laundry is boring, you know?' She's smiling and blushing some more. When and how do I use that information?

'Okay, Elle, so this is my question. Are you wondering if that's normal? Is this tied to the ADHD question you've had?'

She takes a deep breath. 'Yeah, kind of. I mean, it's not a big problem or anything.'

'Okay,' I say slowly, 'and yet, you're bringing it up here, so there must be something concerning to you about it.'

'Yeah, I did see on TikTok that can be a sign of ADHD and I still wonder if there's something about me.'

We spend the remainder of the session exploring her online influences, but I know I will need to venture more deeply into this world myself in order to understand where Elle is coming from.

There is so much online about ADHD. Clicking around on the different resource pages can almost make you feel like you have it.

After a good deal of scrolling, I discover the best ADHD content lives on TikTok.

If you click through the world of ADHD hashtags, you'll add to its billions of views* – and find friends there immediately. You'll meet #Catieosaurus, the grown-up theatre kid whose kind eyes grab you as she walks you through her kitchen fails and body image crises; you'll want to take a nap with her rescue doodle. On the YouTube channel *How to ADHD,* the fresh-faced Jessica McCabe deftly breaks

* There were 11.4 billion views as of 2022, according to Children and Adults with ADHD (CHADD).

it all down, from dopamine chemistry to neurodivergent romance. And for those in the late-diagnosis community, the Arkansas mother Kristen Bandy (#yourADHDmom) brings you into her home, office and car as she 'hits the wall of boredom', has 'bad sensory days' and 'desperately needs to be somewhere on time but [is] frozen in place researching which animals don't fart'.

PREACH, say the zillions of comments.

Googling, you'll quickly encounter *ADDitude,* the only cheerful magazine I know of that's dedicated to a mental condition. (*Generalised Anxiety Disorder!* would probably not attract as many readers.) Its articles teach how to overcome impostor syndrome and perfectionism, how to get things done, how to make friends. It's like an instruction manual for life.

Even Etsy offers its own quaint kind of support. You can order sweatshirts that say 'ADHD (noun): A superpower that turns everyday tasks into a thrilling rollercoaster'; and 'If you can't handle my executive dysfunction, then you don't deserve my HYPERFOCUS'; and my favourite, 'Officially Diagnosed with *Slay*-DHD'.

I text the links to Eloise and Zach. Eloise writes back immediately 'SMDH' (shaking my damn head). Zach does not write back at all.

My group left a lot unresolved in our last meeting, and I'm glad we're back.

'So,' I say as we start, 'I loved our ADHD conversation last time.'

'Why do women always say they "love" things?' Zach says. 'I mean, yeah, we got into some issues. I actually found it to be a frustrating conversation.'

'So did I,' says Eloise.

'I'm just glad we're getting into it,' I say, recognising that Zach is right about my own Girl Self-Defence System.

'Not to be annoying,' Zach says, 'but isn't there also this thing – like a part of therapy culture – where we pat ourselves on the back just for talking about things? This idea that talking is some kind of huge achievement.'

'Zach, why are you being weird?' Eloise asks.

'I don't know, I just think we need to be better than that,' Zach says loudly. 'Like, endless talking about things is not necessarily productive. I think that's why people don't trust therapy.'

'Who says this is endless?' I say. 'I think we are confronting the issues honestly for the purpose of resolving something.'

'Fine,' Zach says. 'But Eloise, you seem to believe ADHD is not a real diagnosis.'

'I think it's situational anxiety a lot of the time.'

'Okay, fine. But what if people are just born how they are?' Zach is fierce in the eyes. 'Aren't you a believer in temperament?'

'Of course . . .' Eloise says slowly.

'Well, have you guys heard of the hunters and farmers theory? That some people are born more like hunters: impulsive, energetic, like to go in spurts. And they struggle in school because the world is made for farmers – being steady, focused, all that shit.'

Eloise and I exchange WTF glances.

'All that shit?' I say softly. 'Zach, are you okay?'

When Elle comes back for her next appointment, she tells me she has been thinking.

'You know, I feel like the ADHD stuff is mostly related to work, and to . . . I don't know, like how people see me.'

This is so interesting. 'Tell me more.'

'Well, I was kind of upset at my roommate yesterday,' she tells me.

'Oh, what happened?'

'Well, we were both working from home, and at one point I decided to take a quick break to exercise, and she asked if I was having a "staycation".'

'The question bothered you?'

'Yeah. I felt like she was saying I wasn't serious, that I'm not a diligent person.'

'Does she think that about you?'

'No, it was just me assuming. I worry that I'm not actually a serious, hardworking person.'

'It's good that you recognise that's your own fear. That helps us.' A pause. 'How long have you felt that way?'

'I guess since high school. Like in tenth grade, physics was really hard for me, and I didn't do well. At some point I just realised I wasn't driven by school – it wasn't for me.'

We discuss Elle's current job, and how she's been surprised at how well she's performing despite feeling like she procrastinates too much.

As we talk, she eventually mentions – head down, almost in a whisper – that she would like to make more money. I ask what her dream job would be.

'Well, I don't even know if this exists, but . . .'

And she describes a job that totally exists.

I've been observing things about how Elle handles herself in the room with me. She makes her voice small, she apologises, she giggles, she looks down. It's time to call her attention to this behaviour. Does she see it?

'Yeah,' she says, smiling. 'That's just – how I am, I guess.'

I ask her if that's a problem for her. After all, she's here because she believes people don't take her seriously. Is it possible she's contributing to that impression?

Elle makes full eye contact with me for the first time since I've met her – real, deep eye contact. 'I see that,' she says. And yes, she would like to see if there's anything we can do about it.

About ten years into my practice, I developed a game some patients find useful. When we start to explore their defence mechanisms – the behaviours that get in their way – we write down each one on a note card and agree to watch as they pop up during our conversations.

When the defence appears, we race to see who can hold up the note card first.

This method has some disadvantages – it can be cumbersome, and it can temporarily lower the emotional intensity of the therapy session. But I find that if we spend a few weeks doing this, patients start identifying them on their own. This new awareness increases flexibility, which is a major way therapy helps people change.

'How about this,' I say. I hand Elle a small stack of note cards from the box on my side table and a marker, and take some for myself as well. 'Let's write down some of the defence mechanisms you just used in that story. Did you observe any?'

'Giggling,' she says. 'I giggled, I guess.'

'Okay, great – let's write that one down.' And we each make a note card for 'giggling'. And another for 'apologising'.

'Now,' I say, 'try retelling the story of your dream job without taking so many of those off-ramps: giggling, apologising, all that stuff.'

She takes on the tone and posture that seems like a kid imitating a grown-up, or a college student trying to sound professional at a job interview: *In my future role, I'd be hoping to leverage my experience with the blah blah blah for the client to blah, blah blah.* I don't even process the whole thing.

I invite Elle to reflect on what defences might be at play.

'I don't know . . . sounding corporate?'

'Great,' I say. 'Let's make a card for "sounding corporate". Now try retelling it as just yourself, without the giggling, apologising or sounding corporate. Just as a person who wants something.'

And she does.

At the same time as I'm thinking with my psychodynamic hat, I can't help but have some practical thoughts as well – for example, that she could use a mentor. I don't want to be too coachy and say so, because this would play into her passivity, or whatever other defences have prevented her from having that idea (or taking action) herself. So instead I point to the fact that she hasn't sought one out.

She identifies the perfect person, the CEO of the company she interned for last summer, who is nice and teaches at a university.

'Hmm,' I say. 'I wonder what's been in the way of reaching out to that person, or even imagining you could.'

'I'd just be so worried about asking for his time . . . I don't know why I'd be justified in requesting that.'

I sit still, waiting for her to see what just happened. A light goes on in her eyes and she sorts through the stack of cards. With a big smile, she holds up 'apologising'.

'Right!' I say. We are quiet for a moment as the mood settles. 'You know, Elle, you are so worried about taking up any space.'

She looks down. 'Yes.'

Her eyes well up with tears.

'What's that feeling coming up right now?'

'Sad. Sad that I'm so scared. I think I've known it for a really long time.'

This is a breakthrough of grief, a moment where a person realises they've been harming themselves, getting in their own way. The grief can only happen when the person finally takes a step away from the thing they've been doing.

She cries some more, and smiles. 'I feel a bit better.' And then looks serious. 'But I don't know what to do about this now.'

I remain silent, setting her up to answer that for herself.

'I assume how I speak about myself has a large impact. Both in here and outside.'

I smile and give a sombre nod. The language piece is huge. With the note card game, she's learning to label her defence mechanisms. As we go on in the treatment, she'll get better at labelling the feelings underneath. Moreover, the fact that she now recognises that the way she communicates about herself actually shapes who she is – that's half the battle.

'And I guess I should do things outside my comfort zone, like maybe one thing that's a little scary or challenging for me every week?'

When a patient has an important insight about themselves, they often get their own ideas for tools and tricks and behavioural change. A therapist doesn't need to prescribe what they should do, and in fact, it's way more impactful if it comes from the patient herself. I give an approving nod.

'I do feel better,' she said. 'Nervous, but hopeful.'

This kind of hope is the real deal: she is recognising something so deep and true about herself that she can imagine changing for real.

I wonder if we have answered her question about ADHD. In my mind, we are getting closer. One of the items in the big, overflowing grab bag we call ADHD is neurotic suffering. This does not explain everybody, but I do suspect it explains Elle.

Uphill Battles

'Zach, you may be disappointed, but I don't think it's ADHD,' I say at our next supervision. 'I think it's emotional for this patient. We had a very interesting session.' I fill them in.

'You see?' Eloise says. 'All you had to do was dig deep enough. Aren't you glad you didn't just send her out with a Ritalin prescription?'

Indeed I am.

Eloise goes on. 'It's such a shame it's come to this. Everyone having to claim this illusory disease to feel okay about themselves.'

That wasn't my sentiment, exactly. But as I'm thinking about how to respond, I notice Zach is sitting there in a full-body clench.

He finally stirs, eyes scrunched shut, and speaks in a quiet voice that must scare the shit out of his kids: 'Eloise, I'm a little tired of your attitude.'

Eloise turns and looks at him, stunned. 'I'm sorry . . . what?'

He takes a tight deep breath. 'I haven't exactly felt comfortable about bringing this up here. But we are getting Julian tested, and Marisol thinks she has it, too.' Marisol is Zach's wife.

Eloise shakes her head earnestly. 'Zach, that's – I mean, I'm so sorry to hear that Julian is struggling – and Marisol, and whatever, but that's fine! I mean, whatever! I have no judgements about that at all, I mean' – Eloise squeezes her temples with one hand – 'I just . . . it's fine. I'm so sorry you feel like I have an attitude.'

'Look,' Zach says. 'It's not that you don't mean well – I think you're a wonderful therapist and you are a dear friend and a dear colleague. But I don't feel like you understand what it's like when people really struggle with this, and I've been hesitant to tell you about what's going on in my life because of it.'

Eloise just sits there mournfully shaking her head.

'Zach,' I say, 'what's going on with Julian and Marisol?'

Zach clicks the pen in his right hand in a steady rhythm. 'Well, we had a few incidents with Julian at school. Teachers have been complaining about his behaviour for the past few weeks – I don't know, just like being super silly during reading time and clowning around. Apparently he was' – a smirk creeps across Zach's face – 'walking around pretending a pencil was his penis and poking kids with it.'

Eloise snorts a laugh. We all just take a moment and enjoy this image, as well as the fresh, clean air of relief in the room.

'And then another time he got mad at a kid who was talking shit about the Mets,' Zach says, 'so he kind of pushed the kid into a desk. We are not proud of this.'

Eloise grimaces.

'Plus,' Zach goes on, 'it's actually been pretty bad at home – for a while now. He doesn't listen. He's having meltdowns all the time. Can't come off Roblox without full-on Armageddon. Marisol and I have started dreading the weekends . . . So we set him up for an evaluation. I don't want to see this situation get any worse. I can already see him feeling bad about school and really digging his heels in with us . . . it's awful.'

'Zach,' I say, 'I'm so sorry. It's unbearable to see your child suffering and it's so good that you are jumping on this and catching whatever it is early. I mean, who knows – he's goofing off during reading time. Maybe he's having difficulty with reading, right? This could be your moment to catch a learning disability and get him some support.'

'Right,' Eloise says. 'Or maybe he's finally acting out whatever ambivalence he has towards Eric [his twin]. I mean, it must kind of suck to always be associated with another human.'

'Right, I mean, who knows,' says Zach. 'But the truth is, I think they're going to say it's ADHD. I think he's going to have it. And Marisol thinks so, too. Honestly, it would be kind of a relief.'

'Yeah,' I say. 'And what's going on with her?'

'Well, she's been feeling totally scatterbrained lately. She says she feels like she's failing at everything. She forgot to pick Eric up from soccer practice the other day. She – God, this sounds so sexist so please forgive me – she burned dinner the other night. Not that she's always the one who makes dinner. I promise, I do the cooking on the weekends.'

'I can really empathise,' Eloise says. 'I literally spent an hour and a half this morning clearing the dirty dishes out of the sink, returning everyone's hoodies to their drawers, and picking up damp towels off the floor. And folding my husband's pyjamas. And running the Dustbuster through the fine sheet of crumbs that upholsters our dining chairs after every meal. And collecting empty soda cans for the recycling bin. Does Marisol do all that stuff in your house, too?'

Zach looks confused. 'Um, I guess? I never really thought about it. We have a housekeeper once a week.'

Eloise and I look at each other and laugh out loud.

'It makes sense that she is totally overwhelmed,' I say. 'The question is why is it hitting a breaking point now? Is she going through something?'

'I don't know, I mean . . . yes? No? She has a lot on her plate, for sure. The twins are a handful, especially with everything going on with Julian. Her mother recently fell and broke a hip, and her dad is a basket case. And her job is nuts as usual – that never lets up. But all of that aside, she says she thinks she's always had it.'

'ADHD?' Eloise asks.

'Yes,' Zach says.

'Huh. Based on what?'

'Oh, I don't know.' Zach glazes over for a moment. 'She says school was always an uphill battle. She did well by studying a lot more than everyone else. She says she developed all these systems for keeping herself together but that she always just had this sense that things were harder for her than they were for other people. Plus, there's a heavy genetic component, so it makes sense she would be connecting the dots.'

'Wow,' I say. 'That's pretty classic.' I'm also wondering if Marisol is not failing but feels underappreciated and worthless, which can make a person feel like a failure.

'Is she talking to someone?' asks Eloise.

'Yes,' Zach says. 'She has been in and out of therapy for a long time and recently started again. In fact, it was the new therapist who said she should get tested.'

Steady

Zach's story leaves me wondering if I'm heading down the wrong path with Elle. It sounds like Marisol is really suffering, and I would hate to be responsible for missing an ADHD diagnosis and landing Elle in a similar place down the line.

In our next few appointments, I take extra care assessing her, not just through direct questions, but observing her. This is what psychiatrists call a 'mental status exam'. We systematically appraise a patient's speech, thought process and emotional state as well as their mannerisms and what's on their mind. I'm confident that Elle's thought process is steady and focused. She's present and engaged with me. Her body is calm and quiet.

She has grown very interested in the defence mechanisms we reviewed in the note card game, and she catches herself using them. She has been able to notice her anxiety when it creeps up for all kinds of reasons – like when she talks about a guy who keeps cancelling plans with her, and how her sister is being annoying about Thanksgiving, and when she's worried about upsetting me by asking for a schedule change.

Elle has become aware of her lifelong pattern of dodging conflict and ignoring her feelings, and is engaged in modifying the mean way she talked to herself about mistakes. She has been getting more confident: looking, talking and feeling more like an adult. She's more compassionate towards the child who was so afraid of burdening her parents. She no longer believes there is anything wrong with her brain.

So one day, I decide to check in about it. 'Elle, I just want to make sure we are on the same page. Do you still wonder about ADHD?'

'Oh, no, I've forgotten about that,' she says.

Aware that Elle is likely to skirt around conflict, I check to make sure she means it.

'Okay. So in your own words, what would you say are the main reasons you had considered that diagnosis for yourself, and how have we done at addressing them, so far?'

'Hmm.'

I wait.

And then she talks. 'I guess the problem I wondered about was like not being serious, like a serious student, and we traced that back to tenth grade when I had kind of a hard time academically.'

'Mm-hmm,' I say. I don't want to overencourage her, but so far this matches the story I believe, too.

'But I think, looking back, that I was scared to ask for help. I'm still scared because I don't like being a burden on people.'

'I'm with you.'

'And,' she sighs, 'I guess I didn't believe in myself, and I don't like confrontation, so I'm working on those things.' She looks me in the eye, confident: 'But I think I'm getting better.'

I double back to the first things she had mentioned when we met, just to make sure.

'And what about getting distracted during the laundry, procrastinating at work?'

'Oh, the work stuff is . . . well, I still procrastinate sometimes. But I'm able to get myself out of it faster now.'

'That's great. And the laundry?'

She laughs. 'I don't know . . . I guess I just had ADHD on my mind so I was seeing it everywhere. I think I just need to get off TikTok sometimes!'

I agree with everything Elle has said. And it looks like we have our answer.

Neurocosmopolitan

Marisol and Julian have both received ADHD diagnoses.

'Can we talk about neurodiversity for a moment?' I ask, the next time I meet with Zach and Eloise. I've been doing more homework.

'Please,' says Zach. 'Let's.'

'Okay,' I go on. 'So are you guys familiar with the concept of neurocosmopolitanism? It's an idea from Nick Walker, a professor who's on the spectrum and is a sapphic BDSM sci-fi romance novelist. The theory is all about depathologising "neurominorities", like people with ADHD and autism. That the notion of "treating" or "curing" them is futile and harmful in much the same way that it's futile and harmful to try to "cure" someone's ethnicity or sexual orientation. So in a "neurocosmopolitan" world, school and work environments would flex to meet the needs of human beings, without requiring medical diagnoses. I'm kind of into it.'

'So am I,' Zach says. 'That these are differences, not disabilities.'

Eloise gets squirmy in her chair. 'Okay, but the whole "superpowers" thing is a bit cloying though, right?'

Zach sits up tall. 'Actually, I just saw this study showing that ADHD makes you better at this berry-collecting video game. They might have an advantage when it comes to fast-paced technology.'

'I think perhaps the point here is that that "superpowers" narrative is not fully correct,' I say. 'Because as anyone knows who is suffering with these issues, ADHD does not feel like a special gift. It's genuinely distressing. Which is why I find myself thinking about this adage that I picked up from the neurodiversity community: *Treat distress, not difference*.'

Eloise nods. 'It is kind of cool to think of ADHD as an adaptation, even if it can cause challenges. Like maybe all the kids with ADHD now are being set up for the tech landscape of the future. Like those traits are weirdly being selected for?'

Zach smiles. 'It sure makes me feel more hopeful for Julian.'

'But wait,' says Eloise. 'Zach, this is so complicated. I feel this pressure to come fully over to your side. And because I care about you and your family so much I feel even more compelled to just agree – to say "Sure whatever helps you" and "So glad you've found relief in this possibility". But I'm having a hard time reconciling that with what I really think, which is that ADHD has become a catchall for all of our neurotic problems.'

I recall that psychoanalyst Habib Davanloo famously said, 'The most common condition in medicine is not the common cold – it's neurosis.'

Eloise goes on. 'It's kids who are stressed-out, anxious, whose brains don't yet have the capacity to articulate what they feel. And we do them a disservice by telling them they're not normal kids.'

'Eloise' – I put a hand on her arm with only the slightest irony – 'we don't say "normal" anymore; we say "neurotypical".' Sometimes around Eloise I feel like I'm talking to my grandmother.

'Fine.' She shakes me off.

'But also,' Eloise says, 'think about all the young women who are self-diagnosing with this. The *Slay*-DHD girls. I mean, is it really empowering for them to claim that something is defective about their brains when they may just be neurotypical people with psychological conflict and anxiety?'

'I don't know about what's good for all girls or women,' Zach says flatly.

'Fine,' Eloise continues, 'but what about Marisol? I mean, she's so high-functioning and impressive. Does this really feel like a win for her? To say she's got this condition?'

'That's why I like the neurodiversity paradigm,' I say. 'Who knows if she's sick or not. But she feels there is something different about her that's causing her pain. Treat distress, not difference.'

'Well,' says Eloise, 'I guess the point is that at the end of the day, we just conceptualise problems based on what offers practical solutions.'

'Maybe so,' says Zach, 'but what's wrong with that? If the hammer fixes it, who cares what is or isn't a nail?'

'In a sense, that's what defines the *dominant culture,* right?' I say. 'When all the other narratives feel impractical and exhausting.'

'So, fine,' Eloise says. 'Then what should we do now that everyone has ADHD? Put Ritalin in the water?'

'Very funny,' Zach says. 'But truly maybe we should just take it out of the *DSM* and just say a certain portion of the population is built differently and they should tailor their lives to match who they are.'

'I'd be in favour of that,' I say. 'Sounds like the neurocosmopolitan dream. Except for the fact that it's completely impractical.'

'Why is it completely impractical?' Zach says. 'Isn't that us just being lazy then about modifying the culture to match people's needs?'

'Maybe, but how is that supposed to happen in the workforce?' I say. 'Half the people get different expectations? Don't have to meet deadlines? Get more breaks? Isn't that unfair to the so-called neurotypical people? Isn't that why people are all so up in arms about ADHD? Because if half the people have ADHD and get a boost, everyone else feels left behind?'

'Yes,' says Zach, 'until you see what it looks like when a kid starts to get left behind because of what's hard for him.'

'Isn't that the whole reason for polarisations in America?' I go on. 'The fight for who is left behind, who gets an advantage, who deserves sympathy and attention and care? And everyone is so afraid and so angry that someone else is getting an advantage they don't have?'

Eloise jumps in. 'And we therapists are the people who believe everyone does deserve sympathy and attention and care. In a truly neurocosmopolitan world, everyone gets to be neurodivergent and have their particular needs accommodated. But . . . that would be insane.'

'It's true,' I say. 'I mean, imagine trying to be an employer in a world where everyone's individual quirks must be considered. Nothing would ever get done.'

Eloise turns to me, slightly irritable. 'But the minute you say "employer", you're talking about capitalism. The minute you say "get things done" you're talking about productivity and the Protestant work ethic that we're all about in this country. That's the reason everyone has ADHD in the first place!'

'It is true that ADHD is less diagnosed in other countries where similar behaviours are just considered to be normal,' I say.

'You mean, *neurotypical*.' Eloise pokes me in the thigh.

'Indeed,' Zach says. 'But for whatever reason – our gene pool, our chemicals, the age at which we have children – in America, we make people with ADHD.'

Eloise shakes her head. 'In America, we make stressed-out kids and put them in front of *Bluey* to decompress and tell them it's all okay because they have ADHD. And we give girls and women too much to do, including keeping a permanent smile on their faces, and then we tell them it's totally understandable that they're falling apart because they've had ADHD all along.'

Zach drags the stained ottoman over and puts his feet up. 'This is exhausting.'

We all look at our phones.

After a moment, I'm moved to respond to Eloise. 'Actually,' I say, 'I think that in America, we're taking all different kinds of problems – brain problems, emotional problems, environmental mismatch problems – and putting them under one simple headline: ADHD.' I look at both of them. 'We offer a single solution, and the narrative of redemption,' I say. 'Like every religion has done, ever.'

Done

That night, I go home and find myself on TikTok.

The same middle-aged woman with curly grey hair and glasses keeps popping into my feed. She looks both exhausted and relieved, after having found a digital health company that provides ADHD treatment to participants who have completed an online survey. The service is dedicated to reducing stigma and improving access to care for people with ADHD. The name says so much: *Done*.

Done's leadership was found to be committing healthcare fraud by offering easy access to stimulants online. For people who have difficulty completing tasks, 'done' is the holy grail – the word you wish you could say but always evades you. It conveys the yearning for narrative certainty, a definitive answer and solution.

The internet may be riddled with danger zones like this, but I've had to become aware of judgements I held about self-diagnosis, too: the paternalistic notion ingrained somewhere in me that we doctors are experts and we know best. Of course, we do know some things. But I always return to Osler: *The patient is telling you the diagnosis.* Sometimes in this era, it feels like a negotiation, but other times it can feel like a true partnership. That's the way it should be.

After many more conversations like the one I just rendered, I've come to have a few firm beliefs about ADHD.

The first is that ADHD is a style of temperament. Some people are born with greater impulsivity and less ability to self-regulate – like my patient Sloane. But it is not unequivocally a disease. It's a difference in people's brains that manifests across a spectrum and causes trouble in certain settings. But it's good to feel proud of your own unique brain. Being different does not have to mean something is wrong with you.

My second observation is that the medicines will help anyone. This is a problem, because the stimulants are not always benign. They can cause side effects, can be misused, and once you've tried them, can be hard to stop. The medicines have been problematic from the start, they remain problematic today – and yet, I prescribe them when I feel they will produce the best results given what's available in an individual patient's total situation, as I did for Chloe and Sloane, each for totally different and highly personalised reasons. I'll try medicine if there's an off-the-charts result from a neuropsych evaluation, or if a person who meets criteria backwards and forwards is really suffering. Sometimes it's when I see a family at a breaking point for all sorts of reasons: a kid is about to get kicked out of school; parents are on the brink of divorce; a patient's self-esteem is in the toilet. Sometimes it's when I see someone developing symptoms of a secondary anxiety disorder or depression because of how bad their life is.

The third is that some people who don't 'have' ADHD claim this identity. Often they're struggling to meet the demands of modern life, or they suffer from another problem, like Elle. The ADHD diagnosis confers advantages, including a means of differentiating oneself, being recognised and treated with compassion. People naturally want simple explanations for their difficulties, and they're influenced by information bias and social contagion. Over time, these 'symptom pools' evolve and change.

In seeking the ADHD narrative, millions of young women today willingly submit to the temptations of closure (having one simple answer) despite the perils of foreclosure (missing out on a more personal, and ultimately more helpful, explanation of their struggles). A brain does not exist without the people and expectations the world supplies, and it responds to the stories we tell. As it turned out, ADHD wasn't the right story for Elle. It did, however, make life a lot better for Zach's wife and son, who had undergone a thoughtful journey towards that diagnosis.

I am hoping that taking care with the language we use can help us navigate this treacherous philosophical territory. Perhaps we can move away from a 'deficit disorder', especially now that half the population seems to 'have' it. I used to believe it was the cumbersome name itself, the inelegance of the concept manifesting in the mouthful of double pathologising, that was the problem. But the neurodiversity perspective has guided me towards a different conclusion. I still think it needs a new name – or several new names. But in some cases, if it's often a difference and not a disease, it might be even better to simply reconsider the word 'have'.

9

Toxic, Etc.

There are stories that save us, and stories that trap us.

Rachel Aviv,
Strangers to Ourselves

The limits of my language mean the limits of my world.

Ludwig Wittgenstein,
Tractatus Logico-Philosophicus, 5.6

Extremes

Teenage girls are extreme people. It's a scientific fact. They speak in hyperbole (every single second!). Seriously, though. And thanks to the internet, this style of speech has self-amplified among young women, both online and IRL.

A teenage girl cannot say she likes the new bagel place: if it's any good, she's *obsessed*. If something is funny, to simply say so would be to damn with faint praise: anything less than *literally dying* will not get the point across – or better yet, just the crying emoji with the tears streaming down its face. In response to Taylor Swift posting about a new album, for example, fans did not merely express excitement, but mortality: 'call me an ambulance' and 'I literally had to plan my funeral'.

I often wonder, listening to girls, if their thoughts and feelings are, you know, *literally* as big as they sound. For some, this might be just a style or habit of speaking, just what's cool today, like saying '*Whatever*' when I was twelve. Or, perhaps, it's a concrete or overly simplistic style of thinking. But for others, it might reflect something deeper.

It could be a sign of an involuntary, emotionally driven coping mechanism known as 'splitting'.

As noted earlier, splitting is a mental process that happens outside of our conscious awareness. It's a filtering of the world into an all-or-nothing scheme. It begins in early life as a way we protect ourselves, and it's a normal part of development. Little kids use it automatically and quite often, to make sense of the confusing or overwhelming emotional experiences of everyday life.

When you're three years old and your mom snaps at you for spilling a cup of dry Cheerios and then taking a few crunchy steps through them, you don't have the language or the cognitive machinery to think, 'Oh, Mom is nice but she gets really stressed when dealing with crumbs.' Instead, you think, 'Mom hates me; she's scary, and I'm bad.' You don't understand moods or time. You don't understand other people's thoughts. You don't have the brainpower to see how good people can do bad things like yell at you. So in splitting off the good person from this bad person, you can protect her and all the goodness she brings. Your mind just sends her on a little trip. Then, when Mom puts away the Dustbuster and hugs you out of your tears, she returns. 'Never mind,' you think. 'Mom is nice and I'm good.' And you split off that bad set of memories so they don't intrude on your happiness.

By adulthood, most people have learned to see and *feel* the world in a more nuanced way. But in adolescence, when emotions run high and the rational thought of the frontal lobe is not yet fully developed, thought processes that resemble splitting are still quite common – and can be tricky to separate out from the more pathological kind. For example, teenagers can get heated in their feelings and be driven to black-and-white thinking ('Everyone in my class is stupid', 'Only losers don't have Snapchat', 'Boys suck'). These may be micro examples of splitting, producing a cognitive style that relies on overgeneralisation, idealisation and devaluation. A harsh, us-versus-them mentality is a splitting-based way of moving through the world. True splitting – the clinically concerning kind – requires these patterns to endure and cause problems for a person over a long time. Some kids talk like this but don't fully believe – or *feel* – what they're saying, but others do.

When splitting is going on, anger often manifests as *rage*. When a person is simply angry at someone else, it likely means that the other person injured them. Anger is an alarm that something needs to be corrected, but its goal is resolution of a conflict. Rage, on the other hand, means someone needs to *burn in hell*. To feel that way, we have to see that person as pretty much *all* bad in that moment. If someone relies heavily on splitting as a coping mechanism, her existence will be marked by a lot of emotional chaos and drama. Someone who processes their emotional life this way, solidly into young adulthood, might even be on track to develop a condition like narcissistic or borderline personality disorder.

For me, it can take some time with a teenager to determine whether a patient's hyperbole is normal – just the big feelings of adolescence – or whether she is heading towards a dysfunctional relationship with herself and others.

The Drama

'I've been on edge all day,' Maeve says as she drops her bag on the floor and perches on the chair in my office. 'I literally got in a fight with ChatGPT.'

I laugh. 'What happened?'

'I was asking for it to give me a quote and it wouldn't. I just kept putting like parts of the quote and then ellipses, and it was like, *Here is your quote.* And I was like, You're literally gaslighting me right now. In saying that you're giving me a quote when you're not. So it's like, *I'm really sorry, I'm going to try and provide you the full quote.* And I was like, You're not giving me direct quotes. And they were like, *I'm sorry for the confusion, here's the direct quote.* And they kept putting ellipses. And I'm like, Can you please stop putting ellipses? I need the full quote. And they kept putting the dot dot dot. And I'm like, Do you even know what an ellipsis is? And it told me what an ellipsis is. And so I was like, Do you see how in the quote you put an ellipsis? And they were like, *Oh, we can't ever give you a direct quote.* After all that. So I'm like, I can't. I'm done. I literally just left the library.'

Maeve's rant is hilariously charming. I love that she included every detail of this exchange. I love that she accused ChatGPT of 'gaslighting' her. I've got a sharp partner in this work.

'But actually, what put me in a bad mood was I saw Lanie's phone lying on the kitchen counter and there was a text from Samara making plans to meet up in the library – again! I told you, they're obviously up to something. I decided to confront Lanie about it and she's a total traitor. She said they were working on a project but I know they don't even have any classes together. They're both just *toxic*.'

Maeve and Lanie chose to live together sophomore year after having broken off from their original freshman roommate group of three. They declared the other friend, Samara, to be a backstabbing, manipulative, social-climbing sociopath. Samara had the nerve to steal a girl Lanie was pursuing romantically, and Maeve swears Samara plagiarised one of her essays. Maeve and Lanie were as unified as can be against their common enemy. Lanie, in Maeve's opinion, was 'just the best'. Living with Lanie alone has been 'a dream come true' and 'proof that everything happens for a reason'.

But then, Lanie started acting weird, saying she was busy during times they would usually hang out. Once the season of the Netflix show they were watching together ended, Lanie didn't seem as eager as Maeve was to find a new show.

Maeve asked Lanie over text what was up. Here's what Lanie texted back:

> I know I've been a little distant lately and honestly I just need some space. I'm not that thrilled with the way our boundaries are working, and I think it's healthier for me if we just hang out a little less. I still love you and value our friendship. 🩶🩶🩶

Yeesh, I thought to myself, when Maeve read this to me in an early session. *What a bunch of passive-aggressive bullshit!* I find I am getting pulled into a very strong feeling and a judgement that Lanie must be a terrible person. I know that part of it is my own irritation with how the word 'boundaries' has been deployed by many people recently in the service of being jerks – a phenomenon that received some press coverage years later. One example was the Jonah Hill–Sarah Brady controversy of 2023, when Brady, Hill's then-girlfriend, posted messages allegedly from Hill accusing her of violating his 'boundaries' by posting her own photos of herself on Instagram.

But whenever a therapist gets overtaken by a strong feeling or judgement in a session, it's a good idea to wonder if she is having a countertransference reaction.

Toxic. Traitor. Up to something. The words pop up in Maeve's brain like a flurry of text messages. She believes Samara has turned Lanie fully against her. There is a conspiracy. They are out for blood. For this moment, in her mind, Lanie is *all bad* to Maeve.

Despite Maeve's wry facility with bitch-signalling and therapy speak, I am beginning to suspect that her mind is engaging in lots of splitting. When Maeve is hit by a wave of complex feelings – hurt, anger, sadness, vulnerability – she panics. She tries to get rid of the feeling as fast as possible, and if Lanie is *all bad,* Maeve's mind can throw her out like a bag of trash and not have to deal with any of her own feelings. When she's in this state, Maeve is not considering the whole picture, or the whole Lanie, or the whole Maeve: she's interacting with cartoonish representations of everyone in her mind.

And the problem with being in that kind of state is she's not able to receive the balancing, calming-down kinds of thoughts that a caring listener would suggest. For instance, maybe there are other reasons Lanie and Samara might be hanging out besides designing an evil plot against her. Or, maybe there is something real Lanie is trying to communicate to Maeve about their own friendship, with an eye towards improving it, as she offered in her text. If Maeve could sit and experience the complex feelings she's having, she could separate out the paranoid ideas from the real issues.

I mention to Maeve that despite her invective and her stylish performances of anger, she may actually have some trouble processing her emotions – including anger. I ask her if she agrees.

'Are you effing kidding me?' she says. 'My problem is that I feel anger *all the time*! Anger is not a healthy emotion. I'm trying to feel it *less,* not *more*.'

Like many people, Maeve is confused about what it means to *feel her feelings*. Feeling one's feelings is entirely different from expressing them to others. Just as I discussed with Skylar, 'feeling angry' and 'getting angry' are not the same. The former is a private experience of thoughts and physical sensations; it's productive and important. The latter describes actions between people and is often destructive.

Maeve is reaching for extreme language: *toxic; traitor; up to something.* Those words are appealing because their rough edges match her inner state. In the moment, they are the only words that make sense.

When Maeve uses these words, my instinct is to push back on them. I want to say what most people would want to say: *Maybe it's not that bad; consider other possibilities; take a breath*. But because of the state she's in, that's the worst thing I could do right now. When a person's mind is engaged in splitting, she is exquisitely sensitive to being challenged, or 'invalidated'. She's in no mood to find a 'healthy' or 'reasonable' or 'balanced' way of viewing the situation – not at this moment. Those suggestions would make her feel shamed and misunderstood, and even more alone. Instead, I just listen and hold myself back from making this worse.

Poisoned Arrows

'Toxic' is perhaps the ripest, deadliest fruit of the therapy-speak tree. The term derives originally from the Greek 'toxicon', which refers to 'poison for putting on arrows'. It was not a major part of therapy discourse until the self-help book craze of the 1980s and '90s. But the term really took off after Britney Spears's titular song in 2003. (Interestingly, in that song, 'toxic' simply referred to intense attraction.) The #MeToo movement broadened the term's popularity through the phrase 'toxic masculinity', but like a toxic gas itself, the word diffused across the culture. One need not search extensively online before encountering reports of toxic celebrities, toxic bosses, toxic friends/relatives/ex-girlfriends, toxic assets, toxic fandoms or even toxic positivity. In 2018, 'toxic' was Oxford Dictionaries' International Word of the Year.

The word is empowering, but it has profoundly disturbed human relationships. It's the basis for online articles and listicles encouraging you to purge your life of difficult people. It's deployed readily in the trend to 'go no contact' with parents and other relations. Its wide use has fuelled the notion that in our culture, some people – maybe all people, even your parents, siblings or children – are optional. If someone is emotionally draining, they are 'toxic', and, like a poison arrow, they must be removed in the name of self-care.

It's not that people should never 'take space' or breaks from one another – or even that certain harmful relationships don't need to end. It's just that the casual, self-righteous use of 'toxic' has made that typically difficult decision so much easier.

Take the social media habits of young people. While blocking, unfollowing or unfriending might be useful in cases of true harassment or abuse, most of the time I see people making these moves impulsively when they are angry. 'Toxic' justifies one's immediate reactions and reinforces a black-and-white, judgemental world. Deeming someone toxic can justify 'acting out', a term that refers to behaving in response to extreme, rigid notions rather than thinking, talking and communicating in a more balanced way. 'Toxic' is a splitting-based concept and has energised an ever-more splitting-based culture.

This term is a great example of the difference between *therapy* and *therapy culture*. Most therapists don't casually use words like 'toxic', and don't tend to describe whole people that way.

Therapy ultimately seeks to free people from roles like Victim, Perpetrator and Saviour. These positions, known together as the 'Drama Triangle', tend to generate most interpersonal histrionics. This theory holds that in most situations where there is strife between people, participants assume one of three roles: Victim, Perpetrator or Saviour. Psychological and relational problems become entrenched when people stick in these roles.

A 'Victim' will feel helpless and enraged at a Perpetrator and believe she desperately needs a Saviour. A 'Perpetrator' will feel worthlessness and crushing guilt. A 'Saviour' will feel numb to their own needs. But in therapy, we invite people to recognise when they are putting themselves or others in these roles. Almost no one is *only* a Victim, Saviour, or Perpetrator. People are complex entities, and relationships are dynamic. Often, just helping a person recognise these roles is enough to get her to try stepping out of whichever one she's in.

'Toxic' has the opposite effect. 'Toxic' is not a role; it is an immutable quality, a definition of what someone or something is down to the molecular level. And its easy use worries me – for Maeve and for many members of her generation. Maeve experiences a lot of pain about what's happening with her roommate. She needs someone to help her navigate the turbulence – and metabolise the loss, if that's what's happening, or improve the relationship, if that's an option. But as long as she is splitting, she can't go through the processes that will help her learn, grow and deal.

People exist in a context, and it's not Maeve's fault that she's grown up in a culture that invites splitting. In addition to notions like 'toxic' floating in the air she breathes, other concepts and ideas about relationships are lingering in the back of her mind.

Victims and Perpetrators

'I figured out what I want to do.' Maeve's eyes twinkle with a kind of violence. 'I was looking at the school's code of conduct online, and it specifically prohibits "bullying and intimidation". I mean, I know they're not like, physically threatening me. But don't you think this kind of backstabbing qualifies as *emotional abuse*?'

Okay. I take a breath. *We're not there yet*.

Maeve's words reflect a thought process that sorts the world into Victims and Perpetrators. I wonder where this worldview is coming from. Nature or nurture? And if nurture, how much has to do with what she learned in the broader culture versus her own home? Did she observe this style of coping in her parents? Is she defaulting to black-and-whiteness because no one ever helped her understand and process her own feelings? Or, is the opposite the case: has she been insulated and overprotected? Is she on track to develop borderline personality disorder, or is she just immature?

I don't know much about her primary relationships or her home environment yet, but there's no doubt she's soaked up a casual use of extreme language. And it's impacting her ability to accurately assess the current situation.

I'm struck by Maeve's term, 'emotional abuse'. A tragic reality of too many people's lives, abuse occurs when someone powerful is violent or cruel towards someone less powerful. Notably, common forms such as child and spousal abuse were not on the radar of the public or even the medical community until fairly recently. Despite the high prevalence of child abuse throughout human history, it was not until the mid-twentieth century that it was formally recognised as a problem requiring surveillance and intervention by professionals. Domestic violence was not identified as an urgent social ill until the 1970s, when the first rape crisis hotlines and domestic violence shelters were opened. The frequency and long-lasting harms of child sexual abuse were largely concealed from public awareness until the 1980s.

Over the last few decades, the word 'abuse' entered the popular discourse for the best possible reasons. The use of the term has since broadened, however, diluting its meaning and confusing many people. For example, when you ask the internet 'what is abuse?' one of the first websites to pop up says the following: 'Abuse is when someone causes us harm or distress.' Many TikToks list common inhibitions as evidence that you may have been abused – like if you 'don't like asking for help' or you're 'scared to put yourself out there'. Infographics on Instagram name 'invalidating your experiences' and 'weaponising silence' as actions that 'count' as abuse.

These definitions are incomplete and can be quite misleading. Abuse is not the same as harm. It's a very specific kind of harm inflicted by a more powerful person on a less powerful person. It's an '*ab*-use', or a misuse, of power.

This expansion of the definition of 'abuse' is itself harmful, undermining the experiences of the many people who are truly abused emotionally, physically and sexually and allowing the term to be freely weaponised. 'Trauma', though also overused, refers to the subjective experience of an individual; 'abuse' always implicates another person. No matter how overused the term is today, it still carries the strong overtone of serious, unforgivable wrong.

The overuse of the term also confuses people about what they have experienced, how upset they should be, and who they are. Take, for example, the notion of 'bullying', a form of abusive behaviour in which a more powerful person – physically or socially – is violent or cruel to a less powerful person. Many of the parents I work with have brought in concerns about bullying. The past two decades have seen enormous progress from the anti-bullying movement, and recent generations of children are far more adept at handling abuses of power in their peer groups than those who came before. Schools take the matter far more seriously than in the tough-it-out days of yore.

But not all social adversity among children is bullying. It's ordinary for parents to witness painful discord and exclusion in their children's social worlds. Some parents have been tempted to hunt for 'bullies' in these situations, hoping that if they call the teacher or the other kid's parent, or the director of the sixth-grade talent show, wrongs will be righted, justice will be served.

The language of Victims and Perpetrators is tempting because as a parent, it can be nearly unbearable to watch your child suffer – even if they are simply enduring the slings and arrows of a normal childhood. We want to fix things for them. But in many situations, if parents hold back, they can offer something much more valuable.

It's helpful to recognise that this pain is a defining feature of parenting. A parent who feels helpless and powerless can take pride in the searing, feverish love for their child that this pain comes from – in the gut-wrenching devotion that is their deepest gift to give.

We can help children process their feelings, with self-respect as a goal. That would mean just being with a child through a range of feelings that might include crying, getting mad and then finding their way towards a position of self-respect. 'I didn't deserve that.' Or 'I'm going to go where I'm appreciated.' Rinse and repeat. A very smart elementary school girl who had been excluded by a friend recently told me, after a long process of working through her feelings, 'I wouldn't want to be friends with someone who doesn't want to be friends with me.' Yes – this is the ideal end point. Taking on the identity of 'victim' can have worse consequences for one's self-esteem than simply recognising that others have behaved badly. In other words, it is more productive to help children process painful losses, rather than always trying to identify punishable crimes and Perpetrators around them.

Of course, again, there are also real villains in this world. And there are powerless people – the children, the elderly, the poor and other weakened and disenfranchised groups – who continue to suffer mistreatment at the hands of those in power. But it is in the service of these groups that we must keep track of what abuse truly means, so that the word will be available – with its full power – when they need it.

An important part of psychotherapy, or any reflection and emotional healing, is to determine whether there has been abuse or trauma in one's life. But even when this is the case, victimhood is a bad psychological place to remain. Being victimised is an event, not an identity. Fortunately, as Maeve and I unpack her situation, her language seems less to reflect her actual circumstances, and more to indicate a different kind of problem.

Late Bloomer

I sit for a moment, reflecting on Maeve's comment about wishing her friends could get busted for emotional abuse. After a long pause, I decide to put my difficulty in responding on the table: 'Maeve, what kind of response do you find yourself expecting, or wanting, from me?'

Maeve is caught off guard by this question. I've shifted the focus from actions and behaviour to what's going on in her mind. But, she's thinking about it – I can see the wheels turning.

I am hoping Maeve will begin to observe what she brings to our interaction. She wants me to support her suggestion. If I do, it would mean I can accept her big, big anger; that I'm willing to feel it along with her and won't judge her for it. I'd be solidly *for her*. If I push back, I might be *against her*. I have to stay out of both of those places.

'I guess I'm just hoping you'll agree with me that this is abusive. Or else do what my mom would do, which is tell me not to freak out.' She says this last part with a weak smile.

This reference to her mother opens the floodgates.

I learn Maeve comes from a loving home and is very close to her parents, especially her mother. Her parents are both small-business owners who seem to like their careers and each other, and the family has been quite happy with their life in a cheerful town. I learn Maeve was hit hard, like many of her peers, by the pandemic. She missed out on a lot of life experiences: graduation, prom and, even more important, the years of resilience-building thrashing around in the social world. She doesn't describe the absence of those experiences as traumatising, exactly; in fact, she really enjoyed the time with her family and remained very dependent on her parents years beyond when a natural separation process would have occurred. To this day, her mom seems to be the one she turns to – every few hours, even as a college student – to handle any adversity. *Should I email this professor and ask for an extension? What should I make for dinner? Is it gross to buy pre-owned leggings?*

And of course, Maeve has not learned to deal with what's much more challenging: her own difficult emotions. I find myself starting to believe Maeve's splitting is a sign of delayed separation, mixed with culturally sanctioned extremism, rather than a psychological disorder.

In either case, a little psychoeducation about the 'Drama Triangle' (Victim, Perpetrator, Saviour) can come in handy. I take a moment to explain it to Maeve.

'So you're saying I'm feeling like a victim?' Maeve says.

Yup, mm-hmm.

Maeve's eyes grow wide. 'I think that's true,' she says quietly.

I invite Maeve to step out of the triangle. Just to see how it would feel.

'I guess that would mean that I have a role in what went wrong, which I know I do. And that Lanie is not necessarily against me – or not *fully* against me, right? Like maybe she meant what she said, that she just wants some space, but she's not like . . . trying to take me down?'

Right.

Maeve's eyes stay pinned open as she takes this in. She lets out a huge, heavy sigh.

This is my big moment. Now that she's moved beyond the splitting and the rage, she can settle into a more grounded anger. And on the other side of that anger, there are deep, vulnerable feelings she's been pushing away.

'Maeve, I bet it hurts, just really hurts, to have your roommate take this step away from you.'

She looks away and tears up. A sniffle, then two.

'Yeah.'

Linguistic Relativity

Splitting is an unconscious process. It is impossible to draw a direct line from cultural trends to a specific individual's psychological habits. But people are affected by culture, and the automatic, or unconscious, parts of our brains – which make up most of our mental life – are particularly sensitive to language.

Language influences our perception of reality and helps to refine our thoughts. Known as the theory of linguistic relativity, or the Sapir–Whorf hypothesis, the classic example is the Inuit culture's 'hundred words for snow', but it's been borne out in many other languages. For instance, the word 'bridge' is a feminine noun in German ('die Brücke'), and German speakers have been found to have classically feminine associations with the word, like 'beautiful' and 'slender'. In Spanish, the word is masculine ('el Puente'), and Spanish speakers associate the term with conventionally masculine qualities, like 'potent' and 'strong'. Greek and Russian speakers are quicker than English speakers in distinguishing light blue from dark blue – because those languages have separate words for the two colours. One's ability to detect odours is directly correlated with how many words describing odours exist in one's language. The features of language are so closely connected to culture that some experts argue that writing – the act of selecting language – is equivalent to thinking itself.

At this moment, the language of extremes has created a culture where one type of thought is growing dangerously common: that it's an act of 'wellness' to trash your relationships. 'Self-imposed solitude might just be the most important social fact of the 21st century in America,' writes Derek Thompson in *The Atlantic,* declaring Gen Z America's 'most isolated generation'. Jean Twenge has described how prior to 2010, the majority of teenagers hung out with friends multiple times a week, and after 2010 there was a sharp drop-off in IRL socialising, which plummeted further during the pandemic and remained just as low in the years that followed. Similarly, *The Guardian* reports that young people are flaking out on social plans – and making videos celebrating this behaviour. They seem to believe people don't need each other. The concern that AI companions might someday replace human relationships is no longer a dystopian fantasy.

Technology and misconstrued ideas about mental health have indeed combined to make Gen Z the loneliest generation, and Gen Alpha is following close behind. Those same videos advertising ways to bail also reference the creators' own anxiety and exhaustion at the thought of leaving the house. But the irony is that social isolation is poison – literally toxic – for the soul. The converse is also true: social contact has immediate benefits on mood, even when people don't believe they want it. Still, today's youth are choosing to stay at home alone. The language of toxicity and condemnation seems to align with this value system, creating a self-reinforcing cycle of distancing, denouncing, disavowing, blocking, unfriending, unfollowing and terminating relationships. All in the name of 'self-care'.

This is perhaps the greatest disservice therapy culture has done to the mental health of our young people. As our legitimate therapeutic concerns have curdled into a cultural obsession with toxicity and abuse, we have unwittingly facilitated freewheeling judgement and rejection of the self and others. We have created a culture of condemnation – and now young people have to live in it.

10

People-Pleaser

> Some women get erased a little at a time, some all at once. Some reappear. Every woman who appears wrestles with the forces that would have her disappear.
>
> **Rebecca Solnit,**
> *Men Explain Things to Me*

> [American females] have been raised to believe that their being likable is very important and that this "likable" trait is a specific thing.
>
> **Chimamanda Ngozi Adichie,**
> *We Should All Be Feminists*

The Answer

Millie's parents tell me the answer at our first meeting.

'She needs to be more selfish.'

They describe a highly competent thirteen-year-old – a strong student and a talented artist with lots of close friends. She puts everybody's needs ahead of her own, and her parents are worried that lately she has been 'giving up' too much.

I ask for an example.

'Well, we think there was a boy she liked,' her mom says, 'but she didn't say very much about it, and then suddenly he was going out with one of her friends, and she didn't seem to mind.'

Her dad looks at her mother, then at me. 'And then there was the time she had a big math test, but we heard her on FaceTime . . . it sounded like she was consoling a friend . . . until after midnight. And that test didn't go very well for her.'

They tell me life at home can be a bit chaotic at times, with two younger brothers who each have issues – one with ADHD, the other with 'no diagnosis yet' but some 'acting-out' behaviour.

'We just don't want her to give up on herself,' her mother says. 'Why does she not, you know, fight for her own interests as much as other people do?'

'To be clear, Millie is a great kid,' her dad says. 'We just wonder if this is a sign that she's developing depression or anxiety, or low self-esteem.'

'And oh,' her mom whispers to her dad, 'we should talk about the climate stuff.'

'She's become quite despairing about the planet,' her father tells me. 'They had some assembly at school about climate change and she got very upset afterwards.'

'Yes, we are all composting now, under her watch.' Her mom smiles.

Her parents chuckle lovingly.

'She's the classic parentified child,' her mom continues. 'We don't want that to cause problems for her attachments later in life.'

Family Stuff, Sometimes

A few days later, Millie arrives and sits down with a pleasant smile and a nervous sigh. She finds the ends of a low ponytail lying over one shoulder, which she begins to twist and untwist, averting her eyes.

'So, I've met one time with your parents.'

'Oh?'

This is not news, but I want to show her I'm not going to conceal the adult back channel.

'And I can share what they said, but let's start by you telling me why you're here.'

'Um . . . well,' Millie says. 'I'm basically fine. Other people have a lot worse problems than me.'

I'm wondering then if Millie thinks there is any reason for her to be seeing a therapist. Sometimes kids don't want to own that they have a problem and it's easier to ask them to speak through their parents.

'Well, what do you think your parents would say about why you're here?'

'Oh.' She lets out an enormous sigh. 'They're always worrying about us.'

'What do you think they're worried about?'

She describes her stress about school and tests, just 'normal stuff'. She looks out the window. 'And family stuff, sometimes.'

I ask what that means.

She looks at me, still fiddling with her hair. 'Like, it's just hard for them, you know?' *Twist, untwist.* 'With Augustus and Jack always getting into trouble, especially my youngest brother, Augustus – he has ADHD – and he struggles a lot in school. And then Jack can be not very nice to my parents sometimes, and they don't always know what to do.'

I notice she has not mentioned anything about herself.

'What's that like for you?' I say.

'Um' – *twist, untwist* – 'I just try to be helpful . . . I guess I'm a bit of a people-pleaser!'

The Secret to a Successful Therapy

As you may have noticed, Millie is different from my other patients: she does not believe she has a psychiatric diagnosis, and she is not sure she needs therapy. She does, however, call herself a 'people-pleaser', as so many girls and women do. It's not clear yet if she views this as a problem – much less a problem she would like to work on with me.

In order for therapy to work, a person has to identify a *problem* they would like to work on. And it can't be just any problem. It has to be an *internal* problem* – something about themselves. The internal problem must be something *psychological* – they have to see themselves as playing an active role in contributing to it. They need not know exactly how or what that role is – that discovery is part of the work of therapy. But some curiosity about their role is essential. This does not discount whatever biological forces they are *contending* with, but the emphasis must remain on how they respond to, react to, process, deal with, metabolise, make sense of, get anxious about, defend against, cope with and generally *handle* whatever is going on inside.

This may seem obvious, but it's easier said than done. This kind of internal focus requires both insight and motivation, which can be especially challenging for teenagers. Often, their parents are sending them to a therapist directly against their will. For many patients, the medical model interferes. If it's just 'how I'm wired', there is little motivation to work hard and change.

My first job with Millie is to figure out whether she wants to be here at all. Does she see being a pleaser as something to work on about herself, or is it just how she is?

Although it's not a psychiatric diagnosis, 'I'm a people-pleaser' may block her in a similar way. The term has grown popular in today's therapy culture, as evidenced by a recent social media fascination with the 'fawning' response. Books on the topic have begun to shed light on this personality type as a response to trauma, adverse experiences and cultural pressures, and to offer suggestions about how to change. But the concept rings so true for so many people that it lends itself easily to identity – and that makes it harder to imagine changing.

* Many people like to come to therapy and vent about others; this can be relieving and even helpful, to a point, but won't ultimately make them better. At least once a day, I find myself reiterating in sessions that, as much as I wish we could, we cannot change your unreasonable math teacher, whiny sibling, controlling friend or critical mother. The only person we can change is *you*.

It's going to be tricky to figure out where Millie stands. Whatever direct questions I ask her, she is likely to tell me what she thinks I want to hear. If she does want my help on some level, she's unlikely to admit that. Girls like Millie also often feel they are not entitled to have real problems, and coming to therapy makes them feel guilty. But if she doesn't want to be here, she's unlikely to tell me, because that might hurt my feelings.

It's hard for almost anyone to admit they have a problem and that they need, or even want, help. For many people, a psychiatric diagnosis justifies asking for it. But even when a problem is identified, people are resistant to changing. Often, they are afraid to examine what goes on with the people they love.

I Feel Bad Saying Anything

I'm eager for our next session.

When she arrives, Millie is dressed in a faded T-shirt and loose-fitting jeans. She sits down in the further away of the twin armchairs. There is a messiness about her that makes the chair, with its plush sandy cushion and its bold wooden arms, seem suddenly fancy. Millie checks back over her shoulder and eyes the large pastel dollhouse on my bookshelf.

'The kids I babysit for have the same dollhouse,' she says, with a smile and a shrug.

I smile and nod, wondering if I should join her in this opening chitchat or not. As I decide, I think how if I were a little kid, I'd want Millie as my babysitter. I bet she's really good. I observe that funny little thought and tuck it away: it must say something about Millie that my mind went there.

She crosses an ankle over her thigh, fiddling with the laces of her sneakers. She wraps and unwraps the loose ends around her finger. I decide to say nothing for now.

That famous silence at the beginning of therapy: it's a hand-me-down from psychoanalysis, where a session typically begins with a space that the patient is meant to fill with their associations, with 'whatever comes to mind'. Most patients vaguely understand that they are supposed to begin, but many don't know what they are supposed to say or why. *Do I report on my symptoms? Can we pick up where we left off? Shall I make pleasant conversation?*

'How was your week?' Millie asks me with a sweet smile.

I am briefly warmed by this unusual opening from a teenager. And it reminds me why she is here.

'It's so thoughtful of you to ask me that,' I say, smiling back. But I don't answer, because I want to let the fact of her question hang in the air for a moment. She's smart. She'll get it.

Millie blushes. *Wrap, unwrap.* 'I know my parents say I need therapy. I'm just not sure what to talk about because nothing really happened this week.'

She got it.

'Well, how would you say your mood has been?'

'Not great, but not like really bad or anything.'

I ask what she understands about why she feels 'not great'.

Wrap, unwrap. 'Climate change? The pandemic? I don't know . . . my life isn't that stressful. A lot of kids I know have *real* problems – like a bad home environment, or like, no coping skills. Sometimes my friends joke that I'm their therapist . . . which is not exactly false!'

'Tell me more about that.'

She perks up slightly and looks at me gravely. 'Well, my friend Willow gets really bad panic attacks, so I try to be there for her with that, and my friend Nova? She's just having a hard time in school – she might be dyslexic or something. All of my friends have so much wrong with them – I think I might be the only one who doesn't have a mental illness!'

In a sense, Millie has positioned herself against therapy culture. Or at least, it's guided her more towards the role of therapist than patient – a role she seems to enjoy. I certainly don't want to talk her out of the idea that she's okay, if she is. So I make sure to land on the positive, before I push.

'You sound like a really good friend.'

She blushes.

'It seems like there's a lot of good in your life. Would it be okay with you if we look a little at why you're here?'

She takes a deep breath. 'Okay . . .'

'So you mentioned in passing you generally feel "not great". Can you tell me more about what "not great" means?'

A heavy sigh again. 'Oh, just tired sometimes. But I have to get up early for school . . . And sometimes just, like, I get sick of people.'

Oooh, we might be getting somewhere. I try to be casual – 'Oh yeah?' – and look at her expectantly but not too expectantly.

'I don't know.' She looks away. 'It's nothing major.' A pause. She kicks her feet a little like she's swimming. 'I just feel bad saying anything . . . I guess I'm a pretty guilty person.'

Sometimes floating an interpretation can come in handy. 'Millie,' I say. 'I don't know you very well, but I've noticed some things about you in our short time together. You've mentioned a few times that your problems are not so bad, that maybe other people have worse problems, and that you're not sure yours are severe enough to warrant therapy. You're very thoughtful about others – like when you asked me how my week was. That's a nice, normal thing to do, but it's also a little noteworthy at the beginning of *your* therapy session.'

I pause for a moment to make sure she's not feeling criticised.

'I bet that's something people appreciate about you, how kind and considerate you are . . . Am I right about that so far? Way off base? What do you think?'

'No! You're totally right!' Millie smiles and plants her high-tops back on the floor.

Is what I'm saying actually resonating? Or is she managing *my* emotions? (Like a good babysitter, and of course, a people-pleaser!)

I decide to stop talking and wait. In the interim, I notice I'm holding my legs straight out, ballet flats going *point, flex, point, flex.*

'That's all definitely true.' Now her body is still.

'Okay!' I clear my throat and tuck a leg under me. 'Okay. But –

maybe I'll go on a bit here, if I may. I am also noticing, like right here for example, that thinking about other people might make you minimise your own problems. You know what I mean?'

'Um . . . maybe?'

'Well, you mention you don't feel great, but when I ask about it you seem to believe it's wrong or bad to focus on that, even though this is *your* therapy session.'

She's making eye contact with me now.

'Maybe yeah, a little.'

I notice that my feet are back on the ground now, too.

'Like, how you called yourself a *people-pleaser*. I wonder if that's something you see as a problem for you?'

Millie sits very still, but she is looking at me. 'That's a good question. To be honest . . . I'm not sure.'

The Wisdom to Know the Difference

Millie may actually believe that some people just naturally are how they are. Some people might just be born guilt-ridden, accommodating and nice.

She's right that one's personality is highly influenced by temperament. But overvaluing temperament and ignoring other factors breeds two possible attitudes: acceptance and hopelessness. Acceptance is a good thing. Some schools of psychotherapy even dictate 'radical acceptance' as one of the most important life skills. But is acceptance always the correct path? If we are too quick to accept the way things are, we give up on the possibility of change.

Years ago, my family went through an especially difficult period. During that time, a relative and I were consoling each other about the circumstances, and he quoted the baseball player Mickey Rivers: 'Ain't no sense worryin' about the things you got control over, 'cause if you got control over 'em, ain't no sense worryin'. And ain't no sense worryin' about the things you don't got control over, 'cause if you don't got control over 'em, ain't no sense worryin'.'

This is an adaptation of the famous Serenity Prayer, written by theologian Reinhold Niebuhr in the 1930s and popularised by Alcoholics Anonymous: 'God, grant me the serenity to accept the things I cannot change; the courage to change the things I can; and the wisdom to know the difference.' In my work, I don't think there is any deeper guiding light. In fact, the task of a therapist is to ask what can or should be changed about a person, based on what they want and what is possible.

Defence Mechanisms, Redux

It takes a few years before Millie actually wants to be here. *Years*. Or rather, it's years before she can *let* herself be fully present and engaged in our therapy. At each step of the way, I have to meet her where she allows me to. Of course, it is not that nothing happens in the intervening time. We develop a comfort, a rapport with each other. We track her moods and discuss some behavioural strategies to increase her energy: getting enough sleep, making sure to eat something for breakfast, taking 'active breaks' when she's draggy during the homework hours. And I become familiar with all of her defence mechanisms.

Each person's constellation of defence mechanisms gives shape to their personality. Some of them, like intellectualisation, humour, altruism and sublimation, help us transform our impulses into positive human enterprise. Others, like projection and denial, can interfere with our grip on reality. Still others, like minimisation, distractibility, vagueness and rumination, can be either helpful or harmful, depending on how and when they are used.

Sigmund Freud developed the notion of defence mechanisms and his daughter, Anna Freud, elaborated and refined it. Without defences, people would be roiling lava pits of feeling and impulse: we need them. In fact, sometimes therapists think of them as 'protectors', because they are doing a job. They are just not always doing that job very well.

A big one for Millie and girls like her is 'minimisation', or making something seem smaller than it is: *'nothing really happened this week'; 'other people have worse problems than me'; 'maybe a little'*. Here is how minimisation works as both a helpful and an unhelpful defence mechanism in different circumstances. Let's say you're living in a dorm and someone repeatedly eats your leftovers in the fridge without asking. You might be really mad. That's so inconsiderate, and plus, time and again, you're stuck feeling hungry. But it might be diplomatic to tell the person you're 'a little frustrated', especially if you don't know them very well and you have to live together. You would be using good social skills. But if you're in your therapy session and you are describing the situation that way, truly convinced that all you felt was 'a little frustrated', that would be a sign that you're not in touch with your feelings. As you've seen throughout this book, lots of work in therapy focuses on identifying defence mechanisms, understanding what function they serve in different contexts, and becoming more flexible in how you use them.

Millie is seventeen by the time she is interested in learning about her defences. She takes eagerly to the note card game (the one I played with Elle). In addition to minimisation, other defences we observe include passivity and hopelessness/helplessness. She carries each of these with a pleasant veneer, taking care to keep things light – another defence mechanism we put on a card. When we start labelling and pushing back on some of those defences, it becomes clearer what feelings lie underneath.

Family Vacation

The call from the precinct came around 10:00 pm, an hour after the general store had closed. In the small town in the Catskills where Millie's family was renting a house for the summer, everything goes quiet and dark by 9:00 pm, except for the steady flashing of fireflies in the trees, and the occasional pickup truck rolling down the dirt roads.

Millie had heard the whole story just moments before. How her brothers had thought the plan was airtight. How Jack sat at the wheel of the family's Subaru while Augustus slipped the slim, dusty bottle of Grey Goose under his Knicks hoodie. How merchandise was not exactly flying off the shelves at the Ulster General Store & Trading Co., but how Augustus had been sure nobody was counting the bottles.

How when the sheriff walked through the door, big hat and shiny star badge and everything, Augustus realised why the clerk had taken so long ringing up his beef jerky.

It was Millie they called first. 'You need to get an Uber and come take the Subaru home. Augustus and I are in kind of a situation,' Jack said. Now eighteen years old, she was the one who could understand how scared shitless they were. Nice kids from Cobble Hill don't run into much trouble with the law. Was this going to be on their 'permanent records'? Were colleges going to have to know? Were they going to have to do time?

It was Millie who helped her parents to stay calm, who implored them not to scream or threaten or punish, who reassured her brothers. It was a first-time offence; they were minors; it was going to be okay, she told her brothers; they should just be honest and apologise. Above all, she reminded them that this would be really tough for their mom and dad.

A Little Upset

A few sessions into processing this experience, Millie comes in tense.

'I'm still thinking about how this all went down,' she says. 'It still makes me nauseous.'

'What's coming up about it?'

'Just that moment when I got the call, and the way my parents looked. So pale and stricken. I gave them hugs, told them Augustus and Jack were just stupid boys and they would grow up one day. But the truth was I was also scared. And I was supposed to go back to the

city to my friend Katie's art show, but I offered to stick around, just to help deal with the fallout. Which was necessary.'

I picture this. 'What were you hoping for from your parents?'

Millie tears up. 'I just wish . . . I don't know, this is stupid, but –'

I give her a glance that has come to replace the note card.

She takes a deep breath. 'Fine. I just wish . . . that they would have been like, "We've got this."'

More tears. She takes a tissue and dabs both of her eyes.

'I feel bad, but . . . I mean, they're really good parents. They must have been so freaked out . . .'

A raised eyebrow from me.

'Oh, my stomach again . . . Okay, I know that's just me getting anxious.' *Deep breath.* 'Yeah, I guess I was a little upset.'

I send her a warm stare.

'Okay, fine. I was upset.'

We push further. Over many sessions, Millie becomes able to see she is *really* upset. Mad, even. We work to help her feel this anger more fully, instead of pushing it away or covering it up with depressive defence mechanisms. She teaches herself to listen to what the anger is trying to tell her: that something is not right about the way she, as a child, is treated like a caretaker in her family. She learns to tap into this feeling as a source of power, to help her keep a clear head during tense family moments, and to ask for something different. She becomes able to stand up for herself, to set some healthier boundaries with family and friends, and to ask for the care and the consideration she now knows she deserves.

The Girl Self-Defence System

'This is stupid.' 'I feel bad, but . . .' 'A little upset.'

Listening to some girls talk is like walking through a museum of classic feminine defence mechanisms. As I mention earlier, this is what I call the Girl Self-Defence System (GSDS).

Minimising and apologising for one's negative feelings – especially anger – is so typical in girls that we often don't even notice it's happening. Not only does it come off as normal, but this behaviour makes girls appealing. Girls like Millie live by these rules, with many successes to show for it. It's typical for girls to play caretaking roles in their families. Parents often expect that daughters will be the ones to tend to them when they are old. Girls learn from a young age that being likable is the most important thing. In Millie's family, they were aware this work fell disproportionately to Millie, but the dynamics just kept playing out. Change is harder than staying the same. Even for Millie, the short-term costs of the status quo – some depressive and anxious symptoms, maybe some missed opportunities – were for a long time easier for her to deal with than the conflict that might follow from asserting herself.

Is the Girl Self-Defence System attributable to nature or nurture? Although I argue in this book that psychiatry has leaned too heavily on biological determinism, it is also true that biology matters. While there is a tremendous variation within groups born male and groups born female, there are meaningful differences in brain development between the sexes. Whether these are driven solely by biology or by social learning is one of the most hotly and eternally debated issues of all time, and I'm not going to solve it here.* We know that teenage girls are about a year and a half ahead of boys in language development. Cognitive science has also shown that girls from a young age (including infants) tend to be more socially driven. Baby girls make more eye contact and produce more sad looks and empathetic vocalisations in response to the distress of another. Baby girls look longer at faces and baby boys look longer at machines. Some researchers

* Gina Rippon, author of *The Gendered Brain,* rejects 'neurosexism', arguing brains contain both male and female elements that have great 'plasticity', or the ability to develop when cultivated. Brain scans, she writes, do not reveal much in the way of structural differences between women and men – or at least not more than is found within groups of women or groups of men. Furthermore, the effects of *experience* (what has been socialised) are often impossible to differentiate on a brain scan from natural hardwiring.

have used these findings to argue that the female brain tends towards 'empathising' while the male brain orients towards 'systematising'. On the nature-nurture question, infant studies do point towards biological forces, but infants are also subject to culture. Hence these discussions are best used as food for thought rather than as a reason to direct, to limit, to judge or to predict the traits of any given individual.

But one needn't turn to science to know that, in general, girls are better at sharing, taking turns and playing with dolls, whereas boys are more likely to want to build weapons and ram plastic cars into each other, or to note that the social world and its emotional nuances are more salient to a thirteen-year-old girl than a thirteen-year-old boy. As I discussed earlier, this social focus serves girls in the task of making meaningful connections outside the family as they move into the (gendered) social roles of adulthood. But at the macro and micro levels, society pressures girls into people-pleasing and sweeping away aggressive feelings.

Let's think about how this all plays out for Millie. Defence mechanisms help people navigate between their internal, biologically informed reactions and the social world, fending off both internal and external dangers. For girls like Millie, the interplay is synergistic. Whenever she has the impulse to be selfish or feels annoyed, she senses she's in danger. This is psychological: we all feel conflict in the presence of mixed emotions, and to Millie, these feelings are a threat to her self-concept as a kind and helpful person. But it's also social: she is indeed expected by the culture to be all of these things. It's not just in her head! The message comes from the macroculture of her school, her peers and the media – and also from the microculture of her (caring, well-intentioned) immediate family. So Millie is careful not to burden everyone with her feelings.

But they build up. A vicious cycle ensues where she does not feel free to express her needs and opinions, or even to acknowledge them to herself. Whatever the roles of nature and nurture, Millie cares about those around her. But the more she cares, the higher the stakes of pushing back, and the more intense the frustrated feelings become. Her GSDS kicks into high gear on a regular basis, allowing her to continue to be the caring friend and family member she wants to be and contributing to an ever-growing mountain of internal stress.

If left untreated, Millie's GSDS symptoms could have put her on the path to clinically significant depression or anxiety, as well as to unfulfilling relationships. Fortunately, her parents identified early that something was going on in the family that was taking a toll on their daughter.

Millie has learned to spot her GSDS over the years, and we've searched for the correct label to describe her overall problem. Is Millie simply 'a people-pleaser'? 'A martyr'? 'A masochist'? A masochist is a person who is gratified by pain – who feels best about herself when she is suffering. This does not feel quite right. 'Martyr' is a bit closer, but not perfect because it does not explain exactly what goes on inside Millie's mind, or why. We have also considered whether Millie is 'a pushover'. On the surface one could say people take advantage of her selflessness and generosity, but it is neither weakness nor spinelessness that is causing this dynamic to repeat itself.

Moreover, 'martyr', 'masochist', 'pushover' – and 'pleaser' – are all problematic because they are *identity* labels. Although Millie exhibits these traits, she is not finished growing and developing, and her identity is not fixed. As Millie starts to understand herself better, these behaviours can change; what seem like inborn traits might actually transform or disappear. In the end, Millie and I come to focus on words that describe her *behaviour, emotional states* and *psychological processes*.

One idea that has been more helpful with Millie is the aforementioned 'Drama Triangle' of Victims, Perpetrators and Saviours.

Millie has been stuck in the Saviour role. Many people have difficulty giving up this role because being a Saviour is a generally positive social identity. Millie also worries that if she steps out of this role, others will get hurt.

'Saviour' doesn't fully capture it, though. The term is a bit extreme (it's from the *Drama* Triangle, after all) and does not exactly reflect what occurs hundreds of times a week – in Millie's mind and in her actions – that perpetuates her problem.

Emotional Labour

One day in the spring of senior year, Millie comes in looking happy. It's a warmish day in April, and she's still got that messy look, but today it's a dressed-up version: long skirt and Birkenstocks, concert T-shirt, hair all twisted up like a *Star Wars* princess.

'I think I figured out what my problem is,' Millie announces.

I look at her expectantly – just plain expectantly this time.

'Well, there's this term that's trending on TikTok, "emotional labour".'

At that point, this term was new to me, although I could infer its meaning. I nod my head yes. 'Yes,' I say.

She goes on to explain it, to give examples. 'It's how girls are caretakers about everything. Like how my brother was going on a weekend trip and I checked before he was leaving if he packed underwear and he was like . . . *uh, wait a sec*. Or how my friend Jared was applying for a summer job and was like, *I don't know, they didn't ever write me back,* and I was like, *Well, did you send a follow-up email?* Or how my boyfriend was getting really frustrated with his physics homework and was about to rage quit and I was like, *Just take a breath*. And like every conflict I mediate with my parents and my brothers. And even how I sometimes have to explain to my dad about giving a feedback sandwich instead of just telling us we are doing things wrong. That's all *emotional labour*! And I was like, That's what I've been doing for *everyone* – I just never knew it was a thing.'

'Correct.'

In a rare moment, I am grateful to the internet and to therapy culture.

What I like about this term is that, like the Drama Triangle, it's a *process* term. It describes something a person can step in or out of, participate in or not – a position, not a fixed identity.

In fact, in my opinion, this principle is a useful road map through therapy culture. Therapy speak that describes *processes* or *states* within oneself or between people is generally useful. If employed thoughtfully – and that's a big 'if' – these notions can increase our ability to observe ourselves and to grow. There are so many examples of these terms: 'impostor syndrome', 'gaslighting', 'presence dysmorphia', 'weaponised incompetence', 'shame spiral' – and, in this case, 'emotional labour'.

Through process terms, therapy culture has helped society by increasing our casual awareness of how people's minds work. By the time Millie applies to a competitive art school (undeterred by the fact that several friends of hers are also applying), she can recognise when she is being a good friend and when she is labouring too hard. She has come to see her personality not as something fixed, but as an ever-evolving series of choices.

You don't need to be in therapy to benefit from a concept like emotional labour, or any other process term. In fact, these offerings from therapy culture can help anyone seeking to move through the world a bit differently, even those who have been stuck in their ways for a long time.

PART THREE

What Now?

11

Three Anxious Mothers (and One Confused Dad)

> The business of raising children became something so difficult as to drive both mothers and children if not altogether mad, then certainly to seek out help.
>
> **Lisa Appignanesi,**
> *Mad, Bad and Sad*

> 'Real' women all are mothers – but once you're a mother, anything that goes wrong is your fault.
>
> **Phyllis Chesler,**
> *Women and Madness*

My Heart of Hearts

I am Zooming with a patient I've seen for a few years, a mom with young kids. Like many women in Heidi's demographic, she is in therapy to deal with stress from all of the demands of her life.

Heidi's upset about a fight she had with her husband over the weekend. She lashed out at him, criticising the way he had disciplined their four-year-old. Her husband is a good guy, she says, and it's not that his methods were abusive or anything – just a bit too harsh.

'So why do you and Gabe have to parent Norman in exactly the same way?' I ask.

She thinks about this for a long time.

'I guess . . . in my heart of hearts, I just hope that someday Norman will want to move back to the same town where we live . . . you know, get a house like a mile away and have dinner with us once a week with his family. I was just scared Gabe would make that . . . not happen.'

Heidi was stunned when she realised this.

'I had no idea that was something I was expecting, or hoping for. Let alone that it was making me so reactive to Gabe.'

22

'Bonnie is just *not* engaging in healthy behaviours', Tracy says to me sharply.

I feel like I've done something wrong, even though we are just meeting for the first time.

'I say, Bonnie: Go to the gym; I say, go outside – get off your phone – but she won't listen.'

Tracy is right, of course; these are good suggestions. But the pressure Tracy emits is almost unbearable: I wouldn't listen either.

Why is Tracy so stressed-out? From what she tells me, her daughter sounds like a relatively functional ninth grader.

'Tracy,' I say, 'what concerns you the most about what your daughter is doing?'

Tracy takes a deep breath, and the worries press forward like air from a punctured balloon: 'I'm concerned she's not making self-care a priority. If she keeps neglecting herself, she's going to end up with so many problems. Science has proven that lack of exercise is connected to depression. And teen suicide is a major concern. Early detection is key. I don't want her to be a statistic.'

I wonder if Bonnie is truly 'neglecting herself', or if she just needs more downtime than her mom thinks is good.

'I know other kids are getting together,' she goes on. 'I talk to the moms. I see what goes on. There are plans. There are parties.'

'Does Bonnie have friends?'

'She has two quiet girls she hangs around with – whatever. But there's a homecoming game on Saturday and I say, "Bonnie, just go to the game!" and she looks at me like I'm from Mars and says, "I don't like football, blah blah blah," but I think this is depression. Any normal teenager would want to go to the homecoming game, go to the party . . . meet boys. It's very concerning.'

I'm beginning to picture a kid whose mother means well, a kid who may in fact be somewhat depressed – but possibly because she's not the kid her mother wants.

'You probably think I'm a total helicopter parent,' Margeaux says with a smile. 'I can only imagine how Rosie portrays me in here.'

Rosie is thirteen and in the two appointments we've had so far, she has only talked about her friends.

'My mom was a classic tiger mom, so that's always been my worst fear,' Margeaux goes on. 'I've tried to be hands-on without snowploughing – you know, like, present and mindful. I think I do an okay job holding an emotionally safe space. But I'm conscious of the dangers there. It's like, I'm your *parent,* not your friend, you know what I mean? But I'm sure that's wrong, too. I'm just bracing to hear about all of my mistakes in a few years. That is, if she's still talking to me. You must see a lot of those "no contact" people.'

I realise I haven't taken a breath since Margeaux started talking.

'Ugh,' she says, 'I live in terror of what Rosie will say about me when she's twenty-five. Whoever *that* therapist is will have a field day!'

I've heard a lot of people diagnose their loved ones and themselves, but I've never seen someone pack so much self-pathologising into one sentence without even needing any psychiatric terms. Pop psychology has furnished today's parents with their own *DSM*.

Being a parent has never been easy, but parents today are more stressed-out than ever. They are drowning in a sea of labels and warnings and conflicting expert advice about the best ways to behave around their children. Furthermore, the expectations about what parenting is even for – what the goals are – also keep changing.

And being a parent brings different challenges for men and women. Mothers face specific pressures and judgements. Also, mothers are typically the main emotional models for teenage girls, showing them what to expect for themselves.

The Never-Healing Wound

Before 'parenting' was a formal discipline, psychiatry had one thing down to a science: mother-blaming. Misogyny has been a faithful nursemaid to Western psychological theories from their first steps. Authorities from St Augustine to the Paris police in the 1700s accused bad mothering of being responsible for society's ills.

When psychology began to formalise in the 1800s, theories organised around how, exactly, the bad mothering did its damage. Freud introduced the notion that early childhood experiences cause mental illness. His theories took into account the psychological function of both parents, but subsequent theorists placed most of the focus on the mother-infant relationship.

To be clear: early experience matters greatly in psychological development. As I've shown throughout this book, who a mother is – as well as who a father is, who grandparents are, who siblings are and who a child is by nature – deeply affects how that child grows up. Contemporary neuroscience has demonstrated that mother-child interactive patterns from infancy through adolescence play a singular role in shaping that child's emotional life and sense of self. Longitudinal studies have shown that infant temperament, maternal distress and mother-infant reciprocity predict how well-adjusted an adolescent will be.

Mothers are important. However, the most influential theories of Western psychology cast mothers as not just formative but omnipotent and, in the end, fully responsible for how a child turns out. For example, John B Watson in 1928 wrote that maternal love 'may inflict a never-healing wound, a wound which may make infancy unhappy, adolescence a nightmare, an instrument which may wreck your adult son or daughter's vocational future and their chances for marital happiness'. The 1930s and '40s saw a new pathogen: 'the overprotective mother'. Around this time, psychiatry popularised the notion of the 'schizophrenogenic mother' (who was allegedly too rejecting towards her children) and the 'refrigerator mother', whose lack of warmth was said to produce autism. Philip Wylie's misogynistic treatise *Generation of Vipers* blamed 'domineering' or 'clingy' mothers for society's moral and cultural problems; his contemporary Edward Strecker, who was president of the American Psychiatric Association (1943–1944), coined the term 'momism' to describe the overprotective mothers who raised men unfit to serve in the army. For decades, male homosexuality was attributed to mothers who couldn't let go. Psychologist René Spitz said in 1951 that when the wrong kind of mother-child relationship develops, 'the mother's *personality* acts as a disease-provoking agent, a psychological *toxin* [italics mine].'* A landmark study decades later found that major clinical journals had held mothers accountable for seventy-two types of pathology in their children, including ulcerative colitis, marijuana use and 'ineducability'.

Attachment theory, which was developed by psychoanalysts using data from severely traumatised children, highlighted the centrality of the mother-child relationship. These theories, however, were easily distorted. In the 1960s, as more women entered the workforce, psychological theories were mobilised to argue working moms violated the natural order of things. Generations of mothers have been

* While it is a fact that a mother's personality undoubtedly makes a deep impact on her child, I include this quotation to highlight the facile equation of a whole 'personality' with a 'toxin' – a relatively crude position for an otherwise sophisticated thinker, reflecting the cultural bias I describe. A similar point could be made offering empathy to the mother, referring to her 'psychological difficulties', for example.

dealing with the fallout and ongoing misunderstandings of this literature. Feminist psychoanalysts have observed that patriarchal culture itself is something men have set up to repress fears of dependency on their own mothers, while yearning for early feelings of connection. Mothers in such a society are objects, not subjects: they are continually defined by what they provide – and whether it is too little or too much.

Helicopter, Snowplough, Therapist, Friend

All of those pressures had taken hold before there was even such a thing as 'parenting'. A parent in the mid-twentieth century was simply someone who had children. But in the 1960s and '70s, as the identity of a mother grew more expansive, the concept of parenting became an area of academic focus. Psychologist Diana Baumrind laid out three parenting 'styles' – permissive, authoritative and authoritarian – and argued that the best-adjusted kids were products of authoritative parenting, in which parents maintain high standards but are warm and responsive to a child's wishes and needs.

In the 1980s, mothers found new reasons to feel anxious and guilty about turning their gaze away from the kids. The world seemed to have become a more dangerous place: media coverage of kidnappings, sexually transmitted diseases and sexual assaults created an epidemic of fearful and even paranoid parenting. 'Stranger danger' became a household slogan. Milk cartons picturing missing children sat on every kitchen table in America. Meanwhile, paediatricians promoted 'attachment parenting'. Mothers were encouraged to hold their children closer than ever and to feel uneasy every time they softened their grip.

The 1990s were dubbed 'the Decade of the Brain', and not surprisingly parents started obsessing over their child's cognitive development from an early age, purchasing products like Baby Einstein's *Baby Mozart* video, which sprang from a popular fascination with neuroscience. Under careful adult supervision, children were pressured to develop skills that would make them promising college applicants in an increasingly competitive system. By the 2010s, the ideology spread from middle- and upper-class parents to working-class parents, creating a parenting attitude that became nearly universal in America and Europe. A good parent hovered overhead, like a helicopter, or pushed her child fiercely, like a tiger. Next came the 'lawnmower', 'snowplough', and 'bulldozer' parents. Phones added a new layer of concern, generating the dystopian notion of 'surveillance' parenting.

Meanwhile, less popular voices complicated the picture. Pamela Druckerman whispered a secret from the French: *benign neglect*. More recently, low-tech 'Free-Range' parenting has offered a refreshing – if often impractical – appeal.

People tend to make parenting decisions based on what they believe worked or didn't work for themselves as kids. High rates of anxiety and depression in millennials made them look back on their own helicopter parents and decide to focus less on safety and achievement and more on psychological well-being. Their kids would be insulated from whatever was too stressful or 'triggering'. They favoured the gentle parenting movement. Also known as 'mindful parenting' or 'intentional parenting', gentle parenting abstains from directives and attends to the child's emotions at all times. While the goal is emotional well-being for all, many have argued that this approach takes a toll on parents, especially mothers. Carrying on in a long tradition of objectifying mothers, the gentle parenting movement judges the child's emotional health as direct evidence of the mother's ability – or lack thereof – to maintain serenity at all times.

Of course, gentle parenting itself has received its fair share of pushback. What about teaching resilience? The wisdom of the proverbial skinned knee? Whatever the answer, Abigail Shrier calls the focus on emotional development 'therapeutic parenting' and argues it's this that is harming kids: 'For at least a generation,' she writes, 'Mom . . . is an *ersatz* therapist, practising bad therapy on kids whose emotions grow increasingly unruly, whose behaviour eludes the traps set by her affected questioning. When she has no patience left to offer, she turns a gimlet eye on her offspring and downgrades her assessment: *Maddie has significant challenges and needs a great deal of additional support.*'

Notice that once again, Mom is to blame for messing up the kids: by failing to provide sufficient tough love, by succumbing to the sappy misdirections of therapy culture. These critiques assume that Mom hasn't thought of these complexities, too – that her brain is not exploding with a cacophony of parenting theories and bifurcated instincts. That she wouldn't be the first to tell you she's probably doing it wrong. Mom has read all the books, all the blogs, all the posts. She can tell you every teachable moment she missed. Every time she intervened when she should have got out of the way. Every time she overindulged or underresponded. She can tell you herself: she's too much, and never enough. So, if pressed, how would she brand her parenting? What's her 'parenting style'? Whatever she calls it, for her, it's a full-body-contact sport in which winning is the only thing that matters, but losing is inevitable. She's an 'intensive parent'.

Intensive parenting is a step past therapeutic parenting. It's everything parenting – helicopter, snowplough, therapist, friend. The psychological costs of intensive parenting run deep, particularly for working mothers, who continue to feel guilt and judgement for every compromise they make. Today's mothers face a typical evening overwhelmed by the tasks ahead: helping their middle schooler build a Lego village for Social Studies; preparing (healthy, locally sourced, organic) lunches for the next day; making sure the uniforms are clean and in backpacks; and responding to the irritating work email about that question she already answered without seeming like a total bitch. (And also getting enough sleep to at least *try* to get to the gym for some 'self-care' the next day.) These mothers come to me asking if, perhaps, they have ADHD (recall Zach's wife, Marisol), because it's all just too much.

Like Tracy, parents have two major fears: that their children will kill themselves or that they will abandon the relationship. All is invested in the nuclear family – which, in turn, is likelier than ever to implode.

Like Heidi, parents are not just paranoid about their kids being screwed up: their expectations of eternal closeness and friendship with their children are at an all-time high. Like Heidi, parents fret more than ever about the kinds of relationships they will have with their adult children and even with their grandchildren.

And like Margeaux, parents have a million reminders, thanks to social media, that they're doing everything wrong. And that doing something wrong violates the mandates of Big Wellness. There are more words for 'bad mother' than ever before.

How many mothers have agonised: *What will my kid say about me in therapy?* The counterproductive idea is that therapy is the ultimate moral verdict, the ultimate judge of the parent's personhood across the child's life.

We All Make Our Choices

How does a mom cope? One way is to look for signs of mental disability in her kids. Our culture offers major incentives to think this way. Take the basic fact that children make parents angry ('Lucas: *Come. On.*'), and add to that the way that parents – especially moms – are told that anger towards one's children is unhealthy and destructive. Nothing vaporises anger (and fear of judgement) more efficiently than telling yourself a child is 'sick' rather than 'bad'.

A good mom doesn't miss early signs of mental illness. Like Tracy, moms are haunted by images of teens in the worst kinds of crisis: the stakes of even the smallest parenting decisions feel like life or death.

For at least the past fifty years, a great deal of a mom's own personal worth has rested on what kind of parent she is, whether that's the right type of mother to be, and how masterfully she does the job. Any sign of deficiency in her children is a fault in her parenting. The only loophole is medical: she gets a pass if the child in fact suffers from autism, ADHD or another psychiatric disorder – any medically accepted category of neurodivergence.

Second, moms cope by pathologising each other. We lock eyes with our most trusted companions, eyebrows raised across the high-top table: *Well, we all make our choices.*

I became aware of this dynamic through personal experience. For me, the various pressures on moms and motherhood played a major role in my own life decisions. I was conscious when choosing medicine and psychiatry that it would be possible to work in a private practice where I could set my own hours. I would be able to do school pickups and sit in the playground, the ice cream truck jingle looping in the background, as kids played kickball and stay-at-home parents mused over Halloween costumes and exchanged strategies about middle school admissions. At the same time, I felt a camaraderie with the working moms; my career did prevent me from chaperoning some field trips or playing a bigger role in the PTA. Those conflicts, though fewer than for many mothers, glued me emotionally to those who worked. (That, and my love for my work.) Inhabiting those two positions gave me a unique window into mom culture: I was part of both worlds, and privy to the delights and doubts that accompany both sets of choices – and to the kinds of judgements moms adopt to make ourselves feel better.

On the park benches at 3:00 pm on a Tuesday, one reliable topic is the moms who are at work. In September, when everyone is new, the conversation goes like this: 'Oh, she's so *amazing;* she runs this incredible nonprofit.' But after some months pass, you find yourself sitting with the same women at cafeteria tables after school, painting cardboard for a class project. Then, it's: 'Yeah, when I was in college I thought I was going to be a screenwriter. *Sigh.*' By early spring, you're spending an afternoon in someone's living room. You all watch googly-eyed as the kids chase the dog around the house: 'It's so sad for her that she's missing this . . . it all goes by so fast.'

At the 7:00 pm gatherings for the working moms, the topic, of course, is the moms who stay at home. At the back-to-school drinks, it's: 'She's so *amazing* – she must have the patience of a saint to do it all without a nanny.' By holiday cocktails, it's: 'I felt so bad – Jaden asked why I could only go to one of the performances. He's confused because Stella's mom is literally backstage doing the costumes for every show.' And at the spring benefit, it's: 'You know, I wonder what she'll do once the kids are out of the house – can you imagine starting from scratch in your fifties?'

Mothers doubt themselves routinely. We turn to one another for fellowship, but there is often an edge: a virtue-cloaked disdain for whoever made the 'other' choice. This compounds the sense of isolation mothers feel – each in our singularly important nuclear family, each the sole participant in our own private Olympic Games, a panel of smiling judges surrounding us at all times, and the harshest one living in our own heads.

A Note from the Surgeon General

In October 2024, the US Surgeon General issued a warning: it is now a risk to your mental health to be a parent. Parental stress has come full circle, as we sacrifice our own sanity on behalf of a commitment to our children's imagined future social-emotional well-being. In the process, we are making them, and ourselves, nuts. If the teen mental health crisis has been at all overstated to this point, this reality is likely to remove any doubt. Kids need healthy parents. The stressed-out, exhausted, desperate, paranoid and literally unhealthy parenting has to stop, and mental health professionals can and must play a role.

Let's start by looking at what's already happening. To deal with feeling not enough, many mothers today are on antidepressants, and increasingly on stimulants. The Prozac feminists are furiously trying to have it all, and their as-yet-unmedicated daughters are looking ahead and feeling like they'll never make it. Maybe we should reassure them that it's just a matter of time until they get their secret weapon: Lexapro.

Or maybe we should actually make the world kinder to mothers, to women, and to girls. Just as 'a child who's giving you a hard time is having a hard time', a mother who's sizing up another woman uncharitably is giving herself even crueller treatment. How do we make a world where women are not powered – and plagued – by self-attack and envy?

What mothers need is to feel that they have, and are, enough. And the best way to achieve that would be to expect a bit less: to strive for more modest expectations of ourselves, our kids and whatever balance or imbalance we find.

Good Enough

That's where paediatrician and psychoanalyst Donald Winnicott's idea of the 'Good-Enough Mother' comes into play. He said, in 1953, that it was better for a baby to have one of these than a so-called perfect mother, because a mother who gradually lets the baby experience disappointments and manageable frustrations is bringing it closer to a sense of reality and a true sense of self. Winnicott introduced this theory, in part, to protect ordinary mothers from what he saw as the encroachment of psychoanalytic expertise on normal life. Revolutionary and clarifying as the concept was, it was not long before the horizon for women expanded, and the conflict between work and home became a widespread source of stress. The very definition of what a good – or even, 'good-enough' – mother was grew multifaceted, contradictory and harder to fulfil. Nowadays, every mother has to be everything. It's the constant toll of 'not enough' – and we wonder why our daughters feel the same way.

Still, in the wake of decades of unkind narratives about women and mothers, the idea of Good-Enough parenting rescued generations of mothers from a potentially worse psychological fate. What we need now is to revive the notion of the Good-Enough Mother, and to animate other related characters: Good-Enough Friends, Good-Enough Daughters, Happy-Enough Marriages, Healthy-Enough Habits, Mentally-Healthy-Enough Teenagers. Perhaps these will become possibilities if our culture opens itself to the notion of a Good-Enough Life.

The hard part is: how do we get there?

Here's something that most mothers find reassuring. Developmental psychologist Ed Tronick revealed in 1989 that in a 'good' mother-infant relationship, only 30 per cent of 'good' interactions could be described as 'closely attuned'. Mothers who are the very best at reading their babies succeed about 40 per cent of the time.

Heidi was able to acknowledge her underlying wish that her son would grow up and live nearby. This allowed her to start grieving the possibility that she likely wouldn't be able to control his long-term decisions, and to accept that they could have a good-enough relationship even if he didn't end up living down the street.

For Tracy, it was a bit more complicated because part of the problem did in fact have to do with her. The medical mission – finding 'signs of depression' in Bonnie – actually served to distract from what was really causing her daughter to be sad. But Tracy needed help with this, not judgement for it. She was so disappointed to have a daughter who was not an extrovert like she was; she felt they were missing out on the enjoyment that comes with shared tastes and interests – the kind of mother-daughter relationship Tracy had enjoyed with her own mom. Tracy needed help seeing how their differences did not have to foreclose a good relationship – that in fact, they could be closer if Tracy let go of who she was still needing her daughter to be.

And for Margeaux, I helped allay her fears about what her daughter's future therapy might mean. That part bears some unpacking.

For one thing, as much as I have critiqued the facile selection of biomedical narratives ('It's just how I'm wired'), I am a big believer in temperament. Anyone with children can tell you that to a large extent they arrive in this world as the people they are. As parents, it is grounding to remind oneself of that. Yes, parent-child relationships provide a foundation for the development of personality, coping skills, relational patterns and expectations. Your early experiences with the people closest to you are, quite literally, formative. But, as parents, we constitute but a fraction of a child's environment. As one writer puts it, 'If parents are the fixed stars in the child's universe, the vaguely understood, distant but constant celestial spheres, siblings are the dazzling, sometimes scorching comets nearby.' And as children grow, who their friends are begins to overshadow the family's influence.

As for what your child will eventually 'say to their therapist': many parents fear that therapy is going to involve a systematic blaming of them. That we are going to find the worst moment of your parenting, the time you lost control or said something childish yourself. We're going to gradually, insidiously, encourage your child to turn against you, maybe ultimately to go 'no contact' in order to preserve her 'boundaries' and 'prioritise her mental health'.

But here's why you can take a deep breath. Any effort to control the narrative is futile – and also not necessary. Things you consider parenting wins may be interpreted by your child as parenting fails; the mistakes you draw on to berate yourself may never have registered. And contrary to popular belief, therapy is not the ultimate judge of your parenting. Good therapy is not about parent-blaming; it's about helping people gain clarity about how they became who they are, how they developed whatever problems stand in their way. Therapists understand that messages that take hold in childhood are filtered through children's brains. It's not only about what you said: it's about how they processed it – and all the other data from their environment. It's about updating the beliefs people adopted as young children that may in fact have been misunderstandings of their parents' ideas or intentions. It's about freeing people from whatever remnants of their childhood adaptations no longer help them. It's, as they say, 'not about you'. To the extent that a person going through therapy may develop insights or feelings about their parents, the goal is to help them come to terms with the fullness of those feelings, which necessarily means ambivalence and rarely amounts to either simple gratitude or a summative rejection. You're not the saviour, or the villain. You're just their mom.

Postscript: One Confused Dad

Walt mostly looks tired. I find him in the waiting room sitting a few seats down from my office door. He's got that faint grey in the face that comes with advancing middle age, five-o'clock shadow and long days in front of a computer screen. I think he manages a contracting business that's done quite well.

He stands up and towers over me, holding out a hand. 'Pleasure to meet you, Doc.'

I'm surprised by the Brooklyn accent.

Walt takes a seat and leans in, elbows on his knees. I see we're going to get right to it.

The power dynamics of being a female doctor in this situation are (still!) amazingly fraught. And yes, lots of dads do refer to me as 'Doc'. I'm always struck and somewhat amused when this happens, and I see it as a reflection of some inherent tensions. They're sweet; they care; they want to do the right thing for their daughter. But there's a part of them that's not so sure they can trust me. Maybe I'm part of the bullshit, the system that overpathologises and overcomplicates matters. 'Doc' is an attempt to show me respect, to be friendly but not too flirtatious, and to make sure we're not forgetting to keep it all a little light, to preserve a sense of normalcy. In other words, 'Doc' is just fine with me.

'She has everything,' he says. 'She's beautiful, she's smart, she has a loving family, every advantage. She had every toy. Every snack. Gymnastics classes. We got a place out in Westhampton last summer.

We let her bring her friends there; we say, *Go. Do whatever you want.* She's a great student. Great work ethic.' He shakes his head. 'I just don't get it.'

I nod sympathetically.

'So, Doc, why on earth is she so upset? What's wrong with her?'

Walt is a hands-on father, and I can tell he and Sage are close. 'I'm the breakfast guy, the homework guy. Didn't miss a softball game. Got up in the middle of the night if she needed me. I think I know my kid pretty well.' Walt is also a beacon of calm when Mom, as his daughter Sage told me during our consultation, 'crashes out'.

I learn Walt indeed grew up in Brooklyn. Played baseball for his high school. Older brother used to give him shit. Parents never knew the half of it.

I'm enjoying hearing about Walt's life. He's warm and caring. I also get how important it is to him that I recognise his commitment to his daughter. A few minutes in, his story slows to a pause.

'Doc . . . I gotta ask you. Do kids have these problems in, you know . . . other places?'

It's clear he doesn't want to say the wrong thing, so I try to read between the lines: 'Are you wondering why kids growing up with so much privilege complain about their mental health?'

'Um, yes.' He looks at me cautiously, sits very still. 'Something like that.'

'You're wondering if perhaps we have overindulged them, taught them to whine about every little thing that's wrong.'

He snickers uncomfortably. 'Exactly. That's right.'

'Well . . .' I clear my throat and share my thoughts. To some extent, he's correct. Kids are culture sponges; they absorb the truth in our world, which is that suffering gets acknowledged when it has a psychiatric name.

'But what are you going to do?' I ask him. 'Take a kid in pain, maybe a kid like Sage who *does* have symptoms of depression, and say, *Don't be depressed*? Good luck with that.'

He gets it: that his only choice is to meet her where she is.

I go on: 'So whether it's big or small or serious or not serious is something only she can tell us, and she will, in time. But if she's saying she's depressed, it's a *something,* not a *nothing*.'

'Maybe so,' he says. 'But aren't we still messing these kids up, you know, by focusing so much on every little concern, every little scratch on the knee?'

I pause on this one. He's not totally wrong, and I don't want to reflexively support Team Therapy and say every feeling requires attention. My goal is to help parents be calmer, not more anxious.

But I think back across the centuries when all female suffering was chalked up to 'hysteria'. To this day, whenever a girl's troubles don't make total sense from the outside, there is a temptation to repeat history – to label, deflect, pathologise. What hysterics needed was to translate their physical symptoms into language that clarified what was bothering them emotionally. Now, instead of convulsions and fainting spells, the symptoms are different – but the young women who have them still need help translating.

So, I say what I believe: 'We are doing them a disservice when we are focused on the wrong things. Look, I'm your daughter's doctor. But right now, let's all be less worried about whether she meets criteria for a depression diagnosis, and more interested in why she's having a hard time.' I pause. 'Does that work?'

Walt nods. That he can do.

12

Returning Girlhood to Girls

In order to see, we must forget the name of the thing we are looking at.

Claude Monet

Hi, I'm Taylor. I write songs about my feelings.

Taylor Swift

Getting Bangs

It's Monday morning. I open my office door and the smell of the room, enclosed in its own air all weekend, hits me hard: the mustiness of old textbooks; an earthy waft off the dog bed, like warm graham crackers; years of my own perfume haunting the upholstery.

I crack open the window: outside, the buzz of a power saw from the endless renovation in the neighbouring townhouse.

Footsteps in the stairwell; a slam of the waiting room door. Hazel's here for her weekly appointment. It's now the spring of her senior year, and she's doing great. She's going to college and it's almost time for us to end our work together.

Hazel sits down with a coy look on her face. 'So . . . I'm thinking about lowering my dose. I mean not today, but . . . maybe soon?'

'Sounds interesting . . . How did this idea come about?'

'Well, this sounds weird, but . . . I feel like I could handle if things were a little harder. Like, maybe it would even be good for me to feel more things, to have more of a struggle. For all of this year, I haven't had intense anxiety, and the emotions I've had felt . . . appropriate. I might be almost functioning more highly than I need to be. Maybe I could afford to function a little less well!' She laughs.

I'm alert to her language here. *Function. Handle.* Of course, it's rewarding when a therapy patient gets better, and the going-off-meds talk is about as concrete a sign of progress as one gets in this work. Plus, life without medicine promises certain advantages. One does not have to access the drugs; one is free of potential side effects or drug-drug interactions. But at the same time, there's an undercurrent of stoicism, even in the idea that going off meds is 'better' than staying on them. I'm not immune to it myself.

When it comes to psychiatric medication, stoicism is evident in almost every patient and family. On the one hand, medicines are so widely used and effective, people are curious about them. But on the other hand, this curiosity is typically tempered by self-judgement, fear of becoming 'weak' and 'dependent' on a 'crutch'. Of course, it doesn't make sense to use more support than you need, but I generally find that stoicism and its assorted judgements do more harm than good.

So when I hear Hazel feels she is ready to decrease her meds – along with the brighter mood, the confidence – I'm delighted. I just want to make sure she's doing it for the right reasons.

'Tell me more,' I say, taking a sip of my iced coffee.

'Well' – she crosses her legs and sits back in the chair – 'all this month I've been doing really well in school, things are going great with my friends. I even got turned down by this guy, who totally seemed like he was into me, over the weekend, and I'm not even that upset about it. I mean, emotionally it just feels a little crazy to be this *super* well-adjusted. I don't want the results of my meds to be like, I'm a better capitalist. You know?'

I carefully hold my face in a half smile. I don't want my pleased reaction to influence her too much. But it's clear that the impulse to lower her meds is not coming from pressure to fulfil society's expectations – in fact, it's the opposite.

When I think about the role of medication in my practice, it's basically a philosophical decision, based in a person's own values and knowledge of themselves. What makes their life most meaningful?

How much of their own emotion do they want to feel? People imagine that a psychiatrist's job is to argue either for or against medication. I see my role merely as providing information about what is likely to happen on or off a medicine. Medicine is not a good choice; it's not a bad choice. It's just a choice.

To be clear: not everyone should discontinue their psych meds. Not everyone can. The stakes are high and these decisions always need to be made in collaboration with a psychiatrist who knows you well and will monitor you carefully. For Hazel, going off meds seems like a safe and reasonable option.

She takes a dreamy sigh. 'I was talking to my friend and she was excited for me to think about seeing what life is like off meds. She was like, "It's the *getting bangs* of psychotherapeutic treatment!"'

At this, I can't help but let a broad smile bloom across my face. What an inspired image: getting bangs! This language conveys a new sense of agency in Hazel. She's understanding that how she feels – and who she is because of it – can be a matter of personal style. And through that lighthearted metaphor, she's translating the language of mental health into her own voice.

I'm glad that when we started the meds, I resisted her narratives of biological essentialism, tying her fate to an illness. I'm glad I didn't say, 'Yes, you have depression and it's a medical condition that runs in your family and it's very serious.' I wish I had articulated my view more clearly, although I think she got the message. If I had to do it over, I would have said this: 'Hazel, you have some *symptoms* of depression because you are grieving, and you're living in a world that doesn't have much patience for people being sad. You also weren't treated very well in this breakup and you have a lot of things to feel angry about. This medicine is going to help you feel less overwhelmed as we work together to help you gain more comfort with those feelings. That will make you feel less hopeless and helpless, and allow you to regain confidence in yourself.'

Now Hazel has come to a place where she welcomes her difficult emotions. She sees them as challenges she can tolerate. She's open to a messier existence because she trusts herself.

Turning Off the Cultural Gaslight

There has never been a time in modern society when girls needed to be stronger. The calm and casual mockery of girls has become normalised and even celebrated at the highest levels. Body positivity has all but disappeared. Some girls are now citing the pleasures of femininity as evidence that *equality* has been making them mentally ill. And among teenage girls, a culture of fear is growing. They are afraid of being sexually assaulted and no one caring. They are afraid of making one misstep on social media and being humiliated. And in their day-to-day interactions, whether they're being rated on a scale of 10, talked over in class, or called a name that's an STD, they are increasingly afraid to speak up. The worst thing a teenage girl can be is 'annoying' and, these days, that bar is easier to clear than ever.

My book is designed to help in one particular way. Girls have been gently offering their own mental deficiencies as 'the problem' to cope with a world that does not see them as fully human. Dual epidemics of pathologising and perfectionism have risen hand in hand, both offering girls the opportunity to cope with every situation by blaming themselves. The girls in this book believed they had to be sick to be heard – which was, in each case, debilitating. And so, the cycle of teenage-girl-as-mental-patient goes on. It's been a long-standing assumption of the patriarchy that teenage girls are crazy, and my greatest hope in writing this book is that girls will be moved to stop inviting this.

Which brings us to the last part: what can be done.

I write these recommendations with mixed feelings. Psychiatrists are not really in the business of telling people what to do. But I recognise this is murky territory and I'm glad to offer some general guidance.

So here are some thoughts for the road. I divide these recommendations into those for girls, for parents and for the psychiatric community.

Suggestions for Girls

The other day, I was talking to someone who owns a small clothing store that has a lot of customers who are young women. We were discussing therapy speak among her clientele, and she said it very well: 'It's like they're all talking *about* themselves, but not *as* themselves.' I hope that by this point it makes more sense when I say: when you reflexively use therapy speak, especially the diagnosis or identity labels, you are borrowing *someone else's* framework – a lexicon with a patriarchal history.

So my first suggestion is this: **Do not abandon your perspective, agency and voice. If you moved past these ready-made clinical terms, what else would you say?**

I know you're scared sometimes. At your age, approval is oxygen. You need it from your friends, your teachers, your coaches, your family and your latest crush. You have to convince them you're cool, you don't care, you don't need them – especially on social media. And if you've pulled that off, you have another problem: living with a big secret. And if you haven't, God help you.

People want you to be so many different things and that will never stop. They'll be mad when you don't play whatever role is expected, or they may just passively reinforce the dynamics that keep you there, even if they love you and know it's not great. People – even good people – will never think about you more than they think about themselves.

So it falls to you to do the very hard work of figuring out what you need and making sure you get it. It can be confusing to know how you feel, to know how to talk about that, and with whom.

One of the things you might be encouraged to do instead is to ask for *care* for whatever you *have*. And that's fine – you should. But I know you need more than treatment for what ails you. Your needs do not begin and end with psychiatric dysfunction. **Don't make your own brain the problem in every situation**. In these times, the most empowering thing a girl can say is the opposite: *I'm not crazy.*

Instead, please **care about your own feelings and listen to them**. If you find it hard to do this, if you keep getting in your own way, please find a therapist who can help you. Or a school guidance counsellor, or a person who is neutral and objective and outside of your day-to-day life who can really listen. **You don't have to be sick to deserve help.**

Please **don't let that person be ChatGPT**. ChatGPT and AI companions cannot really listen to you, and no matter what accurate things the chatbot says, the chatbot cannot be close to you because it has no feelings. It can't help you see what you're *not* seeing. It can't be frustrated, or intrigued, or put off, or hurt by you. It can't really *know* you the way a person can. It does not care if you live or die. Find a human therapist, and one who really cares about getting to know you; who has a sacred, professional commitment to you; who can read your silences; who is willing to participate in the messy, uncomfortable process through which real closeness becomes possible. And if you can't find a therapist, look for an adult – a teacher, a relative, a parent, a friend's parent. Make sure you never stop trying to open up to human beings.

You may, in fact, qualify for a psychiatric diagnosis. Please just remember that **you have always been and will always be more than your diagnosis**.

Don't confuse 'wellness' or 'self-care' – the kind that makes you buy all sorts of stuff – with true mental health. Your soul deserves more than a moisturiser and a scented candle.

I've tried to show what mental health means in this book and how girls can learn things about themselves that the culture isn't teaching them. Do you need to give yourself **compassion** for your deeper vulnerabilities, like Violet, Kaia and Maeve? Do you need to be a better **friend to yourself**, like Eliza, Millie and Becca? Can you cultivate **self-respect**, like Skylar and Elle? Or maybe some of each, like they all did? And perhaps you can learn to **trust yourself and what you have been through**, like Chloe, Hazel and Sloane.

Make friends with your feelings, including angry and aggressive ones, even though they may cause you anxiety. If you're angry, it means that something is wrong. Real anger, which is often the hardest feeling for girls to use effectively, is a power source that gives us the strength we need to make things better. Learn how to manage your anxiety so it doesn't keep you away from yourself. That means learning to recognise it in your body, to understand it's there for a reason, and to settle it – by breathing, distraction, whatever helps – so that you can stay grounded and connected to your feelings. **And if you're someone who is stuck in anger and aggression, ask yourself if that might be covering up some hurt.** Allow yourself to experience that vulnerability. Your feelings are your most trustworthy guide through life.

If you find yourself thinking in clinical language – 'depressed', 'attachment issues', 'trauma' – **keep translating until you've named what you're feeling**. Whatever you feel, learn how to **say it in your own words. So, to repeat: speak *for* yourself and *as* yourself.** You're the only one who can do that.

Or don't! You may not be ready to declare your identity, or your feelings and opinions, to the world. There's a lot of pressure, in a girlbossy way, to be sure of things, to be confident, to take a position. **Finding an authentic identity, though, is a quiet process.** As you get there, take in culture. See what art moves you, what ideas draw you. Translation must be a private act before it becomes a social statement.

To this end, it helps to **read books and poems and listen to songs**. It can be comforting to know that others have felt how you feel, and that not all emotional struggles – even some of the messiest and most upsetting ones – are signs of mental illness.

Viktor Frankl famously said, 'Suffering ceases to be suffering at the moment it finds a meaning.' The Indigo Girls described the experience as getting a 'letter to my soul'. No matter what type of suffering one is experiencing, meaning cannot be found in a medical textbook. Meaning is distilled through other endeavours – the creative arts, literature, religion, philosophy. The landscape of personhood is treacherous, and to traverse it and remain somehow *okay,* people need poetry, in one form or another. Words of wisdom. A connection to someone else in heaven or earth who has said exactly what you feel.

For example, I don't think it's an accident that Taylor Swift grew so popular at a time when the emotional vocabulary of girlhood was shrinking down to a few dull diagnostic categories. At her peak popularity, it almost seemed like there were two major avenues young women were using to convey their distress: the language of psychiatry and the language of Taylor Swift. My sense was that in Taylor Swift, a large swathe of girls seemed to find a translator.

Most people would not recognise Taylor Swift's lyrics as medicine. But to me, cataloguing the female distress-i-verse without pathologising its symptoms was not far from a public health intervention.

Perhaps you've heard of the song 'All Too Well'. In it, she describes a breakup, as zillions of songwriters have done before. It's partly a folk song, partly an introverted rock ballad, but largely, it's a *sleepover*. The kind where you go through the closet. You pick up the objects, feel them, smell them, decide whether to put them lovingly in a drawer or light them on fire. The scarf, the leaves, the refrigerator light. And at the end, the speaker, in her grief, becomes yet another object: 'a crumpled up piece of paper lying here', the rhythm breaking its own rules, going out of its own lines, to make space for the feeling. Anyone who likes this song, who has endured those emotions, would say it's good therapy – maybe even good medicine.

Of course, Taylor Swift does not speak to every girl. She is not the first person to put things well, and she won't be the last. But her example reminds us that art does not overstate or understate a feeling; rather, it honours specificity. A good song, like a good poem, meets life exactly as it is, and can be our best translator – especially when we are at a loss for words.

Suggestions for Parents

In a 2011 episode of the TV sitcom *Modern Family,* supermom Claire Dunphy takes her son, Luke, for an ADHD evaluation. It's not because Luke is suffering. It's because certain traits he's displaying remind her of things she doesn't like about her husband, Phil. The issues this episode presents are so relatable and multifaceted. Is Luke okay? Is Phil okay? What about Claire – is she the one who needs the help? What about their marriage? Or does Claire's concern emerge from a complex interaction of all these moving parts?

So many parents find themselves in a similar predicament. Parenting means thinking, musing and sometimes fretting about your kid – and trying to do everything you can to help them. And in the world of girls and therapy language, specific parenting challenges arise.

So (moms especially), first ask yourself: are you the one with diagnosis terms floating around in your head? Would getting a diagnosis for your daughter help you be less mad at her because it would mean she's not just being lazy, stubborn or selfish? Maybe that's not it – maybe you just don't want to see her suffering, or maybe the way she behaves is causing you distress. Maybe you're scared that she'll fail, or that she's making herself unattractive. **Try to figure out all the things you're afraid of.** They are all valid.

The idea of diagnosis is sometimes appealing because it implies a cure. Sometimes the 'cure' involves modifying a person's environment rather than the person herself. **Before you look to diagnosis and medication, consider other psychosocial or social factors (school placement, activities, family routines) that could be modified.** If a medical 'cure' were not possible, would it still make sense to view your daughter's problem as a medical condition?

Often, we want a diagnosis because it saves us from really uncomfortable emotional work. How do you do when it comes to processing tough emotions in yourself and others? It can be helpful to examine your style of coping, as well as attitudes you've adopted about labels and treatments in your own life.

That said, parents can often be excessively hard on themselves. Are you battling a sense of shame that you have done something wrong, or guilt that you have let her down? In other words: **Are you holding yourself accountable for how your daughter is in ways the culture has taught you to do, but may be incorrect?**

As far as your daughter is concerned, your job is to help her **translate.** Your key question, your North Star, your mantra in the face of therapy speak should be one phrase: ***What does she mean?***

People usually do things and feel things for a reason. If a young woman you know is having a strong reaction, assume it is motivated by a feeling that is understandable. Care about these feelings. **Give her the credit of assuming she's not crazy.**

On the other hand, **'normal' does not mean 'nothing'.** (Hey, some dads – you know who you are.) Do not be dismissive.

It is so hard to respect the full impact of kids' feelings when you know they are so normal. It's easy to minimise, and it's easy to over-pathologise. The way to avoid these traps is through **small acts of translation.** Expand the therapy speak into specific words and stories that are more personal and more meaningful than the autopilot terms. And be patient; this translation can be a long, slow, careful process.

You can start by marking her language, reflecting back that you've been paying attention: *'You've mentioned feeling* **depressed.***'* Or *'I heard you say we were* **giving you a panic attack.***'*

Sometimes therapy speak describes what is actually going on: maybe she *is* having a panic attack.

But if that's not the case (see below about educating yourself), and unless it's being said as a joke, these kinds of statements usually indicate strong feelings. Do not assume you know what she means, or what those feelings are. And do not badger her with questions. Instead, you can make simple observations that highlight her feelings, like 'Clearly, you were really upset', and leave space for her to say more.

She may not want to talk. In that case, you can also do some translating privately, in your own mind, or in conversation with another adult. Does she seem **lonely**? Are you hearing some **despair**? Could she be feeling **overwhelmed**? Try to substitute judgemental terms she may use, like '**toxic**', with more descriptive terms like '**hurtful**' or '**harmful**' or '**unkind**'. When you hear '**trauma**', if it rings hollow or leaves you numb, replace this word in your mind with the word '**burdens**'. When I'm trying to understand what makes someone's life hard, I find that imagining the specific 'burdens' they carry often lights up my own imagination better than 'trauma', which can be quite vague.

When possible, embrace language that takes a developmental perspective. One of therapy culture's main symptoms is its impatience – its impulsivity, if you will. What if we all cultivated more reverence for the passage of time? What if we made an effort to emphasise the long arm of development – and instead of deficient or disordered, thought of more young people as **not yet mature** – **'young'**, even. Whenever possible, look to genuine growing pains you've experienced yourself. You would be amazed how comforted kids feel when their parents say, **'When I was your age, I also had a hard time.'** The most reassuring and wisest advice is almost always: this too shall pass.

Also, try to describe states rather than conditions. Some phrases emphasise biological defectiveness, like 'That's how I'm *wired*.' But people **go through difficult periods.** For example, instead of '*I have anxiety*', a person could say she is simply '**feeling anxious**'.

Your work as a translator requires **educating yourself**. Do you think your daughter is, in fact, having panic attacks? Don't hesitate to consult with a professional, even just once, to have your questions answered. I know it can be very hard to find someone who is available and affordable. All I can say is, high-quality care needs to be made much more accessible and user-friendly, but don't give up on us! A human being can give you personalised guidance that the internet alone cannot. If you can't find a professional, make sure you are talking to another human person. Don't trust ChatGPT to have all the answers.

No matter what your daughter has or doesn't have, never forget that whatever you give to her emotionally is singular. Some parents imagine that they might send their child to be 'fixed' by a therapist. But this is not how it works. Whatever happens with you is always more important than what happens with us, and progress can only occur in the context of a partnership all around.

Suggestions for Psychiatry and the Mental Health Establishment

Psychiatrists represent a small fraction of mental health providers. I focus on psychiatrists here because this is my field, and also because we have historically been the authors of the *DSM* and therefore play a major role in shaping the medical and cultural view of what constitutes mental illness.

There is currently a movement in the United States to reduce the amount of psychiatric medication given to young people. While overmedication is a valid concern, the solution is that the medical system needs more support, not less. Other forms of help need to be made much more accessible. While medications are lifesaving and necessary for many people, they are not always the best option and are often prescribed because other forms of help are unavailable. **Any movement to decrease medication use should be doubly focused on increasing other sources of psychosocial support.**

For the past two decades, American healthcare has seen the erosion of the doctor-patient relationship, beginning with the excessive empowerment of health insurance companies from the 1970s through the 1990s. The psychiatric drug explosion occurred in that context, treating a system that was reeling in withdrawal. This transformation in medicine had just begun when I started my training. *I was there. Managed care. I remember it all too well.*

In an ideal world, primary care physicians could absorb more of the burden of emotional and behavioural problems. This is especially true for child and adolescent populations, when prevention is most effective and when lifelong medical identities are forming. Such a change would require doctors to have sufficient time to get to know their patients, to hear about their problems and to make a meaningful connection. Medication use could be reduced, for example, if paediatricians were in a better position to help parents manage challenging behaviour and family dynamics. **The return of the doctor-patient relationship** would prevent a good deal of overdiagnosis and overmedication.

With artificial intelligence taking over so much technology, a relationship may be the most important thing physicians can offer. We are at a critical moment where the medical system has the chance to operationalise this discrepancy, assigning more of the technical burden to AI and freeing up doctors to do the human work.

In America, insurance companies caused this problem and are the ones best positioned to fix it. They could support a more robust doctor-patient relationship by changing their reimbursement patterns to cover longer visits. This would benefit public health as well as the insurance companies themselves, because a focus on prevention and treatment of subclinical conditions in young people would decrease the long-term burden on the healthcare system.

Insurance companies could also make a big difference by **not requiring diagnoses to reimburse psychiatric care for children and teenagers.** Fewer excessive diagnoses would save costs for insurers as these generate treatments that may not be necessary. In the meantime, clinicians might make a standard practice of informing patients that we are required to give them a medical diagnosis and take time to talk about what that means and doesn't mean. Many people just see the diagnosis on their bill and assume it is literal and fixed.

Beyond insurance issues, we in psychiatry can be more vocal about how **we do not see our patients as walking diagnoses**, nor should they see themselves that way. We can do this by expanding the definition of normal suffering, limiting the weight we give to the *DSM,* and communicating more effectively with the public.

We have seen what happens when people take our symptom checklists out of context, and we might consider the rising importance of the public interface with the *DSM*. This might require changing the *DSM* itself, making it clearer that **a handful of symptoms is not necessarily a disease**. Other dimensional and integrative models* of mental disturbance and illness may align better with clinical realities and even with the most current findings in neurobiology. In future versions of the *DSM,* it might help to bring back the term 'reactions' from its earlier editions.

Right now, our diagnostic system focuses on labelling illness first and considering degree of impairment as an afterthought. This has blurred the line between health and illness and made more healthy variants understood as illnesses. The *DSM-5* does require a severity marker, but in my experience, this has not fundamentally impacted the way clinicians think. We need to find a way to place degree of impairment closer to the centre of our formal thought process.

Whatever changes are made, **we should no longer live in a world where people carry diagnoses of seven different mental disorders**. It just doesn't make sense. The Critical Psychiatry movement and those generating alternative models for the *DSM* add essential voices to this conversation. Early reports indicate the next edition of the

---

* Several dimensional models have been proposed: The Research Domain Criteria (RDoC) organises mental disorders according to basic scientific concepts with the goal of streamlining research. The Hierarchical Taxonomy of Psychopathology (HiTOP) and the *DSM-5*'s Alternative Model for Personality Disorders (AMPD) view mental health as a spectrum and look at traits that traverse categories.

DSM will integrate 'transdiagnostic factors and contextual elements', like quality of life, suicide risk and social, cultural and environmental determinants of health into the diagnostic formulation. This sounds like a good development, but the real test will be to see how it changes the way clinicians think.

Psychiatry has historically been threatened by encroachment from other professions. It has responded to turf wars by expanding diagnostic categories and 'bringing more existing disorders into its sphere of influence'. It is up to psychiatrists to **push back on the expansion and proliferation of diagnostic categories** and focus more on functionality and symptom-focused care. As Allen Frances described in a 2025 *New York Times* essay, this drive to expand our categories explains a good deal of the panic about the rise in autism.

We also need to **get real about medication**. Clinicians and insurance companies should embrace the reality of how people use psychiatric drugs, and separate medicine from the diagnoses we stretch to justify their use – often for years or even decades on end. Patients should know that these medicines sometimes relieve discomfort whether disease is present or not. Having a diagnosis does not necessarily mean you need to take medicine, and taking medicine can be a valid choice, even without a diagnosis.

That said, returning illness to the margins and expanding our definition of normal would impact our interventions. This would allow us to **put medication lower on the list of therapeutics**. Requests for medications would be heard, but it could become more of a universal practice to try other things first.

Finally, debates about the nature of mental illness – from philosophical ideas to concrete clinical decisions – tend to hinge on one main question: whether a person *can't* or *won't*. Are they ill or lazy, sick or bad? Psychiatrists are currently expected to be the arbiters of that question. For example, we are the ones who write letters justifying accommodations at school and work based on medical necessity – as if that were the only valid reason someone might not be set up for success in a given situation. There are no easy answers here, but the neurodiversity movement is working hard to develop a world where **medical failings and moral failings are not the only possible explanations of human variation**.

Currently, most of psychiatry training is about diseases and medications. That sets us up to be diagnosers and prescribers, and to play a remote and hands-off role in patient care. Most mental health services are provided by professionals who are not psychiatrists: psychologists, social workers and counsellors. We doctors often work in teams with these other professionals, but the system has set us up to play a role that is disconnected from patients and families as well as from other members of our team who are often much more clinically engaged. Psychiatry can reimagine itself to be useful in other ways besides simply writing prescriptions.

There is very little psychotherapy taught in residencies, and no training is required in art, literature, religion, music or spirituality. In order for mental health to reorient towards treating the whole person, practitioners must be trained to do so. We have spent the last several decades training technicians; now **let's train healers**.

Perhaps if psychiatry embraced what makes it truly unique within medicine and did not feel the need to be like other specialties, even more doctors would want to be psychiatrists and our scarcity in the healthcare system would improve. With different training, psychiatrists could move away from our unfortunate stint as 'pill pushers' and get better at treating the whole patient. This change from within psychiatry would also help patients understand that, whether or not their problems are medical in nature, their suffering is legitimate and warrants our help.

Psychiatry trainees should be well-versed in the thousands of years of wisdom on human emotions contained in the **arts, literature, philosophy and religion**. In practice, we draw from these tools, but when we turn to nonscientific sources we feel we are going off book. There is already a dwindling supply of supervisors trained in psychodynamic therapy, which will be a further loss for the next generation. Dynamic psychotherapy is informed by humanistic sources of wisdom and healing, and facilitates deep understanding of the human condition.

Finally, the medical humanities have provided a well-recognised space for doctors to become healers. **Engagement with the arts and humanities** fortifies physicians with the ability to use themselves as therapeutic instruments. The world needs this kind of help from us.

Now What?

I've been in practice throughout this teen mental health crisis, and as I look back on more than a decade of watching girls fall apart, I am reminded of a scene from *Girl, Interrupted.* This film heralded the modern era of the 'teen girl as mental patient'. Based on a 1993 memoir by Susanna Kaysen, the film features Susanna, the searching, edgy protagonist played by Winona Ryder. She has stabilised over a lengthy inpatient stay following a suicide attempt, and she's received a diagnosis of borderline personality disorder. Unlike my patient Hazel from earlier in this chapter, Susanna is indeed very sick. However, the same discussion about agency and choice applies.

'You're torn between two opposing courses of action,' says Dr Wick, Susanna's regal psychiatrist, played by Vanessa Redgrave. It's nearing the end of the film and Susanna sits on the sofa in Dr Wick's hospital office, disdainful and smoking a cigarette. She's asking to leave, but Dr Wick says she's not ready. She observes that Susanna is facing important choices – not just 'will I stay or will I go', but . . .

'Am I sane, or am I crazy?'

'Those aren't courses of action,' Susanna spits.

'They can be, dear,' Dr Wick replies, 'for some.' Witchy music begins to play. The camera zooms in on Redgrave's face as her incantation spills forth:

> *Quis hic locus? Quae regio? Quae mundi plaga?* What world is this? What kingdom? What shores of what worlds? It's a very

> big question you're faced with, Susanna. The choice of your life. How much will you indulge in your flaws? What are your flaws? Are they flaws? If you embrace them, will you commit yourself to hospital? for life? Big questions, big decisions!

This is a quote from Seneca (a Stoic philosopher, interestingly) describing a hero's disorientation upon returning home. These lines were also made famous in T S Eliot's poem 'Marina', and have been invoked to portray the displacement and disembodiment that follows travel, trauma and whenever the world turns upside down. The phrase conveys both the stammering of madness and the wonder of discovery.

In using these words, Dr Wick is flagging Susanna's participation in her own problem. She's interrupting the siren call of helplessness that beckons Susanna. She's urging her to take the path of agency. This gesture is all the more powerful because Susanna is navigating a serious mental illness – she's sick enough to be in a hospital. But Dr Wick will not let Susanna define herself by that illness. She is saying yes, these are the treacherous conditions of being you, and yes, *it's up to you alone* to decide how to move forward. She's urging Susanna to author her own story.

In every single moment that we are alive, we have choices. Within every mental illness, every stuck brain place, every combination of temperament and life experience – there are whispers of options. What are you feeling, and what reasons might explain it? Have you told yourself change is impossible, or do you want to try? *Quae mundi plaga?*

Translating Towards Health

Years of meditating on the Serenity Prayer have taught me that it's good for people to imagine that they can change, especially in the case of young people, whose identities are forming. Even if certain things about oneself are fixed and ultimately require acceptance, the gaining of that acceptance is itself a form of change. Psychiatric disease is complex in ways that other diseases of the body are not, and that's a good thing – it's to the advantage of the human soul to acknowledge the dark spaces in what we know, and to fill those spaces with hope.

To that end, I hope I've shown in this book that people grow and change in therapy, but no one gets all better overnight. I remember when I was still years away from treating patients, reading classic therapy narratives like Freud's *Studies on Hysteria,* which curated stories of healing that made it look easy. For other therapists just starting out, or for those who wished therapy moved along more quickly, I wanted to offer a counterpoint. Brains have more neuronal connections than there are stars in the sky, and as much as someone enters therapy wanting to change, human beings are naturally resistant to the process. When we write about our work, therapists necessarily omit hours (days, weeks, months, sometimes years) of sessions where progress is slow. Change is messy, nonlinear and gradual. Be very sceptical of anyone who tells you otherwise.

The question *Now what?* has very different answers for different people. As psychologist Abraham Maslow writes, human beings have a hierarchy of needs. Without food and shelter, physical safety and access to medical care, there can be no solid mental health. Self-diagnosis is not just a misguided trend: it's a reaction to the inaccessibility of help for so many people due to waiting lists, cost, stigma or lack of family support.

But some things are universal. All girls can become aware of the Girl Self-Defence System, the ways in which they automatically anticipate sexism and stoicism (don't be *hysterical;* just *deal*) and present themselves as post-wounded females who need to disown their pain. In a healthier culture, girls would be able to relax. Their feelings would not be minimised, scoffed at, objectified, explained away through biological essentialism, or weighed against how hot they are. Girls could live uninterrupted.

A healthy culture would be like a healthy person. It would resist pathologising and self-objectification. It would promote more interest in the wide and rocky landscape of ordinary pain. It would acknowledge that an individualistic society is set up to make a lot of people feel bad, and that it leaves us all symptomatic, to some extent – and intolerant of our limitations. A healthier culture would support the reality that everyone has 'stuff to work on', and that a person shouldn't need a diagnosis to access support: that we 'treat distress, not difference'. It would recognise that suffering is not usually a sign of illness, and that illness cannot substitute for identity. It would be common knowledge that you help someone not by highlighting the part of them that is wrong, but by connecting with the part that makes perfect sense. In a healthier culture, girls would recognise that history has dismissed them as crazy, and they would know that a more humane world fosters resilience. Ultimately, a healthy culture, like a healthy person, would ask a bit less of the therapy world, recognising that for all of its useful concepts, therapy was never meant to provide a complete framework for how or why to live. It would care that a good story avoids platitudes. It would find some answers in songs.

There's a garden near where I live – a little sanctuary behind a library near a busy intersection in Greenwich Village. It's lush and junglelike: broad-leaved ferns, an embarrassment of roses, giant hydrangeas bobbing like cauliflower. As I walk along its circular path midday in August, I pass wood benches, each hidden in its own shady enclave. To my right, there's a man, mid-twenties, FaceTiming with (I assume) his parents; he found a place in New Jersey that's small but affordable. To my left, there are two construction workers having lunch. And further down the path, there's a girl in her mid-teens wearing sunglasses. She's got a big notebook open on her lap, a pen in hand, and she's writing.

In this book, I have written stories of girls whose native language was therapy speak. There was Violet, whose singular brand of cool hid her terror of needing other people; Chloe and Kaia, desperate for control when life delivered chaos; and Hazel, who was reeling with grief in a system that urged her to move on. There was Millie, doing her best to avoid anger at the people she loves; and Becca – like so many teenagers, stuck in a social malaise she was unable to name. There was Skylar and Maeve, who sought cover in a bitchery that disguised their hurt. And Sloane, Eliza and Elle – who apologised, doubted, deflected and smiled when, despite talents and efforts, gifts and success, they were not yet convinced that they had what it takes.

After months and sometimes years of work, we were able to translate their adopted language into a new, more descriptive, more personal language that fostered compassion, resilience and health. They were able to recognise that their psychiatric symptoms were mostly the result of anxiety from feelings they couldn't tolerate. Ultimately, therapy helped them regulate their anxiety, broaden their tolerance for difficult feelings, and get better. The key to that process was to stop pathologising themselves and start finding their own words for what was going on inside.

The ends of stories about girlhood tend to circle back to the same question: when can girls be fully human? In the movie *Enchanted,* the princess finally lets herself feel anger towards a person for the first time. The *Barbie* movie concludes with Barbie choosing the real world and making her first visit to a gynaecologist. *Harriet the Spy* ends with Harriet writing, 'Now that things are back to normal, I can get some real work done.' Melissa Febos begins the final paragraph of her memoir, *Girlhood,* with 'The more I know my own worth, the less I have to fling myself against anything.'

I don't know what the girl in the garden is writing about, but I do know that those college-ruled handwritten pages have deeply absorbed her. I hope whatever story she's telling is pouring forth in a voice that belongs to her. Because that's an answer, too. Girls should be the authors of their own lives. It's time to hand the pen back to them.

Acknowledgments

It's been my dream since childhood to write a book. Be a doctor, be a mom and write a book. But it was not until about three years ago that it seemed like the book part could actually come true. I have so many people to thank for helping me along the way.

Laura Tucker. Sister-in-law, writer, editor, book-shaper extraordinaire: thank you for taking me seriously when I said over coffee seven years ago that I'd like to write something about my work. You have asked me the key questions at every step, and you are just very, very good at this. Thanks also to your pal Susanna Einstein for taking an early and formative interest in me and in this book.

Ariel Kaminer. Thank you for catching me mid-fever-dream and giving my writing an ear and a platform. None of this would have happened without you.

Brettne Bloom. Obviously, I have plenty of words, but I'm not sure I have the words for this part. Thank you for dropping out of the sky and changing my life. You're not just the dream agent, but – let's see if I can say this – that friend who really believes in you, even when you're not so sure, but who you trust because you see how amazing she is, how she is able to make everyone in her orbit feel inspired and motivated and awesome. That friend who makes every daunting step seem clear and doable, and also the one you'd want to be stranded with on a desert island. I can't believe how lucky I am to get to work with you – and the whole team at The Book Group, especially my wonderful international agent, Jenny Meyer.

Gillian Blake. From our first conversation, I knew you really *got* this book. Somehow you managed to see the final product that needed to be created before it was even fully formed in my head. Your vision and brilliant editorial eye truly brought out the clearest and sharpest in me and in these pages. At every step, you were patient and responsive as I navigated the book world as a first-time author. I am so grateful to have worked with the best of the best.

Aubrey Martinson, thanks for dropping in and offering your crystal-clear millennial guidance – so quickly and with such care. Libby Burton, thank you for your enthusiasm and for your beautiful letter. And to Jessica Jean Scott, Allyson Coy, Stacey Stein and the whole team at Crown: thank you for listening, for being so thoughtful and collaborative, and for bringing your editorial, artistic and strategic talents to every aspect of this book's production.

I am but one of many writers in the Feigelson family. Sonia, these complex stories found shape and tone under your keen developmental eye. Dan, thanks for getting me started with the question 'What do you want to write ten essays about?' and for being so willing to dig in and to help me kill those darlings. Zoe, your artful insights guided me towards the beating heart of this book – and replaced some of my blind spots with clear pictures. Matthew, you translated my message for the digital world through SOLNIQUE's marketing and social media genius. And Tom, thanks for being the moon reflecting the sun, for your great catch on the subtitle, and for helping me know I was a writer in the first place. To Liz for helping me become my most confident self as a teenage girl, young woman, therapist, mother and author. And to Jeremy, who always conveyed that I could do things like write a book (even if you still don't think I'm old enough to have my own patients), and that this type of thing was worth doing. And to my late father, Charles Feigelson. This book was nurtured from its prehistory by your lifelong commitment to psychoanalysis, your effervescent warmth and your care for me.

Mom, thank you for teaching me that it's important to be independent, that being a therapist is the most wonderful kind of work there is, and that it's so much fun to be female. You have listened to everything I have ever had to say and always made me feel important and fully loved. Ira, thank you for setting the bar so high as a physician, and for all of your support in my various pursuits over the years, especially the creation of this book. The two of you read every draft of every chapter. It must have been hundreds of drafts. And thank you for being honest when something just wasn't working yet.

I'm so lucky to have yet another family of writers (and therapists). Mimi, thanks for having so many great conversations with me about the work we do. Your commitment to this profession is inspiring, and I'm lucky to have had your expert ear and your open mind as I figured out what to present here. Lily, thank you for blessing this book with your cultural savvy and Taylor Swift expertise, and for leading me to Violet. Thanks also to Doug for your wonderful encouragement and writerly enthusiasm; thanks to Bill for your regular delivery of perfect cookies, and for your warm heart.

Violet Chernoff (who is not the character in the book): you came along at just the right moment to provide research assistance and a sophisticated younger person's perspective. You are mature and professional beyond your years, and this book was sharpened by your wise insights as much by as the academic detailing you did so quickly and so well. And Julie Tate, your expert fact-checking was an essential part of this process.

To my medical humanities colleagues: Anne Fadiman, who encouraged me, long ago, to be a doctor *and* a writer. Rita Charon, for bringing Narrative Medicine to life and helping me find and sustain a 'laboratory' for it at Mount Sinai. Your integrity and friendship means more than you know. And to David Muller, who gave the vision a chance, and who showed me and generations of future physicians what it means to be present. And especially to Jacob Appel. You were the first person to read this whole book, and your ethical expertise guided me, after decades of paralysis, to realise it was possible to write about clinical work.

To my amazing comrades in mental health. There are so many of you who have helped form this book over the years, from my brilliant residency friends and our beloved captain, Ron Rieder, who envisioned a special destiny for each of us, to the probing Experiential Dynamic Therapy community. But a few deserve special mention. Allie Baker and Suzanne Dieter, thank you for the years of 3MCs and all of your commitment and camaraderie finding our way through this work together. Nate Thoma and Carolyn Broudy – thanks for being my nearest and dearest in pursuit of the ultimate technique. Catherine Steiner Adair, thank you for your clinical companionship and guidance to book world – as well as for providing an emotional compass through the new normals of screen time. Ron Taffel, I am so moved by your enthusiasm for my writing and your outpouring of support. And to all of my wonderful teachers and supervisors in psychiatry at Columbia and Mount Sinai, in theoretical psychoanalysis at University College London, and beyond. Stephen Grosz, thank you for helping me in my first writing venture on psychoanalysis and cure and for setting a beautiful example of clinical writing in your own books. To Paul Geltner, who encouraged some of my early work that eventually became this book, and to the late Philip Lister, whose humanity sits with me in the room. A special thanks to the amazing Reiko Joseph, whose clinical wisdom and extraordinary blend of rigour and flexibility has cultivated my attention and compassion, and has touched every page of this book. And, last but not least, to Andrew Gerber: polymath, speed reader, maverick – whose brain is outsized only by his heart.

A big thank-you also to those who have lent their time and expertise about writing books: Catherine Price, Dave Nussbaum and the gang at Team O.

To my friends who have lent special support: Margaret, you are literally the sunshine that makes so many things grow, and your edits make me smile so much I have no choice but to frame them. Your constant enthusiasm kept me going every step of the way, and I'm grateful every day to have ended up in life with a best friend like you. Joanna and Josh: you guys stuck with me in the trenches, providing amazing listening, great ideas and a classy artistic touch through the daunting task of turning to face the public. Engine78 made establishing an online presence feel authentic and meaningful. And a special thanks to Emily for surviving teenage girlhood together (and everything else), as well as to Leslie and Lila for reading early drafts; and to Julia for your shared passion for dedications.

Weirdly, I also feel moved to thank Erica, the automated voice from Speechify, who spent an entire year reading things back to me. We made it, girl!

And, of course, to Trooper: cotherapist, true friend, Cavapoo. Thanks for being physically adjacent to me for most of the writing of this book, and for keeping us all so safe from the people in the hall.

Finally, Aaron. Thank you for asking me not *if* I would write a book, but rather *what* book I was going to write. Everyone should have a partner who cares this much about them. Every writer should have a person in their life who reads first, best and who, with total warmth and the purest kindness, will not say that it's good until it is. Your constant stream of smart, understated silliness makes it a pure delight to go through life together. This book owes so much to your wisdom, your patience, your emotional skill and your great big heart. You are my everything person.

And, last and with the most hugs, to my children and stepchildren: thank you for your perpetual cuteness and for always being your wonderful selves. Special thanks to TLC for your very special kindness and amazingly thoughtful questions, and to MLC for your consistent interest and shockingly mature editorial insights. WJG, I am deeply grateful for your keen sense of feminism, for your guidance through girl culture, and for all the times you let me know what's relevant – and what 'no one cares about'. And TCG: thank you for your endless sweetness, your energy and intelligence, and for keeping me laughing. You've made this time so much fun. Also, that's what she said.

Notes

Epigraphs

vii **'The Lord said, "If as one people"':** Genesis 11:6–8 (New International Version).

vii **'The idea that gives psychiatry':** Gary Greenberg, *The Book of Woe* (Blue Rider Press, 2013), 25.

vii **'She broke up with me':** *Parks and Recreation,* season 3, episode 3, 'Time Capsule', written and directed by Michael Schur, aired 3 February 2011, on NBC.

Introduction

1 **'Let's normalise not calling girls crazy':** Internet meme, origin unknown.

1 **'Every time you call me crazy, I get more crazy':** Taylor Swift, 'Mad Woman', *Folklore*, Republic Records, 2020.

1 **a mental health crisis affecting teens and young adults:** Jean Twenge, 'The Impact of Smartphones, Social Media, and School Laptops on Youth Mental Health and Academic Performance', Congressional Testimony, 15 January 2026.

2 **it has been shown to have an 'engulfing' effect:** Kari M Eddington and Emily Badillo-Winard, 'Mental Illness Identity: A Scoping Review', *Identity: An International Journal of Theory and Research* 25, no. 3 (2025): 412–27.

2 **learning about mental health largely on social media:** Michelle Faverio et al., 'Teens, Social Media and Mental Health', Pew Research Centre, 22 April 2025.

2 **self-labelling with disorders:** Isaac Ahuvia et al., 'Depression Self-Labelling in U.S. College Students: Associations with Perceived Control and Coping Strategies', *Journal of Affective Disorders* 351 (15 April 2024): 202–10.

2 **and then posting about them:** Susanna Y Park et al., 'Digital Methods for the Spiritual and Mental Health of Generation Z: Scoping Review', *Interactive Journal of Medical Research* 13 (February 2024).

2 **one in five Gen Alpha children:** Centres for Disease Control, 'Data and Statistics on Children's Mental Health', https://www.cdc.gov/children-mental-health/data-research/index.html.

5 **they are so dominant in higher education:** Michael T Nietzel, 'Women Continue to Outpace Men in College Enrollment and Graduation', *Forbes,* 7 August 2024.

5 **handing out 'bro-chures':** Susan Dominus, 'There Was Definitely a Thumb on the Scale to Get Boys', *The New York Times Magazine,* 8 September 2023.

5 **Boys and men have their own burdens:** Efua Andoh, 'Rethinking Masculinity to Build Healthier Outcomes', *Monitor on Psychology* 56, no. 8 (September 2025): 49.

5 **In the words of the writer Lisa Appignanesi:** Lisa Appignanesi, *Mad, Bad and Sad: A History of Women and the Mind Doctors* (Norton, 2008): 6.

5 **girls are more concerned about teen mental health:** Faviero et al., 'Teens, Social Media and Mental Health', Pew Research Centre, 22 April 2025.

5 **In recent years, girls have experienced a decline:** Ruling Our eXperiences (ROX), *The Girls' Index™ 2023: The State of Girls' Mental Health and Self-Confidence,* 23–29.

6 **'Hot Crazy-Matrix: A Man's Guide to Women':** https://www.youtube.com/watch?v=pInk1rV2VEg.

6 **In 1994's *Reviving Ophelia*:** Mary Pipher, *Reviving Ophelia* (Ballantine Books, 1994): 'girl-poisoning culture', 12; 'sexism, capitalism, and lookism', 23.

6 **'Progress is confusing'**, Pipher, *Reviving Ophelia,* 27.

8 **As Denis Diderot, who lived in the 1700s:** Denis Diderot, quoted in Pipher, *Reviving Ophelia,* 19.

8 **Simone de Beauvoir called it:** Simone de Beauvoir, quoted in Pipher, *Reviving Ophelia,* 22.

8 **what Betty Friedan called:** Betty Friedan, quoted in Pipher, *Reviving Ophelia,* 12.

9 **Merriam-Webster's Word of the Year:** https://www.merriam-webster.com/wordplay/word-of-the-year-2022.

9 **the expansion of *spaces*:** Frank Furedi, *Therapy Culture* (Routledge, 2004).

10 **As W H Auden wrote:** W H Auden, 'In Memory of Sigmund Freud', in *Another Time* (Random House, 1940).

11 **How many of us have been reprimanded:** Amanda Montell, *Wordslut: A Feminist Guide to Taking Back the English Language* (Harper Perennial, 2019), 120–21.

12 **'fratriarchy':** Montell, *Wordslut,* 107.

12 **young women are about a half generation:** Douglas Quenqua, 'They're, Like, Way Ahead of the Linguistic Currrrve', *The New York Times,* 27 February 2012.

12 **Compared to male speech, which is 'competitive':** Montell, *Wordslut,* 84–123.

13 **As George Orwell describes:** George Orwell, *Politics and the English Language* (Penguin Classics, 2013).

13 **'The role that young women play':** Gretchen McCulloch, *Because Internet* (Riverhead Books, 2019), 34.

13 **Insurance companies require:** Allen Frances, *Saving Normal* (William Morrow, 2013), 85.

14 **The global antidepressant market:** Fortune Business Insights, *Antidepressants Market Size & Share Report [2020–2027]* (Fortune Business Insights, 2025).

14 **Pharma funds most clinical trials in psychiatry:** Paolo Migone, 'The Influence of Pharmaceutical Companies', *Research in Psychotherapy* 20, no. 2 (July 2017): 276.

14 **even more diagnoses that are even easier to make:** Frances, *Saving Normal,* 77–113.

14 **Females turn to psychiatry:** Maria Arenas et al., 'A Systematic Review and Meta-Analysis on Gender Differences in the Treatment of Anxiety and Depression', *International Journal of Social Psychiatry* 71, no. 5 (August 2025): 835–43.

14 **In the present, physicians:** American Psychiatric Association, 'Mental Health Disparities: Women's Mental Health', https://www.psychiatry.org/getmedia/aa325a61-5b60-4c71-80f1-dc80cf83c383/Mental-Health-Facts-for-Women.pdf.

14 **Women are more likely than men to be prescribed:** American Psychiatric Association, 'Mental Health Disparities: Women's Mental Health'.

14 **Women experiencing physical health problems:** Tessa Zirnsak et al., '"I Have to Fight for Them to Investigate Things" : A Qualitative Exploration of Physical and Mental Healthcare for Women Diagnosed with Mental Illness', *Frontiers in Public Health* 12 (30 April 2024): 1–11.

14 **And young women accrue more psychiatric diagnoses:** Yihui Yang et al., 'Sex Differences in Clinically Diagnosed Psychiatric Disorders over the Lifespan: A Nationwide Register-Based Study in Sweden', *The Lancet Regional Health: Europe* 47 (October 2024): 1–11.

15 **The words a girl uses to *describe* herself:** Bryan Denny et al., 'A Meta-Analysis of Functional Neuroimaging Studies of Self- and Other Judgements Reveals a Spatial Gradient for Mentalising in Medial Prefrontal Cortex', *Journal of Cognitive Neuroscience* 24, no. 8 (August 2012): 1742–52.

15 **people have been weighing in on therapy culture:** Frank Furedi, *Therapy Culture* (Routledge, 2004).

15 **Popular books:** Abigail Shrier, *Bad Therapy: Why the Kids Aren't Growing Up* (Sentinel, 2024).

15 **discussions on forums like Reddit:** Rosie Underhill and Lucy Foulkes, 'Self-Diagnosis of Mental Disorders: A Qualitative Study of Attitudes on Reddit', *Qualitative Health Research* 35, no. 7 (2025): 779–92.

17 **'Fuck Around and Find Out (FAFO)':** Amanda Katz, 'Why the Scary, Funny, Profane "FAFO" Was 2022's Word of the Year', *The Washington Post,* 17 January 2023.

17 **women, in their focus on feelings:** Helen Andrews, 'The Great Feminization', *Compact Magazine,* 16 October 2025.

17 **number one social issue:** Made of Millions, *Remapping Recovery: How Gen Z's Quest for Better Care Is Pioneering New Paths Forward in Mental Health,* 2024; Institute of Politics at Harvard University, 'Harvard Youth Poll' (Fall 2025).

17 **Access to care and affordability:** Able Partners and Springbank Collective, 'Gen Z: Healthcare Just Hits Different', genzhealth.com.

18 **to know and express one's mind and to engage:** Anthony Bateman and Peter Fonagy, *Handbook of Mentalising in Mental Health Practice* (American Psychiatric Association, 2019).

19 **teenagers can derive some of the same benefits:** A-L van Harmelen et al., 'Adolescent Friendships Predict Later Resilient Functioning Across Psychosocial Domains in a Healthy Community Cohort', *Psychological Medicine* 47, no. 13 (2017): 2312–22.

Chapter 1: Diagnosed

23 **'Sometimes it's good to know and to name things':** Esther Perel, host, *Where Should We Begin?,* podcast, season 8, episode 8, 'Is It Our ADHD, OCD, and PTSD? Or Is It Us?', season 8, episode 13, 6 October 2025.

23 **'Translation takes time':** Cristina Rivera Garza, 'A Stacking of Translations and the Affect of the Here-and-Now', in *Best Literary Translations 2025,* guest ed. Cristina Rivera Garza (Deep Vellum Publishing, 2025), 21.

25 **Birth control would also probably help:** Iñaki Lete and Oihane Lapuente, 'Contraceptive Options for Women with Premenstrual Dysphoric Disorder: Current Insights and a Narrative Review', *Open Access Journal of Contraception* (2016): 117–25.

25 **For her OCD, the most evidence-based treatment:** Jonathan S Abramowitz, 'The Psychological Treatment of Obsessive–Compulsive Disorder', *Canadian Journal of Psychiatry* 51, no. 7 (2006): 407–16.

26 **Adolescence was first named:** G Stanley Hall, *Adolescence: Its Psychology and Its Relations to Physiology, Anthropology, Sociology, Sex, Crime, Religion and Education* (D Appleton, 1904).

26 **adolescence ushered in the final stages:** Bärbel Inhelder and Jean Piaget, *The Growth of Logical Thinking: From Childhood to Adolescence,* trans. A Parsons and S Milgram (Basic Books, 1958).

26 **Lawrence Kohlberg and Carol Gilligan:** Lawrence Kohlberg, *The Philosophy of Moral Development: Moral Stages and the Idea of Justice* (Harper & Row, 1981); Carol Gilligan, *In a Different Voice: Psychological Theory and Women's Development* (Harvard University Press, 1982).

26 **Anna Freud noted:** Anna Freud, 'Adolescence', *Psychoanalytic Study of the Child* 13 (1958): 175.

26 ***'sturm und drang':*** Hall, *Adolescence,* xii.

27 **over the span of a week:** Amanda E Guyer et al., 'The Neurobiology of the Emotional Adolescent: From the Inside Out', *Neuroscience and Biobehavioural Reviews* 70 (August 2016): 74–85.

27 **The adolescent brain develops:** Guyer, 'Neurobiology of the Emotional Adolescent'.

27 **the central task of adolescence:** Erik Erikson, *Identity and the Life Cycle* (International Universities Press, 1959).

29 **Occam's razor:** *Britannica,* 'Occam's Razor', https://www.britannica.com/topic/Occams-razor.

31 **'Transference' is when:** Patricia Hughes and Ian Kerr, 'Transference and Countertransference in Communication Between Doctor and Patient', *Advances in Psychiatric Treatment* 7, no. 5 (2001): 417–24.

32 **'Listen to your patient':** Nada Khan, 'Listen to Your Patient', *British Journal of General Practice* 72, no. 725 (November 2022): 555.

41 ***The Body Keeps the Score*:** Bessel van der Kolk, *The Body Keeps the Score: Brain, Mind, and Body in the Healing of Trauma* (Viking, 2014).

41 **rose to number one on *The New York Times*:** 'Paperback Nonfiction', *The New York Times,* 3 August 2025.

41 **Thousands of podcasts:** Listen Notes, 'Podcasts with "Trauma" in the Title', 2025, https://www.listennotes.com/search/?q=trauma&sort_by_date=0&scope=episode&offset=0&only_in=title&language=Any%20language&len_min=0.

41 **Social media reverberates with trauma:** Julie Fenwick, 'The Rise of "TraumaTok" : When Does Sharing Trauma Online Become Unhealthy?', *Vice,* 19 May 2022.

41 **'the word of the decade':** Lexi Pandell, 'How Trauma Became the Word of the Decade', *Vox,* 25 January 2022.

41 **Journalist Abigail Shrier makes this case rather bluntly:** Abigail Shrier, *Bad Therapy: Why the Kids Aren't Growing Up* (Sentinel, 2024): 114.

43 **Trauma was first defined by psychiatry:** American Psychiatric Association, *Diagnostic and Statistical Manual of Mental Disorders,* 3rd ed. (APA, 1980).

43 **'outside the range of usual human experience':** Matthew J Friedman, 'PTSD History and Overview', US Department of Veterans Affairs, https://www.ptsd.va.gov/professional/treat/essentials/history_ptsd.asp.

43 **in the *DSM-IV*, qualifying events had to involve:** American Psychiatric Association, *Diagnostic and Statistical Manual of Mental Disorders,* 4th ed. (APA, 1994).

43 **coining the term 'complex post-traumatic stress disorder (c-PTSD)':** Judith Lewis Herman, *Trauma and Recovery: The Aftermath of Violence – from Domestic Abuse to Political Terror* (Basic Books, 1992).

44 **a person could now be traumatised:** American Psychiatric Association, *Diagnostic and Statistical Manual of Mental Disorders,* 5th ed. (APA, 2013).

44 **'intergenerational trauma':** Vivian M Rakoff et al., 'Children and Families of Concentration Camp Survivors', *Canada's Mental Health* 14 (1966): 24–26.

45 **the impact of maternal stress hormones:** Nasrin Jahan et al., 'Untreated Depression During Pregnancy and Its Effect on Pregnancy Outcomes: A Systematic Review', *Cureus* 13, no. 8 (August 2021).

47 **Historically, OCD has been considered:** American Psychiatric Association, *Diagnostic and Statistical Manual of Mental Disorders,* 4th ed. (APA, 1994).

51 **'transitional objects':** D W Winnicott, 'Transitional Objects and Transitional Phenomena – a Study of the First Not-Me Possession', *International Journal of Psycho-Analysis* 34 (1953): 89–97.

Chapter 2: A History of the Emotional Female in Two Breakups

54 **'The determining male gaze':** Laura Mulvey, 'Visual Pleasure and Narrative Cinema', *Screen* 16, no. 3 (October 1975): 6–18.

54 **'In truth, naming a disease':** Alexander Kriss, *Borderline: The Biography of a Personality Disorder* (Beacon Press, 2024), 34.

60 **'a condition of helpless stupor':** William Styron, *Darkness Visible: A Memoir of Madness* (Random House, 1990), 17–18.

60 **the *DSM-5* removed the bereavement exception:** American Psychiatric Association, *Diagnostic and Statistical Manual of Mental Disorders,* 5th ed. (APA, 2013).

60 **a misplaced depression diagnosis:** Allan V Horwitz and Jerome C Wakefield, *The Loss of Sadness: How Psychiatry Transformed Normal Sorrow into Depressive Disorder* (Oxford University Press, 2007), 20.

62 **a buildup of bad humours:** C Tasca et al., 'Women and Hysteria in the History of Mental Health', *Clinical Practice & Epidemiology in Mental Health* 8 (2012): 111.

62 **the womb of a young female grew 'vexed and aggrieved':** Elinor Cleghorn, *Unwell Women: A Journey Through Medicine and Myth in a Man-Made World* (Dutton, 2021), 22.

62 **Plato was famous for his hatred of women:** Kriss, *Borderline,* 29.

63 **The Greco-Roman physician, Galen:** Galen, *On the Natural Faculties,* trans. Margaret Tallmadge May (Harvard University Press, 1916), in Kriss, *Borderline,* 27–31.

63 **'A woman is a failed man':** Tasca et al., 'Women and Hysteria in the History of Mental Health', *Clinical Practice & Epidemiology in Mental Health* 8 (2012): 110–19.

63 **Even a woman's sadness:** *Malleus Maleficarum* (Bradford, 1948), 44–45.

64 **Thomas Sydenham led the charge:** John M S Pearce, 'Sydenham on Hysteria', *European Neurology* 76, no. 3–4 (2016): 175–81.

64 **'those to whom either nature has given':** Pearce, 'Sydenham on Hysteria', 179.

64 **'alienists', from the French:** Andrew Scull, *Desperate Remedies* (Harvard University Press, 2022), 3.

64 **the term 'psychiatry':** *Britannica,* 'Psychiatry', https://www.britannica.com/science/psychiatry.

64 **Psychiatrists found themselves perpetually on the fringes:** Edward Shorter, *A History of Psychiatry* (Wiley, 1997), 67.

65 **Maria Theresia von Paradis:** Allan Ropper and Brian Burrell, *How the Brain Lost Its Mind: Sex, Hysteria, and the Riddle of Mental Illness* (Atlantic Books, 2021), 36–40.

65 **Mesmer and Maria were a good team:** Ropper and Burrell, *How the Brain Lost Its Mind,* 35–36.

65 **found its way to a physician in Paris:** Shorter, *History of Psychiatry,* 137–38.

65 **In addition, entering a trance state:** Ann Williamson, 'What Is Hypnosis, and How Might It Work?', *Palliative Care: Research and Treatment* 12 (January 2019).

66 **Enter: Blanche Wittman:** Asti Hustvedt, *Medical Muses* (Simon & Schuster, 2010), 35–41.

66 **a 'dynamic lesion' of the brain:** Julien Bogousslavsky, 'The Mysteries of Hysteria: A Historical Perspective', *International Review of Psychiatry* 32, no. 5–6 (June 2020).

66 **Hysteria had reached its 'golden age':** Elaine Showalter, *The Female Malady: Women, Madness, and English Culture, 1830–1980* (Pantheon, 1985), 129.

66 **Most women carried a bottle:** Tasca, 'Women and Hysteria', 114.

66 **A woman would unravel because of her *nature*:** Janet Oppenheim, 'Neurotic

Women', in *'Shattered Nerves': Doctors, Patients, and Depression in Victorian England* (Oxford University Press, 1991).

67 **Charles Darwin and his followers:** Showalter, *Female Malady,* 101–20.

67 **British alienist-psychiatrist Charles Mercier:** Showalter, *Female Malady,* 131.

67 **The sanitorium, previously home to the male lunatic:** Kate Moore, 'Declared Insane for Speaking Up: The Dark American History of Silencing Women Through Psychiatry', *Time,* 22 June 2021.

67 **But psychiatry was still not keeping up:** Scull, *Desperate Remedies,* 40.

67 **Perhaps it was 'horseback riding':** Cleghorn, *Unwell Women,* 101.

67 **the famous nurse Florence Nightingale:** Showalter, *Female Malady,* 63–65.

68 ***globus hystericus*:** Showalter, *Female Malady,* 154–55.

68 **In 1880, Bertha Pappenheim:** Showalter, *Female Malady,* 155–58.

68 **it was therapeutic for his patients:** Juliet Mitchell, *Psychoanalysis and Feminism* (Pantheon, 1974).

68 **psychological symptoms were produced:** Josef Breuer and Sigmund Freud, *Studies on Hysteria* (Deuticke, 1895).

69 **psychiatrists were dealing with a crisis:** Shorter, *History of Psychiatry,* 65–67.

69 **'Who becomes a psychiatrist?':** Shorter, *History of Psychiatry,* 67.

69 **German psychiatrist Emil Kraepelin had an idea:** Shorter, *History of Psychiatry,* 100–112.

70 **a predominantly female patient population:** Phyllis Chesler, *Women and Madness* (Palgrave, 1972), 173–79.

70 **Fun fact: the term 'shell shock':** Showalter, *Female Malady,* 172.

70 **the field of psychiatry was still under threat:** Jonathan Metzl, *Prozac on the Couch: Prescribing Gender in the Era of Wonder Drugs* (Harvard University Press, 2002), 43.

70 **a series of accidental discoveries:** Shorter, *History of Psychiatry,* 248–58.

71 **With the arrival of these blockbuster drugs:** Shorter, *History of Psychiatry,* 239–87.

72 **'psychological justice':** Allan V Horwitz and Jerome C Wakefield, *All We Have to Fear: Psychiatry's Transformation of Natural Anxieties into Mental Disorders* (Oxford University Press, 2012), 223.

74 **'Chill' means someone who:** Naomi Beinart, 'As Boys Shift to the Right, We Are Seeing the Rise of the "New Chill Girl",' *The Guardian,* 18 September 2025.

74 **a dating book that came out:** Ellen Fein and Sherrie Schneider, *The Rules: Time-Tested Secrets for Capturing the Heart of Mr. Right* (Warner, 1995).

78 **In 1912, when phenobarbital came on the market:** Shorter, *History of Psychiatry,* 203.

78 **The 1950s ushered in 'minor tranquillisers':** Metzl, *Prozac on the Couch,* 73.

78 **'Now she can cope':** McNeil Laboratories, 'Now She Can Cope' advertisement, *Medical Economics,* 13 January 1964.

78 **Miltown became the most popular drug:** Metzl, *Prozac on the Couch,* 73.

78 **In 1967, there was 'more mental illness among women':** Showalter, *Female Malady,* 3.

78 **'whatever the cause, it helps to add Miltown':** Cleghorn, *Unwell Women,* 262–63.

79 **'catecholamine hypothesis':** Mark L Ruffalo, 'The Story of Prozac: A Landmark Drug in Psychiatry', *Psychology Today,* 2 March 2020.

79 **In the 1970s, Eli Lilly began experimenting:** Ruffalo, 'Story of Prozac'.

79 **Within a few months, sales took off:** Ruffalo, 'Story of Prozac'.

80 **80 per cent of its consumers were female:** Jacquelyn N Zita, *Body Talk: Philosophical Reflections on Sex and Gender* (Columbia University Press, 1998), 62.

80 **Prior to the 1990s, the FDA maintained:** Horwitz and Wakefield, *All We Have to Fear,* 227–30.

80 **it even required pharmaceutical companies:** Horwitz and Wakefield, *All We Have to Fear,* 227–29.

80 **'What few people know is that Susan':** 'The Personality Pill', *Time,* 10 May 1993; quoted in Shorter, *A History of Psychiatry,* 323.

80 **They could be 'empowered health-care consumers':** Metzl, *Prozac on the Couch,* 169.

80 **In the 1993 bestseller *Listening to Prozac*:** Peter D Kramer, *Listening to Prozac* (Viking, 1993), 271.

81 **'cosmetic psychopharmacology':** Kramer, *Listening to Prozac,* 15.

81 **constant self-surveillance and discipline:** Rosalind Gill, 'Postfeminist Media Culture: Elements of a Sensibility', *European Journal of Cultural Studies* 10, no. 2 (2007): 14.

81 **'Mental health' was now considered a feminine issue:** Fredrika Thelandersson, *21st Century Media and Female Mental Health: Profitable Vulnerability and Sad Girl Culture* (Palgrave Macmillan, 2023), 62.

Chapter 3: Identity and the Internet Age

84 **'The tradition of psychological curiosity':** Daniel Carlat, *Unhinged: The Trouble with Psychiatry – a Doctor's Revelations About a Profession in Crisis* (Free Press, 2010), 45.

84 **'Now we are never not posing':** Melissa Febos, *Girlhood* (Bloomsbury, 2021), 248–49.

86 **more than half of the original users:** John D Haltigan et al., 'Social Media as an Incubator of Personality and Behavioural Psychopathology: Symptom and Disorder Authenticity or Psychosomatic Social Contagion?', *Comprehensive Psychiatry* 121 (2023): 2.

87 **'breathing room':** Elizabeth Wurtzel, *Prozac Nation: Young and Depressed in America* (Houghton Mifflin, 1994).

87 **'We weren't bad or lazy or stupid':** Laura Delano, 'Reading Elizabeth Wurtzel's "Prozac Nation" 30 Years Later', *The Washington Post,* 12 December 2024.

88 **No line was drawn between mental *illness*:** Anne-Sophie Bine, 'Social Media Is Redefining "Depression",' *The Atlantic,* 28 October 2013.

88 **took a toll:** K J Mitchell et al., 'Linking Youth Internet and Conventional Problems', *Journal of Aggression, Maltreatment & Trauma* 15, no. 2 (2007): 39–58.

88 **Tumblr banned blogs encouraging:** Haltigan, 'Social Media as an Incubator of Personality and Behavioural Psychopathology', 2.

88 **The hypnotising algorithms:** Jonathan Haidt, *The Anxious Generation* (Penguin Press, 2024), 163.

88 **It was a living experiment:** Anima Shrestha, 'Echo: The Romanticization of Mental Illness on Tumblr', *Undergraduate Research Journal of Psychology at UCLA* 5 (Spring 2018): 70.

88 **From the halls of academia:** Cathy Caruth, *Unclaimed Experience: Trauma, Narrative, and History* (Johns Hopkins University Press, 1996).

89 **'Emotional contagion', a subset of social contagion:** Elaine Hatfield et al., 'Emotional Contagion', *Current Directions in Psychological Science* 2, no. 3 (1993): 96.

89 **'Stimmungsübertragung':** Christian Keysers et al., 'Emotional Contagion and Prosocial Behaviour in Rodents', *Trends in Cognitive Sciences* 26, no. 8 (August 2022): 689.

89 **women are more given to emotional contagion:** Ian Tucker, 'The Five: Emotional Contagion', *The Guardian,* 24 January 2021.

89 **some of the first documented copycat suicides:** David P Phillips, 'The Influence of Suggestion on Suicide: Substantive and Theoretical Implications of the Werther Effect', *American Sociological Review* 39, no. 3 (1974): 340–54.

90 **Suicide rates increased by 28.9 per cent:** Jeffrey A Bridge et al., 'Association Between the Release of Netflix's *13 Reasons Why* and Suicide Rates in the United States: An Interrupted Time Series Analysis', *Journal of the American Academy of Child and Adolescent Psychiatry* 59, no. 2 (2020).

90 **'TikTok Tics':** Azeen Ghorayshi, 'How Teens Recovered from the "TikTok Tics",' *The New York Times,* 13 February 2023.

90 **Heavier users of TikTok were found to be prone:** Haltigan, 'Social Media as an Incubator of Personality and Behavioural Psychopathology', 3.

91 **Indeed, self-diagnosis became the rule:** Sarah Armstrong et al., 'Self-Diagnosis in the Age of Social Media: A Pilot Study of Youth Entering Mental Health Treatment for Mood and Anxiety Disorders', *Acta Psychologica* 256 (June 2025): 1–9.

92 **the less likely they are to feel confident:** Ruling Our eXperiences (ROX), *The Girls' Index™ 2023: The State of Girls' Mental Health and Self-Confidence,* 7.

92 **the more likely they are to be depressed:** Jean Twenge, 'The impact of smartphones, social media, and school laptops on youth mental health and academic performance', Testimony before US Congress, 15 January 2026.

93 **80 per cent of teenage girls said that they compared themselves to others:** Thomas Curran, *The Perfection Trap* (Scribner, 2023), 135.

93 **decreasing social media use dramatically improves:** Jean Twenge, US Congressional testimony, 15 January 2026.

93 **social media use is a more powerful risk factor:** Curran, *Perfection Trap,* 135.

93 **Smartphones have also made the social world:** Freya India, 'Social Media's Not Just Making Girls Depressed, It's Making Us Bitchy Too', *The New Statesman,* 22 July 2022.

93 **Teens will be the first to tell you:** Michelle Faverio et al., 'Teens, Social Media and Mental Health', Pew Research Centre, 22 April 2025.

93 **Image-based sexual abuse (IBSA):** Leora Tanenbaum, *Sexy Selfie Nation: Standing Up for Yourself in Today's Toxic, Sexist Culture* (Bloomsbury, 2024), 107–11.

94 **In 2024, the U.S. Surgeon General:** Cristiano Lima-Strong and Aaron Gregg, 'Surgeon General Calls for Social Media Warning Labels', *The Washington Post,* 17 June 2024.

96 **They are craving a way to sort:** Made of Millions, *Remapping Recovery: How Gen Z's Quest for Better Care Is Pioneering New Paths Forward in Mental Health,* 2024.

97 **Known as 'operationalised criteria':** American Psychiatric Association, *Diagnostic and Statistical Manual of Mental Disorders,* 3rd ed. (APA, 1980).

97 **Whereas the *DSM-I* had listed:** American Psychiatric Association, *Diagnostic and Statistical Manual of Mental Disorders,* 1st ed. (American Psychiatric Association, 1952).

98 **the new metaphors were about *optimising*:** Kriss, *Borderline,* 197.

98 **Cognitive behaviour therapy:** Alexander Kriss, 197.

98 **A patient was not just a patient:** Institute of Medicine (US) Committee on Health Literacy, Lynn Nielsen-Bohlman et al., eds., *Health Literacy: A Prescription to End Confusion* (National Academies Press, 2004).

98 **Insurance companies were happy to pay:** Gregory Erickson, 'Managed Care and the Mental Health Professions: History and Effects on Outpatient Care', *Graduate Student Journal of Psychology* 12 (2010): 5.

98 **'In an earlier era':** Carlat, *Unhinged,* 45, 60.

98 **'The sad thing that I saw with my trainees was':** 'Daniel Siegel on Interpersonal Neurobiology,' video, https://www.psychotherapy.net/video/interpersonal-neurobiology.

100 **the case of major depressive disorder:** Allan V Horwitz and Jerome C Wakefield, *The Loss of Sadness: How Psychiatry Transformed Normal Sorrow into Depressive Disorder* (Oxford University Press, 2007), 72–123.

101 **'Making Up People':** Ian Hacking, 'Making Up People', in *Reconstructing Individualism: Autonomy, Individuality, and the Self in Western Thought,* ed. Thomas C Heller et al. (Stanford University Press, 1986), 222–36.

101 **notion of 'concept creep':** Nick Haslam, 'Concept Creep: Psychology's Expanding Concepts of Harm and Pathology', *Psychological Inquiry* 27, no. 1 (2016): 1–17.

102 **Depression diagnoses exploded:** W M Compton et al., 'Changes in the Prevalence of Major Depression and Comorbid Substance Use Disorders in the United States Between 1991–1992 and 2001–2002', *American Journal of Psychiatry* 163, no. 12 (2006): 2141–47.

102 **'prevalence inflation':** Lucy Foulkes and Jack L Andrews, 'Are Mental Health Awareness Efforts Contributing to the Rise in Reported Mental Health Problems? A Call to Test the Prevalence Inflation Hypothesis', *New Ideas in Psychology* 69 (2023): 2.

102 **According to Foulkes, it follows a typical pattern:** Foulkes and Andrews, 'Are

Mental Health Awareness Efforts Contributing to the Rise in Reported Mental Health Problems?', 1.

102 **Carlat describes a moment where he realised:** Carlat, *Unhinged,* 61.

102 **82 per cent of people with schizophrenia:** Morten Dybdahl Krebs et al., 'Associations Between Patterns in Comorbid Diagnostic Trajectories of Individuals with Schizophrenia and Etiological Factors', *Nature Communications* 12, no. 1 (November 2021): 6617.

102 **80 per cent of patients with depression:** Keming Gao et al., 'Should an Assessment of Axis I Comorbidity Be Included in the Initial Diagnostic Assessment of Mood Disorders? Role of QIDS-16-SR Total Score in Predicting Number of Axis I Comorbidity', *Journal of Affective Disorders* 148, no. 2–3 (June 2013): 256–64.

103 **psychiatric labels have a way of reifying themselves:** Kenneth S Kendler, 'DSM Disorders and Their Criteria: How Should They Inter-Relate?', *Psychological Medicine* 47, no. 12 (2017): 2054–60.

103 **They can change and overlap:** Cliodhna O'Connor et al., 'Diagnostic Trajectories in Child and Adolescent Mental Health Services: Exploring the Prevalence and Patterns of Diagnostic Adjustments in an Electronic Mental Health Case Register', *European Child & Adolescent Psychiatry* 29, no. 8 (2020): 1111–23.

103 **this is especially true in girls:** E Jane Costello et al., 'Prevalence and Development of Psychiatric Disorders in Childhood and Adolescence', *Archives of General Psychiatry* 60, no. 8 (August 2003): 837–44.

103 **Sarah Fay describes her Kafkaesque journey:** Sarah Fay, *Pathological: The True Story of Six Misdiagnoses* (HarperOne, 2022), 2.

103 **'A finger pointing at the moon':** Martyn Pickersgill, 'Stalling or Oiling the Engines of Diagnosis? Shifting Perspectives on the DSM and Categorical Diagnosis in Psychiatry', *Sociology of Health & Illness* 46, S1 (2024): 140.

103 **also known as 'neuroessentialism':** William Schultz, 'Neuroessentialism: Theoretical and Clinical Considerations', *Journal of Humanistic Psychology* 58, no. 6 (2018): 607–39.

104 **Those who hold anxiety disorders as central:** Isaac Ahuvia et al., 'Anxiety Identity Centrality Is Associated with Avoidant Coping in Anxious Adults', *Journal of Social and Clinical Psychology* 44, no. 1 (February 2025): 1–15.

104 **People with depression have been shown to feel:** Joshua J Kemp et al., 'Effects of a Chemical Imbalance Causal Explanation on Individuals' Perceptions of Their Depressive Symptoms', *Behaviour Research and Therapy* 56 (May 2014): 47–52.

104 **when pathological gambling was made:** Natasha Dow Schüll, *Addiction by Design: Machine Gambling in Las Vegas* (Princeton University Press, 2012), 15.

Chapter 4:
Anxiety Girlies

109 **'Indeed, it is not at all unusual for a girl to say to me':** Lisa Damour, *Under Pressure: Confronting the Epidemic of Stress and Anxiety in Girls* (Ballantine, 2019), 27.

109 **'It just seems like, you agree to have a certain personality or something':** *My So-*

Called-Life, Season 1, Episode 1, 'Pilot', directed by Scott Winant, produced by Bedford Falls Productions and ABC Productions, aired 25 August 1994.

110 **clinical diagnoses of anxiety have increased:** Thea L Anderson et al., 'Contributing Factors to the Rise in Adolescent Anxiety and Associated Mental Health Disorders: A Narrative Review of Current Literature', *Journal of Child and Adolescent Psychiatric Nursing* 38, no. 1 (December 2024).

110 **girls experience higher rates of anxiety:** Chad Sylvester and Joan Luby, 'Gender Differences in the Neurobiology of Childhood Anxiety: The Need for a Developmental Perspective', *American Journal of Psychiatry* 181, no. 4 (April 2024): 262–64.

111 **the 'post-wounded voice, a stance of numbness':** Leslie Jamison, *The Empathy Exams* (Graywolf Press, 2014), 213.

112 **One in five people:** Luis-Joaquin Garcia-Lopez et al., 'Behavioural Inhibition in Childhood as a Risk Factor for Development of Social Anxiety Disorder: A Longitudinal Study', *International Journal of Environmental Research and Public Health* 17, no. 11 (June 2020): 3941.

112 **Parental behaviour makes a big difference:** Nathan A Fox et al., 'Annual Research Review: Developmental Pathways Linking Early Behavioural Inhibition to Later Anxiety', *Journal of Child Psychology and Psychiatry* 64, no. 4 (April 2023): 537–61.

112 **'highly sensitive person (HSP)':** 'Understanding the Highly Sensitive Person', interview with Elaine Aron, Psychwire, https://psychwire.com/free-resources/q-and-a/1t3wsdt/understanding-the-highly-sensitive-person.

112 **Anxiety is a physical experience:** Allan Abbass, *Reaching Through Resistance* (Seven Leaves Press, 2015), 11–23.

114 **leading individuals to believe erroneously:** Allan V Horwitz and Jerome C Wakefield, *All We Have to Fear: Psychiatry's Transformation of Natural Anxieties into Mental Disorders* (Oxford University Press, 2012).

114 **anxiety diagnoses have been generating more requests:** Rose Horowitch, 'Accommodation Nation', *The Atlantic,* 2 December 2025.

120 **'The fact that literally anyone':** Nana Baah, 'We're All Girlies Online . . . It's Not That Deep', *Refinery29,* June 16, 2022.

121 **Parents, especially fathers:** Daniel Freeman and Jason Freeman, *The Stressed Sex* (Oxford University Press, 2012), 123.

121 **the 'Year of the Girl' (2023):** Jess Bacon, '2023: The Year of the Girl', *Dazed,* 12 December 2023.

124 **During adolescence, the amygdala:** Frances E Jensen with Amy Ellis Nutt, *The Teenage Brain: A Neuroscientist's Survival Guide to Raising Adolescents and Young Adults* (Harper, 2015), 232.

124 **The onslaught of oestrogen:** Daniel Freeman and Jason Freeman, *The Stressed Sex* (Oxford University Press, 2013), 100–101.

124 **which may explain why the HPA axis:** Jensen, *Teenage Brain,* 173.

125 **the rational, 'thinking' parts:** Jensen, *Teenage Brain,* 202.

125 **'They kind of get together':** Jack Andrews, quoted in Ellen Barry, 'Are We Talking Too Much About Mental Health?', *The New York Times,* 6 May 2024.

126 **Neurotic people are inclined:** 'What It Means to Be "Neurotic",' *Talkspace,* 23 March 2019.

126 **transform 'neurotic misery into common unhappiness':** Josef Breuer and Sigmund Freud, *Studies on Hysteria,* trans. and ed. James Strachey, in *The Standard Edition of the Complete Psychological Works of Sigmund Freud,* vol. 2 (Hogarth Press, 1955).

126 **It's one of two major personality traits:** Yanna J Weisberg et al., 'Gender Differences in Personality Across the Ten Aspects of the Big Five', *Frontiers in Psychology* 2 (August 2011), no. 178.

126 **what 'neurotic' meant was operationalised:** Otto Kernberg, 'Borderline Personality Disorder and Borderline Personality Organisation: Psychopathology and Psychotherapy', in *Handbook of Personality Disorders: Theory and Practice,* ed. JJ Magnavita (Wiley, 2004), 92–119.

127 **'Strong minds discuss ideas':** https://quoteinvestigator.com/2014/11/18/great-minds/.

127 **a vital system of social connection:** Phyllis Chesler, *Women and Madness* (Palgrave, 1972), 322.

127 **Girls attach more importance:** Freeman and Freeman, *Stressed Sex,* 113–14.

127 **Girls are stronger in empathy:** Freeman and Freeman, *Stressed Sex,* 114.

127 **'girls discuss while boys distract':** Lisa Damour, *Untangled: Guiding Teenage Girls Through the Seven Transitions into Adulthood* (Ballantine, 2016), 102.

127 **girls who co-ruminate have closer friendships:** Amanda J Rose et al., 'Prospective Associations of Co-Rumination with Friendship and Emotional Adjustment', *Developmental Psychology* 43, no. 4 (2007): 1019–31.

127 **Their brains show heightened reactivity:** Jensen, *Teenage Brain,* 202–3.

127 **Anxiety-ridden as it may be:** Sarah-Jayne Blakemore, *Inventing Ourselves: The Secret Life of the Teenage Brain* (PublicAffairs, 2018), 24–36.

128 **trigger a 'tend and befriend' response:** Freeman and Freeman, *Stressed Sex,* 104.

Chapter 5: Too Much

132 **'NELL: that's funny':** Kimberly Belflower, *John Proctor Is the Villain* (Dramatists Play Service, 2024), 65.

134 **'much too much to handle':** 'CANCELLED!', Taylor Swift, *The Life of a Showgirl,* Republic Records, 2025.

138 **'Is Your Team Struggling?':** Jarret Jackson, 'Is Your Team Struggling? Their Dysregulation May Impact Your Performance', *Forbes,* 29 September 2021. From https://www.thecut.com/article/mental-health-managing-dysregulated-nervous-system-essay.html

138 **'Signs You Need to Rebalance Your Nervous System':** *Vogue*, 5 August 2025, https://www.vogue.com/article/dysregulated-nervous-system.

138 **'Oversensitive and Overreactive?':** *Guardian*, 4 March 2024, https://www.theguardian.com/wellness/2024/mar/04/what-is-nervous-system-dysregulation.

139 **'weird behaviours you think are normal':** https://www.tiktok.com/@theworkoutwitch/video/7447510837469646122.

139 **Gen Z's top goal in life:** Rachel Janfaza, 'Welcome to the Chaos, Class of 2025', *The Up and Up,* 10 June 2025.

141 **'rejection-sensitive dysphoria (RSD)':** William Dodson, 'New Insights into Rejection Sensitive Dysphoria', *ADDitude,* 9 May 2025.

142 **Brains are 'anticipation machines':** Dan Siegel, *Mindsight* (Bantam, 2011).

143 **Doctors and laypeople alike:** Alexander Thomas and Stella Chess, *Temperament and Development* (Brunner/Mazel, 1977).

143 **'goodness of fit':** Thomas and Chess, *Temperament and Development.*

145 **Too Fat, Too Slutty, Too Loud:** Anne Helen Petersen, *Too Fat, Too Slutty, Too Loud: The Rise and Reign of the Unruly Woman* (Plume, 2017).

145 **'A weeping woman is a monster':** Rachel Vorona Cote, *Too Much: How Victorian Constraints Still Bind Women Today* (Grand Central Publishing, 2020), 1.

145 **'mental illness is too muchness with a diagnosis':** Cote, *Too Much,* 139.

146 **something deeper and less sympathetic:** 'The Truth About Being "Too Much" Trope, Explained', *The Take,* https://www.youtube.com/watch?v=t_YGF9U_bjw.

147 **After puberty, the stakes of excess:** Rachel Aroesti, 'How Messy Millennial Woman Became TV's Most Tedious Trope', *The Guardian,* 9 June 2022.

147 **Whether it's the disintegration of a pop star:** Sophie Gilbert, *Girl on Girl: How Pop Culture Turned a Generation of Women Against Themselves* (Penguin, 2025), 187–202.

147 **'a whore', 'a bore':** Kacey Musgraves, 'Follow Your Arrow', *Same Trailer Different Park,* produced by Kacey Musgraves, Luke Laird and Shane McAnally, Mercury Nashville, 2013, streaming audio.

147 **'scream[s] inside to deal with it':** Olivia Rodrigo, 'all-american bitch', *GUTS,* Geffen Records, 2023, streaming audio.

147 **'rude', 'a ho':** Megan Thee Stallion, 'Anxiety', *Traumazine,* Go Grizzly, 1501 Certified Entertainment / 300 Entertainment, 2022, streaming audio.

148 **nearly 10 per cent of human beings:** Jana Volkert et al., 'Prevalence of Personality Disorders in the General Adult Population in Western Countries: Systematic Review and Meta-Analysis', *British Journal of Psychiatry* 213, no. 6 (December 2018): 709–15.

148 **almost *one quarter* of psychiatric outpatients:** Falk Leichsenring et al., 'Borderline Personality Disorder: A Comprehensive Review of Diagnosis and Clinical Presentation, Etiology, Treatment, and Current Controversies', *World Psychiatry* 23, no. 1 (January 2024): 4–25.

148 **Criteria include impulsivity:** American Psychiatric Association, *Diagnostic and Statistical Manual of Mental Disorders,* 5th ed. (APA, 2013).

148 **they often receive worse medical care:** Kellyann M Navarre, '"You Sure She's Not Making This Up?" : A Qualitative Investigation of Stigma Towards Adults with

Borderline Personality Disorder in Physical Healthcare Settings', *Personality and Mental Health* 19, no. 1 (November 2024).

148 **almost four times more likely:** Paola Bozzatello et al., 'Gender Differences in Borderline Personality Disorder: A Narrative Review', *Frontiers in Psychiatry* 15 (January 2024).

148 **Men who display similar features:** Dawn M Johnson et al., 'Gender Differences in Borderline Personality Disorder: Findings from the Collaborative Longitudinal Personality Disorders Study', *Comprehensive Psychiatry* 44 (July–August 2003): 284–92.

149 **this modality serves a young, primarily female:** Peggilee Wupperman and Emily Edwards, 'Dialectical Behaviour Therapy and Gender', in *The SAGE Encyclopedia of Psychology and Gender,* ed. Shannon E Davis and Jeffrey J Arnett (SAGE, 2017), 334–36.

150 **it descends from the ancient Greek philosophy:** Derek Beres, 'The Ancient Roots of Psychotherapy Matter Now', https://bigthink.com/neuropsych/cbt-stoicism/.

151 **Skills therapies function as a kind of 'soft police':** Phyllis Chesler, *Women and Madness* (Palgrave, 1972), quoting Dr Nzinga Shaka Zula, 'Therapists are often the soft police of the dominant culture', 24.

153 **complex post-traumatic stress disorder (c-PTSD) describes:** World Health Organisation, '6B41 Complex Post-Traumatic Stress Disorder', *International Classification of Diseases, Eleventh Revision (ICD-11)* (WHO, 2024).

153 **Judith Herman identified c-PTSD:** Judith Lewis Herman, *Trauma and Recovery: The Aftermath of Violence – from Domestic Abuse to Political Terror* (Basic Books, 1992), 119–22.

154 **the 'only acceptable diagnosis for women clients':** Dana Becker, quoted in Paula J Caplan and Lisa Cosgrove, eds., *Bias in Psychiatric Diagnosis* (Jason Aronson, 2004), 209.

Chapter 6: Not Enough

156 **'You're too much, and not enough':** Maggie Kang and Chris Appelhans, creators, *K-Pop Demon Hunters,* Netflix, 2025.

156 **'Perfectionism is internalised oppression':** Gloria Steinem, in Ellen Vora, *The Anatomy of Anxiety* (Harper Wave, 2022), 234.

159 **'Socially prescribed perfectionism':** Liv Sand et al., 'Perfectionism in Adolescence: Associations with Gender, Age, and Socioeconomic Status in a Norwegian Sample', *Frontiers in Public Health* 9, no. 688811 (August 2021).

159 **About fifteen years ago, the United Kingdom started to see:** Thomas Curran, *The Perfection Trap* (Scribner, 2023), 82.

160 **79 per cent of girls report they are going to 'explode':** Ruling Our eXperiences (ROX), *The Girls' Index™ 2023: The State of Girls' Mental Health and Self-Confidence,* 7.

160 **the pressure to manage your physical appearance:** Racheli Miller, 'Body Image Pressure on Women and How to Overcome It', The Compassion Practice, 24 November 2024, https://compassionify.com/body-image-pressure-on-women/.

160 **that makes physical activity pretty unappealing:** Jessica Harvey et al., '"I Feel Proper Self-Conscious All the Time" : A Qualitative Study of Adolescent Girls' Views of Menstruation and Physical Activity', *Wellcome Open Research* 5, no. 279 (November 2020).

160 **you sleep less than the boys your age:** Rachel Simmons, *Enough as She Is: How to Help Girls Move Beyond Impossible Standards of Success to Live Healthy, Happy, and Fulfilling Lives* (HarperCollins, 2018), 147.

160 **more stressed than the boys about school – especially tests:** Lisa Damour, *Untangled: Guiding Teenage Girls Through the Seven Transitions into Adulthood* (Ballantine, 2016), 180.

161 **your generation prizes effortless perfection:** Curran, *Perfection Trap,* 157.

161 **Biologically, your brain is focused:** Roberta A Schriber and Amanda E Guyer, 'Adolescent Neurobiological Susceptibility to Social Context', *Developmental Cognitive Neuroscience* 19 (June 2016): 1–18.

161 **'role overload':** Simmons, *Enough as She Is,* 146–51.

161 **498th time today:** Erin Walsh, 'New Report: A Week in the Life of Kids and Their Phones', Spark & Stitch Institute, 29 September 2024.

162 **Feeling threatened is a sign:** Simmons, *Enough as She Is,* 152–53.

162 **'pressure to fit into specific roles or stereotypes':** Ruling Our eXperiences, *Girls' Index™ 2023,* 24.

163 **vague thoughts of suicide:** Curran, *Perfection Trap,* 89.

163 **you're used to making 'internal attributions':** Simmons, *Enough as She Is,* 100–101.

163 **another thing for tests is to get aggressive:** Damour, *Untangled,* 184.

165 **'Would it be okay for me to talk to that part?':** Richard C Schwartz, *No Bad Parts* (Sounds True, 2021).

175 ***Drama of the Gifted Child*:** Alice Miller, *The Drama of the Gifted Child* (Basic Books, 1983).

177 **'Everything is about sex except sex':** Lyle Rosnick, MD, personal communication.

178 **'teenagers being biologically programmed':** Hannah K Lennarz et al., 'Jealousy in Adolescents' Daily Lives: How Does It Relate to Interpersonal Context and Well-Being?', *Journal of Adolescence* 54 (2017): 18–31.

182 **She can use it to connect with people and entities:** Simmons, *Enough as She Is,* 45.

182 **'Good-Enough Mother':** D W Winnicott, 'Transitional Objects and Transitional Phenomena – a Study of the First Not-Me Possession', *International Journal of Psycho-Analysis* 34 (1953): 89–97.

183 **the antidote to envy, to feeling insufficient, is gratitude:** Melanie Klein, *Envy and Gratitude* (Hogarth Press, 1957).

183 **Gratitude journals do help people feel better:** Robert A Emmons and Michael E McCullough, 'Counting Blessings Versus Burdens: An Experimental Investigation

of Gratitude and Subjective Well-Being in Daily Life', *Journal of Personality and Social Psychology* 84, no. 2 (2003): 377–89.

Chapter 7: The Curious Case of the Bitch and the Narcissist

184 **'These girls aren't wounded so much as post-wounded':** Leslie Jamison, *The Empathy Exams* (Graywolf Press, 2014), 198–99.

184 **'Sometimes being a bitch is all a woman has to hang on to':** *Dolores Claiborne*, directed by Taylor Hackford, Columbia Pictures, 1995.

188 **a Ritalin-addled manifesto:** Elizabeth Wurtzel, *Bitch: In Praise of Difficult Women* (Anchor Books, 1998).

189 **the 'dark triad' of narcissism:** Emanuel Jauk et al., 'How Alluring Are Dark Personalities? The Dark Triad and Attractiveness in Speed Dating', *European Journal of Personality* 30, no. 2 (January 2016): 125–38.

190 **As depicted in the bestseller:** Sherry Argov, *Why Men Love Bitches: From Doormat to Dreamgirl – a Woman's Guide to Holding Her Own in a Relationship* (Adams Media, 2002).

190 **Girls who display high levels:** Madeline Levine, *The Price of Privilege: How Parental Pressure and Material Advantage Are Creating a Generation of Disconnected and Unhappy Kids* (HarperCollins, 2006), 23.

190 **Bitchy behaviour – defined as social aggression:** Freya India, 'Social Media's Not Just Making Girls Depressed, It's Making Us Bitchy Too', *The New Statesman,* 22 July 2022.

190 **Half of girls say they don't like school:** Ruling Our eXperiences (ROX), *The Girls' Index™ 2023: The State of Girls' Mental Health and Self-Confidence.*

190 **Bitchy behaviour still makes trouble:** Susan Moeller, 'Mean Girls Are Oh-So-Real at Any Age. Here's How to Deal', *American Association of Retired Persons (AARP),* 6 February, 2025.

192 **the 'dissociative pout':** Rayne Fisher-Quann, 'The Cult of the Dissociative Pout', *i-D,* 4 May 2022.

195 **Most menstruating women experience:** Nadia Kancheva Landolt and Krasimir Ivanov, 'Short Report: Cognitive Behavioural Therapy – a Primary Mode for Premenstrual Syndrome Management: Systematic Literature Review', *Psychology, Health & Medicine* 26, no. 10 (August 2020): 1282–93.

195 **about 15 per cent have clinically significant distress:** Sara Carlini et al., 'Management of Premenstrual Dysphoric Disorder: A Scoping Review', *Focus: The Journal of Lifelong Learning in Psychiatry* 22, no. 1 (January 2024).

195 **there is some disagreement among experts:** Kancheva Landolt and Ivanov, 'Primary Mode for Premenstrual Syndrome Management'.

195 **This may serve an evolutionary function:** Julie Holland, *Moody Bitches* (Penguin, 2015), 25–39.

195 **Those who take this position have advocated:** Jane M Ussher and Janette Perz, 'PMS

as a Process of Negotiation: Women's Experience and Management of Premenstrual Distress', *Psychology & Health* 28, no. 8 (January 2013): 909–27.

196 **like *really* feel it, *physically*:** Allan Abbass, *Reaching Through Resistance* (Seven Leaves Press, 2015), 41–43.

199 **'unconditional positive regard':** Carl Rogers, 'The necessary and sufficient conditions of therapeutic personality change', *Journal of Consulting Psychology* 21, no. 2 (1957): 95–103.

Chapter 8: *Slay*-DHD

204 **'"Cruel optimism" . . . when you take a really big problem':** Johann Hari, *Stolen Focus: Why You Can't Pay Attention – and How to Think Deeply Again* (Crown, 2022), 150.

204 **'Humans come in so many different flavours':** Jenara Nerenberg, *Divergent Mind: Thriving in a World That Wasn't Designed for You* (HarperOne, 2020), 208.

205 **ADHD prescriptions increased by 344 per cent:** Kayla N Anderson et al., 'Attention-Deficit/Hyperactivity Disorder Medication Prescription Claims Among Privately Insured Women Aged 15–44 Years – United States, 2003–2015', *Morbidity and Mortality Weekly Report* 67, no. 2 (January 2018): 66–70.

205 **incidence of the diagnosis in young women nearly doubled:** Jim Russell et al., 'Number of ADHD Patients Rising, Especially Among Women', *Epic Research,* 30 March 2023.

205 **one in four young adults suspects:** Ohio State University Wexner Medical Centre, 'Survey Finds 25% of Adults Suspect They Have Undiagnosed ADHD', 14 October 2024.

205 **the rise of for-profit telehealth platforms:** US Department of Justice, 'Founder/CEO and Clinical President of Digital Health Company Convicted in $100M Adderall Distribution and Health Care Fraud Scheme', 19 November 2025.

206 **A 2021 survey showed roughly 90 per cent:** Samuel R Chamberlain et al., 'Screening for Adult ADHD Using Brief Rating Tools: What Can We Conclude from a Positive Screen? Some Caveats', *Comprehensive Psychiatry* 106 (February 2021).

206 **A video on #MentalHealth receives on average:** Corey H Basch et al., 'Deconstructing TikTok Videos on Mental Health: Cross-Sectional, Descriptive Content Analysis', *Journal of Medical Internet Research* 6, no. 5 (May 2022).

206 **52 per cent of the ADHD content:** Yeung et al., 'TikTok and Attention-Deficit/Hyperactivity Disorder', 901.

206 **it has earned its own moniker: 'cyberchondria':** Brittany M Mathes et al., 'Cyberchondria: Overlap with Health Anxiety and Unique Relations with Impairment, Quality of Life, and Service Utilization', *Psychiatry Research* 261 (March 2018): 20411.

206 **In 2023, almost four million people age twelve:** Centres for Disease Control, Overdose Prevention, 'Stimulants', 17 July, 2025.

206 **take a toll on self-esteem:** Luise Kazda et al., 'Association of Attention-Deficit/Hyperactivity Disorder Diagnosis with Adolescent Quality of Life', *JAMA Network Open* 5, no. 10 (October 2022).

206 **adolescents experience an improvement:** Margaret H Sibley et al., 'Characteristics and Predictors of Fluctuating Attention-Deficit/Hyperactivity Disorder in the Multimodal Treatment of ADHD (MTA) Study', *Journal of Clinical Psychiatry* 85, no. 4 (2024). Cited in Paul Tough, 'Rethinking ADHD', *The New York Times Magazine,* 20 April 2025.

211 **Starting in the 1700s, children:** George Still, 'Some Abnormal Psychical Conditions in Children', *The Lancet* 159, no. 4103 (1902): 1077–82.

212 **the hardly more appealing 'minimal brain damage':** Alan Schwarz, *ADHD Nation: Children, Doctors, Big Pharma, and the Making of an American Epidemic* (Scribner, 2016), 28.

212 **'Ritalin: helps "the problem child" become lovable again':** CIBA Pharmaceutical Company advertisement, *Journal of the American Medical Association* 197, no. 11 (1966), and reprinted in various journals through the 1970s; quoted in Schwarz, *ADHD Nation,* 121.

212 **The condition became known as 'attention deficit disorder':** American Psychiatric Association, *Diagnostic and Statistical Manual of Mental Disorders,* 3rd ed. (APA, 1980).

212 **the attention and hyperactivity components:** American Psychiatric Association, *Diagnostic and Statistical Manual of Mental Disorders,* 4th ed. (APA, 1994).

212 **ADHD was recognised as a disability:** Andrea Tarantella, 'Is ADHD a Disability? Unraveling Facts and Myths', ADHDAdvisor.org, 4 October 2023.

213 **overlooked in girls:** Nicole Crawford, 'ADHD: A Women's Issue', *Monitor on Psychology* 34, no. 2 (February 2003): 28.

213 **those women who had displayed symptoms:** Darby E Attoe and Emma A Climie, 'Miss. Diagnosis: A Systematic Review of ADHD in Adult Women', *Journal of Attention Disorders* 27, no. 7 (March 2023): 645–57.

214 **diagnosis conversations between doctors and patients:** Rose McCabe, 'When Patients and Clinician (Dis)agree About the Nature of the Problem: The Role of Displays of Shared Understanding in Acceptance of Treatment', *Social Science & Medicine* 290 (December 2021).

215 **On the YouTube channel *How to ADHD*:** Jessica McCabe, *How to ADHD,* YouTube, 2017–present, youtube.com/c/HowtoADHD.

215 **11.4 billion views as of 2022:** https://chadd.org/attention-article/adhd-on-tiktok/.

217 **That some people are born more like hunters:** Thom Hartmann, *ADHD: A Hunter in a Farmer's World* (Healing Arts Press, 2019).

226 **'the concept of neurocosmopolitanism':** Nick Walker and Dora M Raymaker, 'Towards a Neuroqueer Future: An Interview with Nick Walker', *Autism in Adulthood* 3, no. 1 (March 2021): 5–10.

226 **'berry-collecting video game':** David L Barack et al., 'Attention Deficits Linked with Proclivity to Explore While Foraging', *Proceedings: Biological Sciences* 291, no. 2017 (February 2024).

227 **Habib Davanloo famously said:** John Rathauser, personal communication.

229 **'ADHD is less diagnosed in other countries':** Beatriz Macdonald et al., 'Cross-Country Differences in Parental Reporting of Symptoms of ADHD', *Journal of Cross-Cultural Psychology* 50, no. 6 (2020): 806-824.

231 **these 'symptom pools' evolve and change:** Edward Shorter, *From Paralysis to Fatigue: A History of Psychosomatic Illness in the Modern Era* (Free Press, 1993).

Chapter 9: Toxic Etc.

233 **'There are stories that save us':** Rachel Aviv, *Strangers to Ourselves: Unsettled Minds and the Stories That Make Us* (Farrar, Straus and Giroux, 2022), 24.

233 **'The limits of my language':** Ludwig Wittgenstein, *Tractatus Logico-Philosophicus,* trans. CK Ogden (Kegan Paul, 1922), 149.

233 **In response to Taylor Swift posting:** Jessica Bennett, 'OMG! The Hyperbole of Internet-Speak?', *The New York Times,* 28 November 2015.

237 **how the word 'boundaries' has been deployed:** Emma Goldberg, 'Is Today's Self-Help Teaching Everyone to Be a Jerk?', *The New York Times,* 26 August 2025.

238 **The term derives originally from the Greek 'toxicon':** John Ayto, *Dictionary of Word Origins* (Arcade, 2011), 538.

239 **'toxic' was Oxford Dictionaries' International Word of the Year:** Oxford Languages, 'Word of the Year 2018: Toxic', Oxford University Press, November 2018.

239 **If someone is emotionally difficult:** Anna Russell, 'Why So Many People Are Going "No Contact" with Their Parents', *The New Yorker,* 30 August 2024.

240 **These positions, known together as the 'Drama Triangle':** Stephen B Karpman, 'Fairy Tales and Script Drama Analysis', *Transactional Analysis Bulletin* 7, no. 26 (1968): 39–43.

241 **Domestic violence was not identified:** Connections for Abused Women and Their Children, 'Things to Know About the History of the Domestic Violence Movement', cawc.org, 7 September 2023.

242 **The frequency and long-lasting harms of child sexual abuse:** David Corwin and Brooks Keshin, 'Child Sexual Abuse – Discovery, Professionalization, and Institutionalization: 40 Years of Struggle in the USA', American Professional Society on the Abuse of Children. https://apsac.org/wp-content/uploads/2023/06/CSA-40-yrs-in-US-Corwin-Keeshin-11-11.pdf, 6–19; John E. B. Myers, 'A Short History of Child Protection in America', *Family Law Quarterly* 42, no. 3 (2008): 449-463.

242 **'Abuse is when someone causes us harm or distress':** Somerset Safeguarding Adults Board, 'What Is Abuse?', somersetsafeguardingadults.org.uk.

246 **particularly sensitive to language:** A Bazan et al., 'Language as the Source of Human Unconscious Processes', *Evolution and Cognition* 8, no. 2 (2002).

246 **the Sapir–Whorf hypothesis:** Manvir Singh, 'How Much Does Our Language Shape Our Thinking?', *The New Yorker,* 30 December 2024.

246 **Greek and Russian speakers are quicker:** Singh, 'How Much Does Our Language Shape Our Thinking?', and *Britannica,* 'Whorfian Hypothesis', https://www.britannica.com/science/Whorfian-hypothesis.

246 **One's ability to detect odours:** Asifa Majid, 'Human Olfaction at the Intersection of Language, Culture, and Biology', *Trends in Cognitive Sciences* 25, no. 2 (2021): 116–17.

246 **writing – the act of selecting language:** Carl Bereiter and Marlene Scardamalia, *The Psychology of Written Composition* (Lawrence Erlbaum, 1987).

246 **'Self-imposed solitude':** Derek Thompson, 'The Anti-Social Century', *The Atlantic,* 8 January 2025.

247 **Jean Twenge has described:** Jean Twenge, *Generations* (Atria, 2023).

247 **young people are flaking out:** Jedidajah Otte, ' "People Feel They Don't Owe Anyone Anything" : The Rise in "Flaking" Out of Social Plans', *The Guardian,* 7 January 2025.

247 **social isolation is poison:** J Christiansen et al., 'Associations of Loneliness and Social Isolation with Physical and Mental Health Among Adolescents and Young Adults', *Perspectives in Public Health* 141, no. 4 (July 2021): 226–36.

247 **Social contact has immediate benefits:** Thompson, 'The Anti-Social Century'.

Chapter 10: People-Pleaser

248 **'Some women get erased a little at a time':** Rebecca Solnit, *Men Explain Things to Me* (Haymarket Books, 2014), 4.

248 **'[American females] have been raised to believe':** Chimamanda Ngozi Adichie, *We Should All Be Feminists* (Anchor Books, 2012), 23–24.

250 **It has to be an *internal* problem:** Allan Abbass, *Reaching Through Resistance* (Seven Leaves Press, 2015), 47.

251 **Books on the topic:** Meg Josephson, *Are You Mad at Me: How to Stop Focusing on What Others Think and Start Living for You* (Gallery Books, 2025).

255 **'Ain't no sense worryin'':** Mickey Rivers and Michael DeMarco, *Ain't No Sense Worryin': The Wit and Wisdom of 'Mick the Quick' Rivers* (Sportspub, 2003), 3.

256 **Serenity Prayer, written by theologian Reinhold Niebuhr:** First published in 1943; widely circulated version adopted by Alcoholics Anonymous, c. 1944.

256 **therapists think of them as 'protectors':** Richard C Schwartz, *No Bad Parts* (Sounds True, 2021), 7–26.

260 **teenage girls are about a year and a half ahead:** Frances E Jensen with Amy Ellis Nutt, *The Teenage Brain: A Neuroscientist's Survival Guide to Raising Adolescents and Young Adults* (Harper, 2015), 228.

260 **girls from a young age:** Simon Baron-Cohen, *The Essential Difference: Male and Female Brains and the Truth About Autism* (Basic Books, 2003).

260 **brains contain both male and female elements:** Gina Rippon, *The Gendered Brain: The New Neuroscience That Shatters the Myth of the Female Brain* (Bodley Head, 2019).

Chapter 11: Three Anxious Mothers (and One Confused Dad)

267 **'The business of raising children':** Lisa Appignanesi, *Mad, Bad and Sad: A History of Women and the Mind Doctors from 1800 to the Present* (Norton, 2008), 284.

267 **'"Real" women all are mothers':** Phyllis Chesler, *Women and Madness* (Palgrave, 1972), 134.

270 **Authorities from St Augustine:** Michael Fitzgerald, 'The History of Blaming the Mother for Psychopathology in Psychiatry', Trinity College, academia.edu.

270 **Longitudinal studies have shown that infant temperament:** Ruth Feldman, 'The Relational Basis of Adolescent Adjustment: Trajectories of Mother-Child Interactive Behaviours from Infancy to Adolescence Shape Adolescents' Adaptation', *Attachment & Human Development* 12, no. 1–2 (2010): 173–92.

270 **'inflict a never-healing wound':** John B Watson, *Psychological Care of Infant and Child* (W. W. Norton, 1928), quoted in Oliver Burkeman, 'The Diabolical Genius of the Baby Advice Industry', *The Guardian,* 16 January 2018.

271 **the 'refrigerator mother':** Mitzi Waltz, 'Mothers and Autism: The Evolution of a Discourse of Blame', *American Medical Association Journal of Ethics* 17, no. 4 (April 2015): 353–58.

271 **Philip Wylie's misogynistic treatise:** Philip Wylie, *Generation of Vipers* (Farrar & Rinehart, 1942), 184–203.

271 **Edward Strecker, who was president:** Edward A Strecker, *Their Mothers' Sons: The Psychiatrist Examines an American Problem* (JB Lippincott, 1946).

271 **'the mother's *personality* acts as':** René A Spitz, 'The Psychogenic Diseases in Infancy: An Attempt at Their Etiologic Classification', *The Psychoanalytic Study of the Child* 6, no. 1 (1951): 257.

271 **major clinical journals had held mothers accountable:** Paula J Caplan and Ian Hall-McCorquodale, 'Mother-Blaming in Major Clinical Journals', *American Journal of Orthopsychiatry* 55, no. 3 (July 1985): 345–53.

271 **working moms violated the natural order:** Elisabeth Badinter, *The Conflict: How Modern Motherhood Undermines the Status of Women* (Metropolitan Books, 2012).

272 **Diana Baumrind laid out three parenting 'styles':** Diana Baumrind, 'Effects of Authoritative Parental Control on Child Behaviour', *Child Development* 37, no. 4 (1966): 887–907.

272 **The world seemed to have become a more dangerous place:** Jonathan Haidt, *The Anxious Generation* (Penguin Press, 2024), 85–91.

272 **paediatricians promoted 'attachment parenting':** William Sears and Martha Sears, *The Attachment Parenting Book: A Commonsense Guide to Understanding and Nurturing Your Baby* (Little, Brown, 2001).

272 **The 1990s were dubbed 'the Decade of the Brain':** George HW Bush, Presidential Proclamation 6158, 'Decade of the Brain, 1990–1999', 17 July 1990.

273 **or pushed her child fiercely, like a tiger:** Amy Chua, *Battle Hymn of the Tiger Mother* (Penguin Press, 2011).

273 **'lawnmower', 'snowplough' and 'bulldozer' parents:** Claire Cain Miller and Jonah Engel Bromwich, 'How Parents Are Robbing Their Children of Adulthood', *The New York Times,* 16 March 2019.

273 **Phones added a new layer of concern:** Haidt, *Anxious Generation,* 95–110.

273 **Pamela Druckerman whispered a secret:** Pamela Druckerman, *Bringing Up Bébé: One American Mother Discovers the Wisdom of French Parenting* (Penguin Press, 2012).

273 **'Free-Range' parenting:** Lenore Skenazy, *Free-Range Kids: How to Raise Safe, Self-Reliant Children (Without Going Nuts with Worry)* (Jossey-Bass, 2009; updated ed. 2010).

273 **the gentle parenting movement:** Sarah Ockwell-Smith, *The Gentle Parenting Book: How to Raise Calmer, Happier Children from Birth to Seven* (Piatkus, 2015).

273 **Abigail Shrier calls the focus:** Abigail Shrier, *Bad Therapy: Why the Kids Aren't Growing Up* (Sentinel, 2024), 169.

274 **She's an 'intensive parent':** Caitlyn Collins, interview by Ezra Klein, 'The Deep Conflict Between Our Work and Parenting Ideals', *The Ezra Klein Show, The New York Times,* 22 March 2024.

277 **In October 2024, the US Surgeon General issued a warning:** US Surgeon General Vivek Murthy, *Parents Under Pressure: The US Surgeon General's Advisory on the Mental Health & Well-Being of Parents* (US Department of Health and Human Services, 2024).

278 **idea of the 'Good-Enough Mother':** D W Winnicott, 'Transitional Objects and Transitional Phenomena – a Study of the First Not-Me Possession', *International Journal of Psycho-Analysis* 34 (1953): 89–97.

278 **the encroachment of psychoanalytic expertise:** Mary Jacobus, *The Poetics of Psychoanalysis: Space, Class, Gender* (Oxford University Press, 2005), 147–48.

279 **only 30 per cent of 'good' interactions:** Edward Z Tronick, 'Emotions and Emotional Communication in Infants', *American Psychologist* 44, no. 2 (February 1989): 116.

000 **Mothers who are the very best at reading their babies:** Eia Asen, Mentalization-Based Treatment (MBT) course, Anna Freud Centre, 2016.

280 **'If parents are the fixed stars':** Alison Gopnik, quoted in Susan Dominus, 'The Surprising Ways That Siblings Shape Our Lives', *The New York Times Magazine,* 6 May 2025.

Chapter 12: Returning Girlhood to Girls

284 **'In order to see, we must forget':** Claude Monet, quoted in https://www.3minutosdearte.com/en/thoughts/claude-monet-to-see-we-must-forget-the-name-of-the-things-we-are-looking-at.

284 **'Hi. I'm Taylor. I write songs about my feelings':** Taylor Swift, quoted in Rob Sheffield, *Heartbreak Is the National Anthem: How Taylor Swift Reinvented Pop Music* (Dey Street Books, 2024), 1.

287 **a culture of fear is growing:** Naomi Beinart, 'As Boys Shift to the Right, We Are Seeing the Rise of the "New Chill Girl",' *The Guardian,* 18 September 2025.

289 **Don't confuse 'wellness' or 'self-care':** Pooja Lakshmin, *Real Self-Care: A Transformative Programme for Redefining Wellness (Crystals, Cleanses, and Bubble Baths Not Included)* (Penguin Life, 2023).

291 **'Suffering ceases to be suffering':** Viktor E Frankl, *Man's Search for Meaning,* trans. Ilse Lasch (Beacon Press, 2006), 67.

291 **The Indigo Girls said:** Indigo Girls, 'Virginia Woolf', track 8 on *Rites of Passage,* Epic Records, 1992.

291 **'All Too Well':** Taylor Swift, 'All Too Well (10 Minute Version)', *Red (Taylor's Version),* Republic Records, 2021.

292 **In a 2011 episode of the TV sitcom:** *Modern Family,* season 2, episode 20, 'Someone to Watch Over Lily', written by Bill Wrubel, directed by Michael Spiller, aired on 20 April 2011.

294 **replace this word in your mind with the word 'burdens':** Richard C Schwartz, *No Bad Parts* (Sounds True, 2021).

296 **Insurance companies could also make a big difference:** Allen Frances, *Saving Normal* (William Morrow, 2013), 85.

296 **clinicians might make a standard practice:** Paula J Caplan and Lisa Cosgrove, 'Is This Really Necessary?', in *Bias in Psychiatric Diagnosis,* ed. Paula J Caplan and Lisa Cosgrove (Jason Aronson, 2004), xix–xxx.

297 **Several dimensional models have been proposed:** Winfried Rief et al., 'Do We Need a Novel Framework for Classifying Psychopathology? A Discussion Paper', *Clinical Psychology in Europe* 5, no. 4 (December 2023).

297 **the most current findings in neurobiology:** Daniel J Siegel and Chloe Drulis, 'An Interpersonal Neurobiology Perspective on the Mind and Mental Health: Personal, Public, and Planetary Well-Being', *Annals of General Psychiatry* 22, no. 1 (February 2023): 5.

298 **next edition of the *DSM*:** Linda Richmond, 'APA Board Considers Strategic Plan, New *DSM*', *Psychiatric News* 60, no. 9 (August 2025).

298 **'bringing more existing disorders into its sphere':** Daniel Carlat, *Unhinged: The Trouble with Psychiatry – a Doctor's Revelations About a Profession in Crisis* (Free Press, 2010), 213.

298 **functionality and symptom-focused care:** Luise Kazda et al., 'Attention Deficit/

Hyperactivity Disorder (ADHD) in Children: More Focus on Care and Support, Less on Diagnosis', *British Medical Journal* 384 (February 2024).

298 **this drive to expand our categories:** Allen Frances, 'Autism Rates Have Increased 60-Fold. I Played a Role in That', *The New York Times,* 23 June 2025.

299 **With different training:** Carlat, *Unhinged,* 219–23.

299 **dwindling supply of supervisors:** Aimee Murray et al., 'Where Have All the Supervisors Gone? Practical Tips for Recruiting Psychotherapy Supervisors', *American Journal of Psychotherapy* 79, no. 3 (2025): 245–52.

300 **Based on a 1993 memoir by Susanna Kaysen:** Susanna Kaysen, *Girl, Interrupted* (Turtle Bay Books, 1993).

300 **the film features Susanna:** *Girl, Interrupted,* directed by James Mangold, Columbia Pictures, 1999.

301 **T S Eliot's poem 'Marina':** T S Eliot, 'Marina', in *Ariel Poems* (Faber & Faber, 1930); reprinted in *Collected Poems 1909–1962* (Faber & Faber, 1963).

302 **As psychologist Abraham Maslow writes:** A H Maslow, 'A Theory of Human Motivation', *Psychological Review* 50, no. 4 (1943): 370–396.

304 **'The more I know my own worth':** Melissa Febos, *Girlhood* (Bloomsbury, 2021), 310.

Index

abandonment, 77, 198, 275
abuse, 69, 241–42
acceptance, 135, 143, 150, 182, 255, 301–2
ADHD
  as adaptation, 227
  COVID-19 pandemic and, 205
  defining, 230–31
  diagnosing, 136, 204–6, 213–14
  dysregulation and, 139–40
  executive function coaching for, 25
  fraud regarding, 230
  history of, 211–13
  as identity, 142, 213, 231
  misdiagnosing, 45, 206
  neurocosmopolitan and, 226–30
  public perception of, 207
  regulation and, 210–11
  rejection-sensitive dysphoria (RSD) and, 141
  self-diagnosing, 206–7, 227
  as situational anxiety, 217
  social media and, 206, 215–16
  stimulants for, 212–13, 230, 231
  superpowers from, 226–27
  symptoms of, 210
  temperament and, 230
  trauma and, 154, 206
  treatment for, 24–25, 40, 154, 205, 212–13, 230, 231
adolescence, overview of, 4–8, 26–28
adolescent boys/young men, 5, 260–61
aggression. *See also* anger
  attitude of, 189
  being stuck in, 290
  bitchiness and, 188
  a lot-ness and, 146
  passive, 26, 237
  relational, 93
  sex and, 69, 177
  social, 190
  stereotypes for, 196
  sweeping away of, 261
  tests and, 163
'All Too Well' (song), 133, 291
Alternative Model for Personality Disorders (AMPD), 297
ambivalence
  cultural, 7
  and diagnosis, 48
  examples of, 26
  internal conflict and, 199
  and mixed emotions, 261
  in parental conflicts, 276
  in relationships, 223
  and therapy, 185
amygdala, 124
anger
  bitchiness and, 195–96
  friendship and, 290
  impulsive behaviours and, 239
  rage and, 235
  regulation of, 237–38
  shame and, 200–1
  splitting and, 235
  suppression of, 33
  vulnerability and, 245–46
anger issues, 76, 194–95
anorexia, 103, 169. *See also* eating disorders
anti-bullying movement, 188, 242. *See also* bullying
antidepressants, 14, 71, 79, 277–78
anxiety
  Anxiety Girlies and, 119–23, 128
  awareness of, 224–25

anxiety (*cont'd*)
behavioural inhibition and, 112
disorders, 113–14
forms of, 74
friendship and, 127–28
function of, 111
as identity, 114, 121
lashing out and, 186
neuroticism and, 125–26
normal, 111
overview of, 7, 110–13
parenting and, 112
as physical experience, 112–13
regulation of, 113, 129–30, 290, 304
as road map, 116
separation, 46–47
situational, 217
sleep and, 109–10
social media and, 119–23
social purgatory and, 114–19
teenage girl brain and, 123–25
tend and befriend and, 127–28
test, 159–60, 162, 163–66, 167
treatments for, 113
truth and, 130
Anxiety Girlies, 119–23, 128
apologising, 219, 220, 259–60
Appignanesi, Lisa, 5, 267
approval, 29, 92, 143, 288
artificial intelligence (AI), 2, 289, 296
attachment, 127–28, 143–44
attachment issues, 290, xvii
attachment parenting, 272
attachment theory, 271–72
attachment trauma, 144
attunement, xvii–xviii, 30, 37–41, 127, 143–44, 279
avoidance. *See also* defences/defence mechanisms
of anger, 304
anxiety and, 114
of conflict, 199
of confrontation, 186
of difficult patients, 148
of emotions, 94, 197
of medications, 45
OCD and, 212
of pain, 39
procrastination and, 162, 181, 208
of reality, 33
of social media, 91
of therapy, 35

Baumrind, Diana, 272
Beauvoir, Simone de, 8
behavioural inhibition, 112
Benadryl, 79
benign neglect, 273
benzodiazepines, 78
bereavement, 60
best friend necklace, 156–57
bingeing, 169–70
biological determinism, 260
biological essentialism, 56, 104, 115, 212, 224, 251, 280, 286, 294, 302. *See also* brain
biopsychosocial approach, 4
bipolar disorder, 138
bitch
All-American, 188–89
anger issues and, 195–96
bullying and, 197–98
example of, 184–88
hidden curriculum and, 189–90
inner child and, 200–2
proto-bitch, 191–92
on social media, 190
body image, 7, 38, 54, 91–92, 96, 110, 114–15, 147, 155, 160. *See also* perfectionism; self-esteem
borderline personality disorder, 138, 148–49, 300
boundary issues, 76
brain, 15, 27, 66, 123–25, 142–43, 260, 302
Bratz dolls, 192
breakups, xvii, 54–83, 93
Breuer, Josef, 68
bulimia, 169. *See also* eating disorders
bullying, 197–98, 242–43
Butisol, 78

capitalism, 2, 6, 104, 177, 180–81, 192, 205, 213, 229
caretaking, 39, 89, 105, 121, 195, 229, 259–60, 263–64, 289
Carlat, Daniel, 84, 98, 102
Charcot, Jean-Martin, 65–66
ChatGPT, 235–36, 289

chemical imbalance, 56, 79–80, 87
Chesler, Phyllis, 127, 267
chillness, 73–78, 82–83, 116, 151, 162, 196, 288
chlorpromazine, 70–71
circumstantial thought processes, 12
cognitive behaviour therapy (CBT), 25, 98, 149150
cognitive dissonance, 162
comorbidities, 29–30, 102
comparison, 15, 92–93, 278. *See also* sizing up
compassion, 18, 61, 155, 201, 225, 231, 289–90, 304
complex post-traumatic stress disorder (c-PTSD), 43–44, 153–54
concept creep, 101
confidence
  decline in, 5–6, 69
  emotions and, 153
  enoughness and, 183
  example of, 40, 118, 180, 190, 225
  medication and, 285, 286
  pressure and, 290
  social media and, 92
control. *See also* obsessive-compulsive disorder (OCD)
  of ADHD, 136, 154
  of anxiety, 113, 124, 129
  behaviour, 27
  birth, 25, 195
  of disease, 196
  of emotions, 94, 146, 150
  example of, 48–49, 66, 73, 76–77, 279
  freak, 47
  impulse, 27, 139
  issues, 10, 76, 81
  means of, 77
  medication and, 154, 195
  moral, 212
  narcissism and, 193
  negative message of, 151
  nervous system and, 164
  parenting and, 280
  regulation and, 151
  Serenity Prayer and, 255
  taking back, 36, 76–77
  tendency for, 47
  in therapy, 82
  words for, 51
coping mechanisms, 33. *See also* defences/defence mechanisms
cortisol, 124
co-ruminating, 125, 127
Cote, Rachel Vorona, 145
countertransference, 31, 32, 35, 126, 137, 168, 187, 237
COVID-19 pandemic, 90, 205, 243, 253
Critical Psychiatry movement, 297–98
cultural gaslighting, 287–88

Damour, Lisa, 109, 111
death, 43, 60, 77, 90, 95
deep fakes, 94
defences/defence mechanisms, 9, 33, 113, 126, 137, 144, 151, 193, 200, 218–20, 224, 261
  Girl Self-Defence System (GSDS) and, 15, 190, 216, 259–63, 302
  overview of, 256–57
Delano, Laura, 87–88
depression, 58, 72, 104, 273, 282
  causes of, 79
  criteria for, 60
  diagnosing, 14, 30, 59–60, 100–1, 102, 279
  grief and, 60, 286
  misdiagnosis of, 35–36, 60
  and mothers, 144
  overdiagnosis of, 100–1, 211
  social media and, 93
  treatment and medication for, 25, 71, 79
Descartes, René, 64
devaluation, 126, 137, 140, 234
diagnosis, 39, 52, 61, 71–72, 97. *See also specific illnesses*
  cost of, 103–5
  desire for, 292–93
  expansion of, 100–2
  fear and, 292
  identity and, 103
  insurance companies and, 296–97
  as negotiations, 214
Diagnostic and Statistical Manual of Mental Disorders *(DSM)*, 14, 43–44, 69–70, 79–80, 97, 113–14, 297–98
dialectical behaviour therapy (DBT), 138–39, 149–50

DiFranco, Ani, 84
dissociative identity disorder, 90. *See also* multiple personality disorder
distraction/distracted/distractible, 7, 150, 205, 226, 290
distress tolerance skill, 150
doctor-patient relationship, 24, 30, 46, 66, 68, 97–98, 101, 209–10, 214, 295–96, 299–300
domestic violence, 241–42
Drama Triangle, 240, 245, 262–63, 281
DSM-think, 102
Dunham, Lena, 147
dynamic lesion, 66
dysregulation, 138–40, 142, 143–44, 145, 151, 210–11

eating disorders, 7, 90, 96, 103, 110, 115, 169, 215. *See also* body image
Election (film), 147
Eli Lilly, 79
Eliot, T S, 301
emotional contagion, 89, 90, 102
emotional impulsivity, 211
emotional labour, 263–64
emotional/internal conflict, 45, 61, 286
emotions/feelings
  care for, 289
  disorientation regarding, 27
  extremes of, 233–35
  fear of, 16
  feeling, 238
  friendship with, 290
  mixed, 261
  war on, 151
empathy/empathising, 10, 59, 89, 127, 223, 260, 261, 271
envy, 162, 177, 183, 278
Erikson, Erik, 27
executive function coaching, 25

Fake Insta, 38
father issues, 43
fawning response, 251
Fay, Sarah, 103
fear
  anger and, 199, 229
  anxiety and, 115
  control and, 36, 51
  culture of, 287
  grief and, 220
  identifying, 292
  naming, 163
  OCD and, 47
  pain and, 74
  in parenting, 7, 225
  relationships and, 252
  tests and, 111, 159
  witches and, 63
Febos, Melissa, 84, 304
feminism/feminist, 6, 43, 68, 80–81, 105, 122, 127, 133, 188, 248, 272, 278
fluoxetine (Prozac), 62, 71, 79, 80, 81, 87, 278
food issues, 177. *See also* body image *and* eating disorders
Foulkes, Lucy, 102
four 'humours', 62–63
Frances, Allen, 298
Frankl, Viktor, 291
Free-Range parenting, 273
Freud, Anna, 26, 256
Freud, Sigmund, 10, 26, 66, 68–69, 126, 177–78, 189, 256, 270, 302
Friedan, Betty, 8
friendship
  anxiety and, 120, 127–31, 186
  approval in, 288
  best friend necklace, 156–57
  boundaries and, 259
  closeness in, 125, 137
  confrontation in, 128–31
  co-rumination in, 127
  drama in, 7, 54–56, 58–59, 96, 109–10, 114–19, 136, 204–5, 236, 237–38, 248–49
  emotional abuse and, 235–38, 241–46
  with emotions, 290
  exclusion in, 239, 243
  focus on, 26
  FOMO and, 91
  imperfections and, 182–83
  jealousy and, 178
  objectifying, 160
  parenting and, 269, 272–75
  social media and, 38, 93, 161–62
  tending and befriending in, 127–28
  therapy from, 19–20, 253

toxic, 239
trauma of, 43
Frozen (film), 146–47
Fuck Around and Find Out (FAFO) parenting, 17

Galen, 63
Gaslight (film), 70
gaslighting, 9–10, 193, 235–36, 263, 287–88
Gen Alpha, 2, 17–18, 247
Gen Z, 2, 6, 17, 139, 247
gender bias, 63, 214. *See also* sexism
general talk therapy, 25. *See also* humanism; psychodynamic therapy; supportive psychotherapy; talking cure
generalised anxiety disorder, 113, 216
gentle parenting, 273
giggling, 131, 156, 165, 208, 219
Gilligan, Carol, 26
Gilman, Charlotte Perkins, 67–68
Girl, Interrupted (film), 300–1
Girl Self-Defence System (GSDS), 15, 190, 259–63, 302
girl-poisoning culture, 6, 8
girlspeak, 11–13
globus hystericus, 68
good-enoughness, 182
Good-Enough Mother, 182, 278–81
goodness of fit, 143–44
gratitude, 183
grief, 60, 220, 286

Hacking, Ian, 101
Hall, G Stanley, 26
Hari, Johann, 204
harm, 24, 45, 91, 93–94, 101, 104, 114, 122, 190, 220, 226, 239, 241, 242, 256, 273, 285, 294
Haslam, Nick, 101–2
health insurance, 28, 295–97. *See also* insurance companies; managed care
health literacy, 98
heartbreak, 54–62, 71–72, 81–83
helplessness, 32, 33, 42–43, 51, 60, 67, 72, 191, 240, 243, 257, 286, 301
Herman, Judith, 43–44, 154
Hierarchical Taxonomy of Psychopathology (HiTOP), 297
hierarchy of needs, 302
highly sensitive person (HSP), 112
Hippocrates, 62
homosexuality, 271
hopelessness, 38, 104, 255, 257, 286
hormones, 4, 7, 27, 195
horoscopes, 84–85
Hot Crazy-Matrix, 6
humanism, 96
humour, 126, 256
hunters and farmers theory, 217
hypnosis, 65–66
hypothalamic-pituitary-adrenal (HPA), 124
hysteria/hysterical, 1, 24, 61, 62–72, 132, 145–46, 147, 151, 283, 302

idealisation, 7, 126, 137, 234
identity
ADHD as, 142, 213, 231
anxiety as, 114, 121
authentic, 290
diagnosis and, 103
flavours of, 84
formation of, 7–8
internet age and, 85–88
replacement, 58
social intimacy and, 127
illness identities, cost of, 103–5
image-based sexual abuse (IBSA), 93–94
imperfections, 182–83
inner child, 200–2
inner critic, 9, 166–67, 170, 174, 178, 206
insecurities, 12, 38, 162, 177, 186
insight, 188, 220–21, 251, 281, 307
Instagram, 6, 38, 56, 74, 88, 111, 115, 161, 190, 237, 242
insurance companies, 2, 13, 97–98, 100, 295–97. *See also* health insurance; managed care
internal attribution, 163
internal focus, for therapy success, 250–52
internet. *See also* social media
abuse and, 242
ADHD and, 213
danger zones on, 230
function of, 86
identity and, 84–105
labels from, 24

internet (*cont'd*)
mental health advocacy on, 95–96, 98
mental health awareness initiatives and, 2
sad girl, 85–88
therapy culture and, 9, 10, 72, 98, 233, 263–64
Internet Sad Girl, 85–88
issues, defining, 76. *See also specific issues*

Jamison, Leslie, 111, 184
jealousy, 55, 172, 177, 178. *See also* envy
Just a Little Girl meme, 121–22

Kaling, Mindy, 147
Kaysen, Susanna, 300–1
Kohlberg, Lawrence, 26
Kraepelin, Emil, 69
Kramer, Peter, 80–81
Kriss, Alexander, 54

language, 238, 246–47, 304. *See also* girl-speak; therapy speak
lashing out, 186, 201, 203
learning issues, 167, 206
Lexapro, 278
'like', 11
linguistic relativity theory, 246–47
lithium, 71
loneliness, 43, 61, 68, 86, 247, 294
lunacy, 64, 67

Machiavellianism, 189–90
madness, 64, 67, 132, 301
major depressive disorder, 100–1. *See also* depression
malaise, 181. *See also* social malaise
managed care, 1, 209
martyrdom, 262
Maslow, Abraham, 302
masochist, 262
maternal love, 270–71
McCabe, Jessica, 215–16
McCulloch, Gretchen, 13
medical model, 96–100
medications. *See also specific medications*
advertisements for, 80
as Band-Aid, 72
developments of, 78–80, 97
gender bias in, 64
life without, 285
misdiagnosis and, 206
overmedication of, 295, 298
as philosophical decision, 285–86
pros and cons of, 285–86
statistics regarding, 14
menstruation, 25, 62, 67, 195
mental status exam, 224
Mesmer, Franz Anton, 65
#MeToo/Me-Too'd, 40, 92, 239
Meyer, Adolf, 69–70
Middle Ages, 63–64
Miltown, 78
minimisation/minimised, 14, 104, 257, 259–60, 293, 302
misdiagnosis, 45, 103, 206
misogyny, 12, 17, 63, 104, 191, 270–71. *See also* gender bias; sexism
momism, 271
money, 176–77
money issues, 185, 188
mood transfer, 89
mother issues, 43
mother-blaming, 270
mother-child interaction, 42, 112, 270, 271–72, 279
multiple personality disorder, 90. *See also* dissociative identity disorder
Mulvey, Laura, 54
Musgraves, Kacey, 147
My Fair Lady (musical), 65
myelin, 15

narcissism, 2, 148, 186, 189–90, 192–93, 202, 235
Nerenberg, Jenara, 204
neurasthenia, 66–67
neurocosmopolitan, 226–30
neurodivergence, 95, 104, 167, 216, 229, 276
neurodiversity, 226, 227–28, 232, 299
neuroessentialism, 103–4
neurology, 64
neurosexism, 260
neurotic suffering, 221
neurotic/neuroticism, 125–26
Nightingale, Florence, 67–68
normalising, 16, 69, 120

not-enoughness
best friend necklace and, 156–57
capitalism and, 180–81
development of, 160
example of, 160–63
inner critic and, 166–67
intergenerational transmission of, 174–80
Mean Coach and, 170–74, 179, 180
self-hating, 170–74
social media and, 181–82
stress and, 157–59
test anxiety and, 159–60, 162, 163–66, 167
wealth and, 176–77
nurturing, 121

obsession/obsessed/obsessing, 27, 56, 113, 233
obsessive-compulsive disorder (OCD), 25, 47, 76–77, 103, 212
obsessive-compulsive personality disorder (OCPD), 47
Occam's razor, 29
operationalised criteria, 97
Orwell, George, 13
Osler, Sir William, 32, 207
overdiagnosis, 100, 296
overinterpretation, 102
overmedication, 295
overprotective mother, 271
oxytocin, 128

pampering, 189
panic attacks, xvii, 74, 113, 253, 293–94
panic disorder, 113
Pappenheim, Bertha, 68
parenting
ambivalence and, 223
anxiety and, 112
attachment theory and, 271–72
attacks in, 142
attunement in, 143–44
authoritarian, 272
authoritative, 272
conflicts in, 261
coping in, 275
depression in, 144
expectations in, 269–70
fears in, 275
Free-Range, 273
friendship in, 272–75
gentle, 273
Good-Enough Mother in, 278–81
helicopter, 269, 272–75
intentional, 273
as mental health risk, 277–78
mindful, 273
mother-child interaction in, 270
overprotective, 271
overwhelm in, 274
pathologising in, 276
perfectionism and, 182
permissive, 272
personal worth in, 275–76
pressure in, 268–69
process of, 267–68
refrigerator, 271
schizophrenogenic, 271
snowplough, 269, 272–75
social media and, 275
stress in, 267–68, 269–70, 274, 277–78
suggestions for, 292–95
therapeutic, 273–74
therapy speak in, 293–94
translation work in, 293–94
parsimony, 29. *See also* Occam's razor
passivity, 32, 36, 141, 194, 197, 219, 257. *See also* helplessness
peer supervision, 30–34, 45–46, 48–49, 123–25, 174–80, 209–11, 216–17, 221–24, 226–30
people-pleasing, 248–50, 256–57, 262
Perel, Esther, 23
perfectionism, 47, 156, 159–60, 166–67, 182
Perpetrator role, 240, 241–44, 262–63
personality, 255, 256, 271
personality disorders, 47, 54, 102, 138, 148–49, 153, 197, 206, 241, 300
personality traits, 47, 76–77, 126, 159, 248, 261–63. *See also* temperament
phenobarbital, 78
phobias, 113. *See also* fear
phones, 2, 6, 44, 57, 58, 88, 92, 93, 109, 117–18, 125, 160–62, 190, 207, 229, 236, 268, 273
Piaget, Jean, 26
Pipher, Mary, 6
placebo effect, 65

Plato, 62
plurals, 90. *See also* dissociative identity disorder; multiple personality disorder
PMS irritability, 195
post-feminist self-consciousness, 105
post-traumatic stress disorder (PTSD), 43, 94, 153–54
pouting, 192
prefrontal cortex, 27–28. *See also* brain
premenstrual dysphoric disorder (PMDD), 25, 195
Pretty Woman (film), 65
prevalence inflation, 102
privilege, 29, 86, 92, 210, 282
process term, 264
procrastination, 162, 204, 207–8, 218, 226
Prozac (fluoxetine), 62, 71, 79, 80, 81, 87, 278
psychiatry
  influences to, 61–62
  medical model and, 96–100
  reductionism in, 1–2, 62
  social media, 94–96
  suggestions for, 295–96
  words in, 3–4
psychoanalysis, 68–69. *See also* Freud, Sigmund
psychodynamic therapy, 126, 178, 219, 299–300. *See also* talk therapy
psychological justice, 72
psychopathy, 189–90
puberty, 4, 27, 110, 124, 127, 147, 160
Pygmalion, 65

radical acceptance, 150, 255
rage, 30, 33, 36, 202, 235, 240, 245. *See also* anger
Rakoff, Vivian, 44
reductionism, 1–2, 62, 100, 209
refrigerator mother, 271
rejection-sensitive dysphoria (RSD), 141
relational aggression, 93
relationships
  breakups, 54–62, 72, 93
  chillness in, 73–78, 82–83
  girl support in, 260
  heartbreak in, 54–62
  social media and, 93
  toxic, 239
Research Domain Criteria (RDoC), 297
resting bitch face, 192
revenge porn, 93–94
Ritalin, 212
Rodrigo, Olivia, 147, 184
Rogers, Carl, 199
role overload, 161
Rosemary's Baby (film), 70
rumination, 125, 127–28, 256

sadness, 33, 48, 63, 70, 85–88, 110, 121, 126, 167, 220, 237, 260, 279, 286
sanitoriums, 67
Sapir–Whorf hypothesis, 246–47
Saviour role, 240, 262–63
schizophrenogenic mother, 271
selective serotonin reuptake inhibitors (SSRIs), 71, 97, 195. *See also specific medications*
self-attack, 58, 278, 287–89
self-blame, 33. *See also* inner critic; internal attribution; superego
self-care, 9, 59, 239, 247, 268, 274, 289. *See also* wellness
self-criticism, 170–74. *See also* self-blame
self-diagnosis, 24, 40, 115, 157–58, 204–5, 206–7, 227, 302
self-esteem, 7, 9, 94–95, 111, 154, 159, 206, 213, 231, 243, 249
self-harm, 16, 42, 88, 90–91, 149, 170, 174, 178. *See also* harm
self-hating, 170–71. *See also* self-blame
self-image, 5–7, 90, 91–94. *See also* body image *and* self-esteem
self-oriented perfectionism, 159
self-punishment, 170. *See also* self-blame; self-criticism; self-harm
self-regulation, 143, 150. *See also* anxiety; dysregulation
self-respect, 243, 290. *See also* self-esteem
self-talk, 220
self-worth, 104. *See also* self-esteem; self-respect
Seneca, 301
sensitivity to judgement, 39, 53, 101, 112, 124, 139, 141, 179
Serenity Prayer, 256, 301–2
serotonin, 79. *See also* chemical imbalance
sexism, 6, 89, 223, 260, 302

sexual abuse/assault, 40, 41, 69, 93–94, 287. *See also* #MeToo/Me-Too'd
sexuality, 7, 10, 41, 43, 69, 77, 177, 188, 271
shame, 7, 77, 84, 126, 142, 145, 162, 167, 177, 187, 199, 200–1, 206, 213, 238, 264, 293
shaming, 17. *See also* slut-shaming
shell shock, 70
Shrier, Abigail, 41–42, 273
Siegel, Daniel, 98–99
silence, in therapy, 28, 130, 177, 220, 252–53
Simmons, Rachel, 163, 181
sizing up, 278
skills culture, 149–53. *See also* dialectical behaviour therapy (DBT)
sleep, 11, 24–25, 30, 44, 60, 109–10, 139, 143, 160, 256, 274
slut-shaming, 93–94
social aggression, 165–66, 190, 235–38. *See also* Anxiety Girlies; relational aggression
social anxiety disorder, 113
social competition, 182, 190
social malaise, 304
social media
  ADHD and, 206, 215–16
  anxiety and, 119–23
  bitchiness on, 190
  comparison and, 92–93
  depression and, 93
  harms from, 162
  as illness incubator, 88–91
  image-based sexual abuse (IBSA) and, 93–94
  impulsive behaviours on, 239
  not-enoughness and, 181–82
  parenting and, 275
  psychiatry and, 94–96
  relationships and, 93
  self-image and, 91–92, 105
  traumatiser, 91–94
Solnit, Rebecca, 248
Spears, Britney, 239
Spitz, René, 271
splitting, 144–45, 234–35, 245, 246
Stefani, Gwen, 121
Steinem, Gloria, 156
stimulants, 212–13, 231, 277–78
Stoicism, 150, 212, 285
Strecker, Edward, 271
stress. *See also* parenting
  behavioural inhibition and, 112
  coping with, 166, 229, 262
  disorders, 14
  emotional, 78
  example of, 109–10, 114, 116, 123–24, 160, 173, 175
  fight or flight response and, 127–28
  insomnia and, 11
  internet and, 86, 96
  masking, xviii
  maternal, 45
  as normal, 250
  overview of, 157–59
  parenting, 267–68, 269, 277–78
  relief for, 74
  splitting and, 144
  storm and, 26
  symptoms of, 94
  too-muchness and, 147
  videos of, 119
Styron, William, 60
suicide, 5, 42, 88, 90, 91, 95, 113, 163, 268, 298, 300
superego, 178–79
supportive psychotherapy, 25, 195
Swift, Taylor, 121, 132–34, 284, 291–92
Sydenham, Thomas, 64
systematising, 261

talk therapy, 25, 126
talking cure, 10, 68–69
teenagers, overview of, 26–28. *See also* adolescence, overview of
temperament, 143, 167, 230, 255, 280
tend and befriend response, 127–28
test anxiety, 111, 159–60, 162, 163–66, 167
Thee Stallion, Megan, 147
therapeutic alliance, 29, 30, 35
therapeutic parenting, 272–75
therapy
  ambivalence about, 281
  function of, 239–40
  history of, 62–71
  internal focus in, 250–52
  purpose of, 122–23
  silence in, 252–53
  successful, 250–52

therapy (*cont'd*)
transformation of, 97–98
types of, 113
therapy culture
backlash regarding, 15–18
impatience regarding, 16, 294
language of, 8–11
process terms and, 264
unsympathetic response to, 17
therapy speak
decoding, 51–53
definition of, 8–11
as harmful, 13–15
in parenting, 293–95
process terms, 264
rise of, 1, 2
self-expression in, 11–13
13 Reasons Why (series), 90
Thompson, Derek, 247
TikTok, 88, 90, 92, 94–95, 215–16
TikTok Tics, 90
Tofranil, 71
too-muchness
being difficult and, 147–49
causes of, 144
example of, 134–38, 140–43
eye of the beholder and, 143–45
in literature, film and music, 146–47
skills culture and, 149–53
Taylor Swift and, 132–34
walking on eggshells and, 138–40
women and, 145–47
Tourette's syndrome, 90
toxic, defined, 238–40
transference, 31, 36, 37, 40, 67, 142–43, 150–51, 218
transitional objects, 51–52
translation work, in parenting, 293–95
trauma
ADHD and, 154
attachment, 144
complex post-traumatic stress disorder (c-PTSD) and, 153–54
culture, 41–42
defined, 43, 242
diagnosing, 49–50, 153
dysregulation and, 139
focus on, 41
intergenerational, 44
police, 44–46
sexual, 42
social media and, 88–89
symptoms of, 40
types of, 42–44
The Trauma Test, 94
tricyclics, 79
Tronick, Ed, 279
trust issues, 76
Tumblr, 88
Twenge, Jean, 93, 247

unconditional positive regard, 199

Valium, 78, 80
van der Kolk, Bessel, 41–42
viciousness, 188. *See also* aggression, bitchiness *and* anger
Victim role, 240, 241–44, 262–63
vocabulary, acquiring, 12–13
von Goethe, Johann Wolfgang, 89
von Paradis, Maria Theresia, 65
vulnerability, 14, 38, 62, 90, 196, 245–46, 290

Walker, Nick, 226
Watson, John B, 270–71
wealth, 176–77. *See also* money *and* money issues
wellness, 2, 95–96, 246, 289. *See also* self-care
Werther Effect, 90
William of Ockham, 29
Winnicott, Donald, 182, 278
witchcraft, 63–64
Wittgenstein, Ludwig, 233
Wittman, Blanche, 66
Wurtzel, Elizabeth, 87, 88, 188
Wylie, Philip, 271

'Year of the Girl', 121–22
The Yellow Wallpaper (Gilman), 67–68

Zoloft, 79, 80

About the Author

Dr Suzanne Garfinkle-Crowell is a psychiatrist who treats children, adolescents and adults. She studied English at Amherst College and received a master of science degree in theoretical psychoanalysis from University College London. She completed her medical and residency training at Columbia University/New York State Psychiatric Institute and the Icahn School of Medicine at Mount Sinai, where she is Founding Director of the Academy for Medicine and the Humanities. She lives with her family in Greenwich Village.